DATE DUE

MAKING
CAMPAIGNS
COUNT

MAKING
CAMPAIGNS
COUNT

Leadership and
Coalition-Building in 1980

DARRELL M. WEST

CONTRIBUTIONS IN POLITICAL SCIENCE, NUMBER 110

GREENWOOD PRESS
WESTPORT, CONNECTICUT · LONDON, ENGLAND

Acknowledgments

Permission to reprint from the following articles is greatly appreciated:
Darrell M. West, "Press Coverage in the 1980 Presidential Campaign," in *Social Science Quarterly*, 64, no. 3, September, 1983, pp. 624–633, published by the University of Texas Press; Darrell M. West, "Constituencies and Travel Allocations in the 1980 Presidential Campaign," *American Journal of Political Science*, 27, no. 3, August, 1983, pp. 515–529, published by the University of Texas Press; Darrell M. West, "Cheers and Jeers," *American Politics Quarterly*, January, 1984, published by Sage Publications, Inc.; Darrell M. West, "Rhetoric and Agenda-Setting in the 1980 Presidential Campaign," in *Congress & the Presidency: A Journal of Capital Studies*, 9, no. 2, Autumn, 1982, pp. 1–22, published by the Center for Congressional and Presidential Studies and the U.S. Capitol Historical Society.

Library of Congress Cataloging in Publication Data

West, Darrell M., 1954–
  Making campaigns count.

  (Contributions in political science, ISSN 0147-1066 ;
no. 110)
  Bibliography: p.
  Includes index.
  1. Presidents—United States—Election—1980.
2. Electioneering—United States. I. Title. II. Series.
JK526 1980d   324.973'0926   83-13021
ISBN 0-313-24235-6 (lib. bdg.)

Library of Congress Catalog Card Number: 83-13021
ISBN: 0-313-24235-6
ISSN: 0147-1066

First published in 1984

Greenwood Press
A division of Congressional Information Service, Inc.
88 Post Road West, Westport, Connecticut 06881

Printed in the United States of America

10 9 8 7 6 5 4 3 2 1

TO ANNIE

Contents

Illustrations

Preface

In this book, I explore leadership and coalition-building in the 1980 presidential campaign. Unlike many studies of elections, which emphasize voters, I concentrate on candidates and their personal advisors. Despite the importance of candidate strategies, research on political leaders virtually has disappeared from library shelves (with the exception of journalistic accounts). Twenty years ago, scholars like C. Wright Mills studied the relations among leaders to see if a "power elite" governed America. Others explored changes in the composition of leadership to determine whether there was a "circulation of elites." But over the last two decades, election analysts have studied voters to the near exclusion of candidates.

Happily, this pattern is beginning to change. Recent work by Richard Fenno demonstrates the importance of candidate "home style" for congressional elections. At the presidential level, Benjamin Page makes the simple but important point that people do not vote in a vacuum; rather they make decisions within the options that candidates present them. And Gary Jacobson and Samuel Kernell argue that potential candidates and financial contributors help to determine the competitiveness of House elections by influencing the quality of challengers.

My analysis falls within this "reemerging" research tradition of candidate studies. I ask the following questions: How have changes in presidential campaigns influenced candidate strategies? What coalitions did presidential contenders try to put together? How did candidates use rhetoric, campaign travels, and symbolism in their coalition-building? What did candidates learn from audiences in their months and years on the campaign trail? And what do these things imply for political leadership and coalition-building?

As befits a project that relied on extensive fieldwork (in-depth interviews, personal observation, and the detailed study of travel schedules, candidate speeches, and audience reactions), I developed many debts. I wish to thank Indiana University faculty member Leroy Rieselbach, for reading countless drafts, making insightful comments, and teaching me (among other things) to never

split infinitives; Alfred Diamant, for giving me the benefit of his broad interests; Jeff Fishel, whose research on presidential campaigns inspired this project;
Marjorie Hershey, who suggested numerous improvements, and James Kuklinski, who led me through the mysteries of research design. To them goes my
deep gratitude for helping to improve this product. In addition, several people
read earlier portions of this work: Richard Fenno, Thomas Mann, Annie Schmitt,
James Sundquist, Roger Cobb, Lee Sigelman, Steven Brams, Delmar Dunn,
Robert Erikson, David Paletz, Patricia Hurley, William Adams, Laurie Rhod-
ebeck, Charles Bonjean, Murray Havens, Adam Clymer, William Haltom, Michael MacKuen, and Laurily Epstein; their suggestions were greatly appreciated. Comments by the editors and reviewers of Greenwood Press also helped
make this work better. In the data collection area, scores of campaign advisors
and staff members contributed to this project through generous gifts of time and
tale; their names are listed in Appendix I. The following individuals also as-
sisted me by providing travel schedules, candidate speeches, audio tapes, and
campaign documents: William Andrews, Andy Carrano, Mark Knoller, Dave
Oakland, Keven Vance, Dan Swillinger, David Spear, Gayle Prousalis, De-
lores Farrell, Jeb Bush, Alixe Reed, Margaret Tutweiller, Michelle Clause, Betty
Meyer, Melodie Miller, Robin Gray, Kim Hoggard, and Greg Newell. A number of research assistants speeded the project through their diligence and hard
work: Regina Germain, Robin Landes, Roxanne Lapointe, Colette Rhoney, Nancy
Rosenberg, Jon Seib, and Mary-Jo Swinimer. Portions of this work were made
possible by National Science Foundation Grant SOC 79–12966, a Brookings
Institution Research Fellowship, and an Indiana University Grant-in-Aid of Research. None of these institutions bears any responsibility for the interpretations
that I present. Finally, Judy Bryan deserves a special thanks for her support
throughout the project.

Some of the material presented in this book originally appeared in: "Consti-
tuencies and Travel Allocations in the 1980 Presidential Campaign," *American
Journal of Political Science* (August, 1983); "Cheers and Jeers," *American
Politics Quarterly* (January, 1984); "Press Coverage in the 1980 Presidential
Campaign," *Social Science Quarterly* (September, 1983); and "Rhetoric and
Agenda-Setting in the 1980 Presidential Campaign," *Congress & the Presi-
dency* (Autumn, 1982).

MAKING
CAMPAIGNS
COUNT

1

Introduction

This book is about the 1980 presidential contest. Few campaigns in recent history have generated the drama and excitement that the 1980 race did: the nomination challenge of a nationally known senator, Edward Kennedy, to President Jimmy Carter; the unprecedented spectacle of "America Held Hostage" in Iran; Kennedy's fumbling performance on the campaign trail; the unexpected emergence of George Bush and John Anderson as challengers to Republican frontrunner Ronald Reagan; Anderson's independent candidacy; the general election debate between Carter and Reagan, and the surprising size (almost ten percentage points) of Reagan's victory over Carter. If for no other reason, the 1980 presidential campaign deserves attention because of its historical value.

But the importance of this race stretched beyond the campaign itself. The most interesting drama came after the election when President Reagan attempted far-reaching changes in federal policies. Working with a Senate that Republicans controlled for the first time since 1954 and a group of Democratic House members known as "Boll Weevils," Reagan sought unprecedented actions. In an effort to decrease the role of government, he proposed major cuts of social programs (health, education, housing, and welfare) and reductions in federal regulatory efforts (such as consumer protection, safety regulations, and environmental safeguards). On defense matters, the president sought massive increases in military expenditures to fight communism and what he saw as a spreading Soviet menace. In the words of Richard Wirthlin, Reagan's campaign pollster and strategist, the chief executive sought these changes because

our feeling was that America was not going down the proper road and that we did need to reassess the national agenda and the policy options that had been tried to deal with what was on the national agenda and to start looking at other alternatives that offered more promise.[1]

Much to the surprise of observers, Reagan successfully pushed many of these proposals through Congress. Soon after the election, the House and Senate followed Reagan's suggestions and cut $40 billion from the budget, including reductions in programs such as food stamps, public assistance, housing subsidies, the school lunch program, public service jobs, college loans, and Medicaid, among others. Legislators also approved tax cuts for individuals and businesses totaling $749 billion over a five-year period and added $18 billion to the defense budget. In fact, Reagan's success with Congress was so phenomenal in the early days of his administration that House Minority Leader Robert H. Michel proclaimed "a new direction for national government and national politics in this country" while Senate Majority Leader Howard Baker said, "this Congress has made more fundamental changes in public policy than any Congress in decades."[2]

In this book, I explore the 1980 campaign and its aftermath, paying particular attention to the subject of coalition-building. Coalitions are important for a number of reasons. They are the building blocks of successful campaigns. To advance to the highest office in the land, candidates must develop and retain the support of voters, contributors, convention delegates, and party activists. Coalitions are also crucial for governance. As President Reagan learned, chief executives sometimes have to explain painful and unpopular choices to the public. At other times, they have to push complex and controversial legislation through Congress. Without strong coalitions—among voters and in Congress—presidents may lack the capacity to exert leadership forcefully. Meanwhile, at the normative level, coalitions supply a vital link between campaigns and governance. Candidates who use their electoral coalitions to develop governing coalitions provide much-needed continuity for the political system. Coalitions enable leaders to muster the legislative majorities necessary for policy actions. And at election time, they simplify voter choices between competing leadership packages. For these reasons, I investigate coalition formation in the 1980 race.

THE STUDY OF COALITIONS

Scholars have studied various features of coalitions. Going back to the early work of William Riker and his successors, researchers have concentrated on the size of coalitions, debating the conditions under which "minimum winning coalitions" emerge.[3] Other writers, such as Robert Axelrod, have devoted attention to the composition of coalitions and found substantial differences in the electoral coalitions of Republicans and Democrats since 1952.[4] A third body of literature has developed around strategies of coalition-building; it investigates tactics by which support is developed.[5] And still others have explored the topic of realignment in an effort to discover the conditions under which party coalitions change.[6]

Although researchers have devoted considerable time to investigating coalitions, many of them have approached the subject from the standpoint of voters. For example, writers generally have analyzed realigning elections at the mass voting level, using aggregate election returns and public opinion surveys to study changes in party coalitions. Similarly, research on coalition formation often emphasizes qualities of the voting public, i.e., citizen beliefs and attitudes. This emphasis on voters is not surprising because voting behavior has dominated the study of American elections for several decades. Scholars have analyzed many features of public opinion and voting behavior: Are voters knowledgeable about or interested in politics? Do they vote on the basis of issues, party identifications, or their perceptions of candidate qualities? Are voters governed by short- or long-term forces? What role does the state of the economy play in elections? While the list could go on, it should be clear that the study of voters has been the overriding concern of election scholars for some time.

This focus has yielded rich dividends, but the preoccupation with American voters has distracted researchers from candidates. Candidates are important in elections. They set the choices available to voters. They influence the rate of political change. And they establish the broad boundaries in which elections take place. In addition, candidates play a crucial role in coalition formation. Contrary to the impressions we get on election day, presidential coalitions do not arise full-blown overnight. Rather, candidates spend months and sometimes years rallying support.

Perhaps no race in recent times illustrated this idea more than the 1980 contest. As I note in following chapters, Reagan's role was crucial in his coalitional efforts. Many commentators (rightfully) have interpreted the election as a protest vote against Carter and the poor state of the economy.[7] But Reagan deserves credit for a strategy that took full advantage of Carter's weaknesses. With his campaign visits, Reagan actively pursued Democrats and social conservatives throughout the nominating process and general election. He also developed rhetorical and symbolic appeals that showed his interest in coalitional change. Furthermore, Reagan's campaign presented voters with a vision of America based on military strength, traditional values, and limited government. Thus, Reagan did not sit idly by. He worked to define the country's problems on his terms. He developed policy proposals (budget and tax cuts) to deal with these problems. And he mobilized popular and legislative support for his programs. Instead of being the lucky recipient of a protest vote (which implies that anyone could have beaten Carter by ten percentage points and gone on to win major victories in Congress), Reagan's contributions to his victory should not be underestimated.

Because of this situation, scholars should study not only the timing and processes by which voters shift their loyalties. It is equally important to consider how (and why) candidates try to bring about those shifts. Many studies have analyzed the composition and determinants of coalitions at the level of voters, but few scholars (with the exception of Fenno) have studied candidates' perceptions of their constituencies and the impact of those perceptions on coalition-building.[8] Since candidates, and their advisors are at the center of coalition formation, it behooves scholars to explore their activities in detail.

COALITIONS AND THE CAMPAIGN ENVIRONMENT

Candidates do not build coalitions in a vacuum. Rather, they make strategic decisions within certain institutional settings. This feature has become especially important in recent elections as the rules of the game have changed dramatically (see chapter 2). Delegate selection and money-raising take place under very different rules than before. Actors who previously were crucial (such as party leaders) have lost importance while others (such as media figures) have gained influence. Although these trends are readily apparent, not everyone agrees on their implications for coalitions. The traditional model of coalition-building and campaign decision-making emphasized its ad hoc and reactive nature. According to Xandra Kayden, Nelson Polsby, Aaron Wildavsky, and others, candidates made decisions on a day-to-day basis.[9] They built coalitions in an incremental and unsystematic manner. Planning was nonexistent. Strategic decisions were made by whoever happened to be in the room at the time.

However, with the rise of the new electoral system, there are disagreements over the validity of this interpretation. On the one hand, some scholars have documented the emergence of scientific approaches to campaigning.[10] With the rise of polling, direct mail, and media consultants, they argue that campaigns have been increasingly well organized. They have become less reactive, more comprehensive in their planning, and more hierarchically structured. Instead of the "disjointed incrementalism" that characterized previous approaches, campaign organizations have become more systematic in their coalition-building. Alternatively, other writers have questioned these conclusions, arguing that coalitions have lost their traditional meaning. Rather than stabilizing elections and providing continuity for the political system, they suggest that these new technologies have contributed to de-alignment and the weakening of party coalitions. If anything, these new techniques have given campaigners more powerful tools for destabilizing old alliances, manipulating voter choices, and increasing the fluidity of modern elections.[11]

While my research cannot settle this dispute, it can contribute some ideas to the discussion. The evidence from 1980 and thereafter indicates that candidates can put together a winning electoral coalition and use that support to make major policy changes. Even though there are many de-aligning features of the new electoral system, coalition formation is not impossible. Reagan's resounding victory (combined with the Republican sweep of the Senate and Reagan's success in attracting votes from Democrats and Independents) gave Republicans unusual opportunities for controlling the government and cementing their electoral coalition (though the recession undermined these efforts). Accordingly, the 1980 race raises the question of what Reagan (and others) did strategically during the campaign to build coalitions in the new electoral system.

COALITIONS AND POLICY MOTIVES

The election of 1980 can also shed light on the motivations of politicians wishing to build coalitions. Rational choice theorists have developed models which place primary emphasis on electoral self-interest. This research (popularized by Anthony Downs and David Mayhew) describes candidates as vote maximizers, motivated generally by electoral incentives.[12] According to this approach, politicians survey the political landscape and "go hunting where the ducks are." Implicitly, scholars utilizing this perspective assume that candidates build coalitions in the most expedient manner, guided only by their single-minded pursuit of victory.

In contrast to this view, one can argue that candidates have policy as well as electoral motivations. As Fenno and Page have noted, candidates are not merely vote maximizers; they also bring substantive concerns to their positions.[13] Therefore, they may build coalitions around issues or constituencies that interest them, even if the political odds look unpromising.

This idea was particularly important in 1980 as Americans elected the most ideological president the country has had in recent times. Few politicians have been more consistent in their philosophies than Reagan has. For twenty years he has played the right-wing dinner circuit. And lest there be any doubt about the sincerity of Reagan's rhetoric, the Californian's presidential actions demonstrated the depth of his commitments. Therefore, students of the Reagan coalition should look to his campaign activities (as well as those of his opponents) to investigate the interplay of electoral and policy incentives.

THE NORMATIVE IMPLICATIONS OF
COALITION-BUILDING

Finally, the 1980 election can help researchers discuss the normative dimensions of coalitions. Despite the importance of a link between campaigns and governance, many writers have belittled the substantive possibilities of presidential races. Scholars such as Murray Edelman have criticized candidates for manipulative strategies.[14] Reporters claim that no one discusses the "issues" in detail. Voters deride political parties, saying there is not "a dime's worth of differences" between them. And even cartoonists have taken potshots; in a memorable series about Jimmy Carter's Secretary of Symbolism, Garry Trudeau (the creator of "Doonesbury") bemoaned the lack of substance in modern campaigns.[15] Taken together, these criticisms suggest limited prospects for coalition formation in American campaigns.

But this portrayal may exaggerate the lack of substance in modern elections. In spite of the fun and games atmosphere that sometimes characterizes presidential contests, substance manages to come through. Research reported later in this book shows that presidential candidates used electoral tactics (rhetoric, campaign visits, and symbolic appeals) in consistent ways. In addition, work by Gerald Pomper and Jeff Fishel notes a significant relation between campaign promises and executive actions in postwar administrations.[16] Douglas Hibbs also has discovered systematic differences in macroeconomic performance across administrations of different parties.[17]

These findings suggest that campaigns are intimately linked to governance.

Rather than being superficial events with few meaningful policy consequences, presidential campaigns serve several important functions. First, they are important for government policy because they shape the country's political agenda—the range of issues deemed worthy of public debate and attention.[18] Prior to the 1980 election, supply-side economics was at the fringe of the political agenda; other than a handful of writers and political leaders, few discussed the idea. But through "entrepreneurial" activities on the part of writers and the campaign speeches of certain politicians (namely Jack Kemp and Ronald Reagan), this idea was publicized, became part of the Republican party platform, and (after Reagan's election) was enacted into law as "Reaganomics." Indeed, one can argue that the most important effect of Reagan's victory (along with the unseating of several liberal stalwarts in the House and Senate) was in shifting the terms of political debate.

In the defense area, Reagan's proposals for massive military expenditures changed the debate between Republicans and Democrats and between liberals and conservatives from "should there be a sizeable increase?" to "how much of a sizeable increase?" And on the domestic side, Reagan's advocacy of major budget cuts changed the debate from "how should the government slow its growth?" to "how deeply should we cut social programs?" Clearly, Reagan's distinctive policy interests—cuts in social programs, reduction in the size of government, opposition to the Equal Rights Amendment, support for a constitutional amendment banning abortions, militant anti-communism, and upgrading of defense capabilities—fundamentally altered the range of acceptable policy options. In fact, no one should have been surprised at the general direction of the Reagan Administration. While few would have predicted the resounding legislative successes of his early administration, Reagan's presidential agenda was remarkably similar to the issues and themes he addressed during the 1980 campaign; his campaign rhetoric also foreordained many of his legislative proposals and administrative appointments. Because of these patterns, the 1980 race represents an unusual opportunity to show how campaigns influence political agendas and public policies (for Reagan as well as other political leaders).

Second, campaigns are important for communication styles—how candidates (and presidents) present themselves and their positions to the public. Reagan gained an extraordinary amount of public sympathy (plus a temporary extension of his presidential honeymoon) for a calm and even humorous reaction to an assassination attempt. Seeing his White House aides the morning after surgery, he said, "Hi fellas, I knew it would be too much to hope that we could skip a staff metting." Told that the government was running smoothly, he asked indignantly, "What makes you think I'd be happy about that?"[19] These bursts of humor were not new to Reagan. Throughout his political career, he has used humor, clever symbolism, and down-to-earth anecdotes to fashion a reputation as a "great communicator." During the 1980 campaign, Reagan often used his wit to make political points, once describing the three Democratic candidates as "Jerry Brown, who's on both sides of every issue; Ted Kennedy, who's on the *wrong* side of every issue, and Jimmy Carter, who still doesn't know what the issues are."[20] In fact, some media reporters attributed Reagan's early popularity as president to the rhetorical skills he developed through a series of campaigns. Although these attributions are difficult to prove, the fact that many influential political participants *believed* them to be true gave Reagan an important resource with Congress—the ability to appeal over its head to public opinion. Combined with an early image of invincibility within the Washington community, Reagan created a reservoir of goodwill and popular support for himself.

Third, as Fenno has noted in his study of House races, campaigns are important for democracy. A race for the presidency requires candidates to make many substantive decisions. With their campaign speeches, they establish a policy agenda—choices of issues, levels of specificity, and direction of appeals. In making decisions on campaign visits, campaigners emphasize certain constituencies while de-emphasizing others. And by their styles of communication, presidential contenders create a public "persona." Campaigns are also relevant for representation because they serve as a means of two-way communication between candidates and the public. Elections require that campaigners demonstrate public support in a variety of settings. Presidential aspirants spend months and sometimes years on the campaign trail—meeting constituents, hearing questions, and articulating their political positions. While their public presentations give them a chance to inform the public, these activities also allow the public to educate candidates. As candidates deliver their messages before diverse audiences, constituencies give them informal feedback through the "warmth" of their reactions. No activity other than campaigning places political leaders in more intimate contact with the general public.

In sum, presidential campaigns have their share of comedy, drama, and horror. But it would be a mistake to conclude that campaigns are useful only for entertainment. Presidential contests have many long-term implications. They influence party coalitions. They mold the political agenda. They shape the communication styles of leaders. And ultimately, they tell us much about the state of American democracy. Because no race in recent history has had more policy consequences than that of 1980, we should learn as much as possible about this campaign.

DATA AND METHODS

This analysis of campaign coalition-building is an exploratory study. By nature of the topic, it lies more in the area of what Fenno calls "soaking and poking" than hypothesis-testing. I chose this approach because little has been written describing the perspectives of candidates and their advisors. Unlike the voting studies field, which has accumulated twenty-five years of data and research, the campaign area only recently has begun to receive the same level of detailed treatment. For this reason, I decided to follow an inductive, rather than deductive, approach (see Appendix II for notes on conducting campaign research).

To study candidate strategies in the 1980 presidential campaign, I collected six data bases about various aspects of coalition formation. First, for the views of campaigners, I relied on published interviews with candidates and personal interviews with candidates' top advisors. I conducted ninety in-depth interviews with advisors to the ten major Republican and Democratic contenders (Anderson, Baker, Brown, Bush, Carter, Connally, Crane, Dole, Kennedy, and Reagan). These interviews, which I undertook between December, 1979 and March, 1981, were open-ended and lasted from twenty to ninety minutes (with the average being forty-five minutes). The interview list (see Appendix I) consisted of campaign managers, national political directors, press secretaries, field organizers, media advisors, pollsters, direct mail specialists, directors of scheduling, and research directors. Unless otherwise attributed, all quotations used in this book come from these interviews. For documentation of the interviews, Appendix I lists the interview date and campaign position for all the advisors.

During these interviews, I elicited responses with direct and indirect questions. For example, I asked about the type of constituencies and the nature of the electoral coalition that the candidate was attempting to bring together and the reasons for choosing that path. For indirect confirmation about their coalitional strategies, I asked about the types of campaign audiences before which candidates appeared and the types of people whom the candidates tried to reach with direct mail and media advertising. In addition, I questioned advisors about the conditions that influenced their coalition-building and the tactics through which they communicated their strategies to the public. Since I interviewed several people in each campaign organization (ranging from four in the Dole organization to fifteen Carterites), I cross-checked all responses for consistency before describing the candidates' strategies. And as a final check on accuracy, I compared the interview responses with published press accounts and unpublished staff memos on campaign strategies when those memos were available.

Second, I spent twenty-four days in the early primaries traveling with various candidates to observe their presentational styles. These travels took me through the early contests in New Hampshire, Vermont, Massachusetts, and Illinois. My aim was to observe candidates in their natural settings. As they campaigned for national office, I studied their rhetoric and symbolism to determine how they were presenting themselves to the public. Although it was difficult to report these observations in this research, the traveling helped give me a "feel" for presidential campaigning.

Third, I supplemented these interviews and observations with "harder" data sources. For a quantitative analysis of campaign rhetoric, I conducted a content analysis of candidate speeches delivered between November, 1979 and November, 1980. These data, described at greater length in chapter 4, allowed me to explore the rhetorical roots of coalition-building, i.e., how candidates used rhetoric to communicate their policy ideas and coalitional strategies.

Fourth, in order to study how campaigners allocated their time among different constituencies, I collected candidates' daily travel schedules from November, 1979 to November, 1980. This research, reported in chapter 5, represents a systematic effort to investigate the relation between candidates and their constituencies, as expressed in campaign visits.

Fifth, I tabulated travel information as reported in newspapers to compare press coverage of campaign travels with the actual visits listed on candidate itineraries. This information, which I also report in chapter 5, is used to show how one gets different impressions of coalition-building from the press as opposed to candidate travel schedules.

Sixth, I analyzed audience reactions to candidate speeches (chapter 7). This investigation relied on audio tapes of 178 speeches taken during the nominating and general election campaigns. These data enabled me to explore the ways candidates receive feedback about their presentations while they are on the campaign trail.

While this research rests on numerous data bases, I would be remiss not to note its boundaries. I do not investigate mass voting behavior in the 1980 presidential campaign. Since scholars have studied voters to the virtual exclusion of candidates and their advisors, I seek to fill this gap by concentrating on campaigners. There also are inherent limitations to studying a single election cycle. While one can compare patterns from 1980 with those that scholars found in previous elections (and I do so when possible), I tried to keep in mind the idiosyncracies of the 1980 campaign when developing generalizations about leadership and coalition-building. Finally, this research discusses electoral coalition-building by major party candidates during nominations and the general election. With the exception of Anderson's independent candidacy, it does not consider the efforts of ''minor'' candidates.

OUTLINE OF THE RESEARCH

The outline of this book is as follows. Chapter 2 describes the changing nature of the nominating process, political parties, campaign technologies, and the mass media. In particular, I show how these changes affect the way campaigners calculate their political opportunities and risks, and therefore how they play out their ambitions in the electoral process. In chapter 3, I discuss coalition-building in the new electoral system. Specifically, what factors did they consider as they devised their coalitional strategies? What was the interplay of electoral and policy motivations? And what do these things tell us about coalition formation and the prospects for realignment? Chapters 4 to 6 cover the variety of electoral tactics that candidates use to communicate their coalitional approaches. Campaign strategies were not simply ''issue-based'' phenomena (although issues were part of the mix); rather candidates communicate through rhetoric (chapter 4), campaign visits to particular constituencies (chapter 5), and symbolic appeals (chapter 6). Basically, I found that the messages delivered through these tactics were quite consistent. Instead of being expedient, manipulative, or inconsistent, they were mutually reinforcing. In chapter 7, I investigate feedback mechanisms and suggest a reason for the lack of policy discussions in presidential campaigns. Candidates do not discuss policy because, relative to other topics, audiences do not reward them for doing so. Finally, in chapter 8, I conclude the research by discussing the broader links between campaigns and governance. Do campaign activities help us predict leader behavior? Is there a relation between presidential campaigns and the policy process? And does this research tell us anything about political leadership and coalition-building, particularly in regard to the election of Ronald Reagan? For those readers who seek a chronological account of the campaign, I list the campaign's major events from 1978 to 1981 (Appendix III) and election results from the nominating process (Appendix IV) and general election (Appendix V).

NOTES

1. Personal interview with Richard Wirthlin, February 19, 1981. In the following chapters, all quotations come from personal interviews listed in Appendix I unless otherwise attributed.

2. The Michel quote comes from Irwin Arieff, "Bowing to Reagan's Wishes, Lawmakers Took Bold Steps to Reduce Government Role," *Congressional Quarterly Weekly Report*, 39, no. 51 (December 19, 1981), p. 2507; Baker's statement is cited in David Hess, "Congress Has Ended New Deal," *Philadelphia Inquirer* (December 18, 1981), p. 6A.

3. William Riker, *A Theory of Political Coalitions* (New Haven, Conn.: Yale University Press, 1962).

4. Robert Axelrod, "Where the Votes Come From," in Jeff Fishel, ed., *Parties and Elections in an Anti-Party Age* (Bloomington: Indiana University Press, 1978), pp. 86–99. Also see John Petrocik, *Party Coalitions* (Chicago: University of Chicago Press, 1981).

5. The classic in this area is Nelson Polsby and Aaron Wildavsky, *Presidential Elections*, 5th ed. (New York: Scribners, 1980).

6. V. O. Key, "Secular Realignment and the Party System," *Journal of Politics*, 21 (May, 1959), pp. 198–210 and "A Theory of Critical Elections," *Journal of Politics*, 17 (February, 1955), pp. 3–18; James Sundquist, *Dynamics of the Party System* (Washington, D.C.: Brookings, 1973).

7. Paul Abramson, John Aldrich, and David Rohde, *Change and Continuity in the 1980 Elections* (Washington, D.C.: Congressional Quarterly Press, 1982).

8. Richard Fenno, *Home Style* (Boston: Little, Brown, 1978).

9. Xandra Kayden, *Campaign Organization* (Lexington, Mass.: D. C. Heath, 1978) and Polsby and Wildavsky, *Presidential Elections*.

10. Robert Agranoff, *The New Style in Election Campaigns* (Boston: Holbrook Press, 1972) and Larry Sabato, *The Rise of Political Consultants* (New York: Basic Books, 1981).

11. Walter Dean Burnham, *Critical Elections and the Mainsprings of American Politics* (New York: W. W. Norton, 1970).

12. Anthony Downs, *An Economic Theory of Democracy* (New York: Harper, 1957) and David Mayhew, *Congress: The Electoral Connection* (New Haven, Conn.: Yale University Press, 1974).

13. Fenno, *Home Style* and Benjamin Page, *Choices and Echoes in Presidential Elections* (Chicago: University of Chicago Press, 1978).

14. Murray Edelman, *The Symbolic Uses of Politics* (Urbana: University of Illinois Press, 1964).

15. Garry Trudeau, "Doonesbury," *Louisville Courier-Journal* (April 18, 1979).

16. Gerald Pomper, *Elections in America*, 2nd ed. (New York: Longmans, 1980) and Jeff Fishel, *From Presidential Promise to Performance* (Washington, D.C.: Congressional Quarterly Press, forthcoming).

17. Douglas Hibbs, "Political Parties and Macroeconomic Policy," *American Political Science Review*, 71 (December, 1977), pp. 1467–1487.

18. The groundbreaking work on agenda formation is Roger Cobb and Charles Elder, *Participation in American Politics: The Dynamics of Agenda-Building* (Boston: Allyn and Bacon, 1972). See also James Sundquist, *Politics and Policy* (Washington, D.C.: Brookings, 1968).

19. Cited in Paul Boller, Jr., *Presidential Anecdotes* (New York: Oxford University Press, 1981), p. 356.

20. Reagan delivered these lines February 18, 1980 at a Federation of Republican Women forum in Portsmouth, New Hampshire.

2

The Changing Nature of Presidential Campaigns

Presidential campaigns have changed dramatically during the past two decades. At the institutional level, primaries have proliferated, the media have gained influence, party organizations have lost control over key resources, and procedural changes have "opened up" the process for more broadly based participation.[1] These changes have been accompanied by increases in the "independence" of voters, a decline in voter turnout, and growth of public mistrust and cynicism.[2] The campaign audience also has fragmented into a bewildering variety of interest groups, political action committees, and "single-issue" lobbies.[3] And to accentuate their dilemmas, presidential contenders must operate within such a complex system with its long campaigns, numerous participants, and confusing rules that campaigns often appear to be more of an endurance contest than a meaningful race for the presidency. So profound have these developments been that we now see titles such as *The New American Political System* and *Parties and Elections in an Anti-Party Age* and find arguments of fundamental shifts in the presidential selection process.[4]

Although writers give these trends considerable attention, they have not devoted much time to the impact of these changes on campaigners. This chapter explores the effects of recent changes in presidential campaigns on candidates and their advisors. What are their views of the contemporary campaign environment? How do they see their political opportunities and risks? To answer these questions, I compared the "old" and "new" electoral systems and found that campaigners were very aware of the rules of the game as well as the overall campaign environment. These institutional settings influenced their strategic calculations and therefore demonstrate the importance of candidate perceptions in presidential campaigns.

THE "OLD" ELECTORAL SYSTEM

From the time of Franklin Roosevelt to John Kennedy (1930s to the early 1960s), presidential campaigns were marked by four qualities: uneventful nominating processes, a stable party system, limited technologies, and compliant media.[5] According to William Keech and Donald Matthews, nominating contests during this period produced few surprises.[6] For the party that controlled the presidency, the nominating process usually served to ratify the incumbent or his handpicked successor. Until 1968, when the electoral system began to change, the only president or "heir" denied renomination was Harry Truman in 1952. More commonly, the rule was a "free ride" to the nomination: Roosevelt in 1936, 1940, and 1944; Truman in 1948; Eisenhower in 1956; Nixon in 1960; and Johnson in 1964. In the "out" party, that is, the one without the presidency, the situation was less clearcut. But generally, prenomination front-runners won their party's nomination: Landon in 1936, Dewey in 1944; Stevenson in 1956; and Kennedy in 1960. Only in cases when there were two strong contenders (Dewey and Stassen in 1948 and Eisenhower and Taft in 1952) or no clear leader (1940 and 1964) did the nominating process determine the nominee. Because of these patterns, it was not surprising that scholars devoted their attention to general elections rather than caucuses, primaries, or nominating conventions; fall elections were the only strongly contested stage of the process.

Political parties during this period also lent stability to elections. At the organizational level, party leaders provided "glue" for the system. Since they controlled key resources—ballot access, money, volunteers, and jobs—party regulars were able to restrict entry to the nominating game.[7] Of course, occasionally there were "dark horse" candidates for the presidency. For example, Wendell Willkie in 1940 swept the Republican nominating convention. At other times (mainly in the late 1800s and early 1900s), party bosses put forth political novices whom they could control. But generally, inexperienced candidates were excluded from presidential competition until they completed the required apprenticeship. Similarly, the strong ties between parties and voters stabilized the "old" electoral system. Following Roosevelt's success in forging the New Deal coalition, Democratic voters provided core support for enduring Democratic majorities in the House and Senate. In fact, the most common explanation of general election voting behavior during this era centered on voters' "party identifications." Using survey data from the 1950s, Angus Campbell, Philip Converse, Warren Miller, and Donald Stokes argued that party affiliations represented the most important determinant of voting.[8] Instead of relying on issue positions or evaluations of candidate qualities, citizens voted their party leanings. There were several reasons for the influence of party in the electorate. Because party identifications constituted longstanding psychological attachments, they were thought to remain stable from election to election. Party support also persisted across generations because parents passed party preferences to their children. And since surveys indicated that many voters made up their minds early in presidential contests (often in support of their party's nominee), voter preferences were not "destabilized" by campaign activities—candidate strategies, media advertising, campaign speeches, and press coverage.[9]

At the same time, candidates in the old electoral system were limited in their campaign technologies. Computerized direct mail, one of the more common modern technologies, was nonexistent; it would not develop until the mid–1960s. Television hit the national scene in 1952 when the networks broadcast party nominating conventions. But it did not supplant radio and print outlets until a decade later. Meanwhile, for much of this era, public opinion polls were in their infancy. Although the polling industry emerged in the 1930s, two well-publicized flops undercut its legitimacy. In 1936, using mass mailings to telephone subscribers, the *Literary Digest* magazine predicted a landslide victory for Republican Alfred Landon, only to see Roosevelt reelected overwhelmingly. And in 1948 several major pollsters erroneously predicted a Dewey victory over Truman. Perhaps with rightful skepticism, it was not until 1960 (in the Kennedy campaign) that candidates began to incorporate polling into their strategic arsenals.[10]

Finally, news organizations in the old electoral system often were nonassertive or compliant (at least in comparison with contemporary news gatherers). While media reporters sometimes uncovered "scandals," such as the *New York Post* exposing Nixon's secret "slush" fund in 1952, more often than not they looked the other way. Presidents Roosevelt and Kennedy were famous for their "collegial" relations with the media, an atmosphere that encouraged narrow definitions of news. Unlike the "adversary journalism" and "new journalism" that developed later, reporters usually stuck to "hard news," the "who, what, where, when, and how" approach. Activities that fell outside this boundary (for example, national security issues, classified materials, news interpretation, extramarital affairs, and drinking problems) were not news. Hence, political leaders were able to engage in unpublicized romantic affairs; more important, they were able to campaign and govern without adversary relations with the media.

In summary, the old system had distinctive features. The nominating process was predictable. There were few primaries; most delegates were selected through caucuses where party leaders exercised considerable influence. Presidents generally had a free ride to renomination; the "in-party" challenge was the exception, not the rule. Dark horse candidates were rare. Party identifications in the electorate were strong and stable from election to election. Voters often followed the dictates of party affiliation at the ballot box. Campaign technologies were relatively unsophisticated. And media reporters restricted themselves to hard news, with little effort at interpretation.

THE "NEW" ELECTORAL SYSTEM

By the mid–1960s and continuing through the 1970s, presidential campaigns underwent a metamorphosis. Because of the proliferation of primaries, the nominating process became less predictable. According to F. Christopher Arterton, the number of convention delegates selected through presidential primaries between the 1920s and 1960s stayed roughly the same (around 35 to 40 percent of delegates); the number of primaries was also stable, with each party averaging about fifteen primaries.[11] But starting in the 1960s, this pattern began to change. Among Democrats, the number of primaries went from seventeen (45.7 percent of delegates) in 1964 to fifteen (40.2 percent) in 1968, twenty-two (65.3 percent) in 1972, thirty (76.0 percent) in 1976, and thirty-five (71.8 percent) in 1980. Although Republicans generally lagged behind the Democrats in party reform, their nominating process followed suit, going from seventeen primaries in 1964 to thirty-six in 1980.[12]

With the rapid increase in primaries, candidates have become willing to contest presidential renominations. Going back to 1968, Eugene McCarthy and later Robert Kennedy used the nominating process and dissatisfaction with the Vietnam War to challenge the incumbent, Lyndon Johnson. Likewise, in 1972 two little-known House members (John Ashbrook and Paul McCloskey) opposed the nomination of President Nixon, while in 1976, Ronald Reagan contested President Ford's renomination. And, again in 1980, a nationally known senator (Edward Kennedy) and the governor (Edmund Brown, Jr.) of a major state tried to take the nomination away from President Carter. In comparing these trends to those that preceded them, one sees that contrary to the conclusions of Keech and Matthews for the nominating period since 1936, presidents (or their hand-picked successors) no longer receive a free ride to the nomination. Presidents now are approaching the point where a challenge is more the rule than the exception. But even more important than the *number* of "in-party" challengers is the *type* of candidates challenging presidents. Excluding Robert Kennedy, in-party challengers during the late 1960s and early 1970s tended to be candidates who were not nationally known, people like McCarthy, Ashbrook, and McCloskey. In part, ambitious but little-known candidates were willing to gamble precisely because they had little to lose. Since they had few chances to achieve national prominence in other ways, they opted for risky and long-shot challenges to presidential renominations. Increasingly, however, in-party challengers are prominent and nationally known candidates (Reagan in 1976 and Kennedy and Brown in 1980). While one can explain Reagan's risk-taking behavior in 1976 on the incumbent's unelected status and Reagan's advanced age, both Kennedy and Brown had political futures that lay far ahead of them. So their challenges suggest a fundamental "opening up" of the nominating process since the mid–1960s.

These changes have led scholars to reassess their research agenda. Owing to these structural changes (more presidential primaries, a greater public role in the nomination stage, and more broadly based participation), writers such as John Aldrich and Thomas Marshall are now investigating the nominating process. Generally, they argue that explanations based on party affiliation are less relevant in the nominating process than the general election, since each party holds separate nomination contests. While the separation is not complete, parties prevent voters from using party labels to discriminate among candidates by listing challengers of different parties on separate ballots. They also are finding that when one approaches the campaign from a one- or two-year perspective, short-term campaign forces appear more important than previously indicated. When voters and activists start the nomination process having few preconceived ideas about presidential contenders, personal campaigning, media appeals, and candidate strategies are more important than in the old electoral system; with the sequential nature of primary and caucus contests (which one columnist referred to as the new American soap opera), candidates have time and feedback from periodic election results to build their "momentum" in a variety of political settings.

Political parties in the new electoral system have also undergone major changes. Party leaders have lost their monopoly over key resources. Candidates now raise most of their own money (with the exception of federal campaign subsidies) and develop their own personal campaign organizations, with staff numbering in the hundreds. "Boss" control of the nominating process has faded before the onslaught of primaries, insurgent delegate challenges, dark horse candidates, and court rulings that outlawed strict ballot access rules; long-shot successes by McGovern in 1972, Carter in 1976, and Anderson and Bush in 1980 all but eliminated the "gate-keeping" functions of party leadership.[13] Furthermore, party loyalties in the electorate have weakened. In the 1950s, three out of four adults identified with the major parties. By the 1970s, this figure had declined to 63.5 percent. Conversely, the number of party "independents" (those not identifying with either major party) rose from 21.8 to 34.8 percent.[14] These contrasts led some observers to conclude that the country had gone from a "two-party" to a "no-party" system.[15]

Along with these changes, new and sophisticated campaign technologies have developed—television, polling, and direct mail. In an article entitled "The Making of the President Ain't What It Used to Be," Theodore White (the longtime chronicler of presidential contests) noted how technologies have transformed campaigns and created new centers of influence:

Specialists now conduct campaigns. The men who understand the Media Map are the media masters. In the back rooms they are joined by other specialists—in public-opinion polling, in direct mail, in street and telephone canvassing, in ethnic analysis. Anyone who has the direct ear of the candidate is now styled a "strategist"; the old-fashioned hatchet man out on the road is now styled a "surrogate."[16]

These technologies have improved the candidates' tools for mobilizing popular support. Television enables campaigners to bypass party leaders and elected officials and communicate directly with voters. Public opinion polls give organizers systematic feedback about voter concerns, candidate standings, and media appeals. And direct mail (what Larry Sabato calls the "poisoned pen of politics") allows presidential aspirants to "target" finely honed messages to particular constituencies. With these technologies, candidates have tools (albeit expensive ones) that were unavailable in the old electoral system.

Although these changes are dramatic breaks in the landscape, no discussion of the new electoral system can be complete without considering news organizations. In various forms, the media have always been important in American politics. But for a variety of reasons, news reporters have unprecedented influence in the election process. The decline of parties (to which the media contributed) has created new opportunities for reporters, especially in the "winnowing" process. Media figures play a crucial role in defining the "serious" candidates, those who are expected to do well in the nominating process. For this reason, candidates usually cater to reporters. As an example, television cameramen at Kennedy campaign appearances usually warranted privileged treatment (even at the audiences' expense). At one small gathering for top insurance executives that I observed, camera crews crowded in front of the audience and obstructed the view of Kennedy. Complaining, one member of the audience shouted, "we want to see him too." Standing firm, a cameraman defended his position with the reply, "so does the nation." Needless to say, the candidate did not overrule the cameraman.

News reporters also have gained influence because of changes in their profession. Unlike the old electoral system where leaders developed collegial relations with reporters, the new system emphasizes adversary relations.[17] With presidential abuses in Vietnam, Watergate, and the Central Intelligence Agency, and the role that reporters played in exposing these scandals, the media became less compliant and more assertive in pursuing political leaders. Rather than sticking to hard news, anything from classified programs to romantic involvements became fair game for press coverage, particularly among those practicing "new journalism."[18] The adversary approach of the contemporary media even led one recent press secretary (Jody Powell) to describe his job as "being eaten to death slowly by worms."

In short, the new electoral system differs dramatically from the old process. With the proliferation of primaries, nominating contests have become long and unpredictable. In-party challenges are the rule, not the exception. Dark horse candidates have multiplied. Party loyalties are weak; short-term campaign forces (like personal campaigning, media appeals, and clever symbolism and rhetoric) enable candidates to build momentum. Party leaders have lost influence while specialists in new technologies have gained. And the media have become assertive power brokers.

CANDIDATES AND POLITICAL OPPORTUNITIES

The switch from an old to a new electoral system has not been lost on candidates and their advisors. Campaign organizers are aware that "system transformations" create new opportunities for candidates as well as new risks. Perhaps no race in recent memory illustrates the opportunities better than the 1980 presidential campaign. The new electoral system influenced candidate strategies in a variety of ways. For example, changes in the nominating process played a major role in the Kennedy and Brown decisions to challenge President Carter's renomination. Advisors to both candidates argued that the primary system (and the expanded influence of voters) provided realistic opportunities for intraparty challenges. According to Kennedy's brother-in-law Stephen Smith, who also served as campaign chairman:

through the primary system, there is an opportunity that gives a challenger a better chance. . . . There's a better opportunity than there was in '56 and perhaps a better one than there would have been in '60. Now as you open it up more with the opportunities to run and go before a primary electorate, there's a degree of chance that's perhaps greater than going before a closed convention party selection process. . . . You're dealing with a larger body of people to make a decision and a chance to put your case to them that's not being made more narrowly in a traditional sense by so-called political leaders that are much more apt to be conservative in protecting the incumbent or staying with an incumbent. . . . The traditional political leader would stay with an incumbent for a longer duration than perhaps the primary voters would.

Tom Quinn, Brown's longtime advisor and campaign chairman, similarly emphasized the opportunities that primaries provided:

It's pretty hard for me to believe that anybody would think it's impossible to challenge a sitting president. I don't believe that at all. I mean, clearly Kennedy and Brown both failed this year but that doesn't prove it can't be done. . . . With the proliferation of the number of direct primaries, it's possible to deny anybody a nomination. Reagan almost did that to Ford four years ago.

Of course, advisors cautioned that the existence of electoral institutions through which challengers could mobilize popular followings against a president was not the only reason for their challenges. Kennedy and Brown considered a variety of things when they thought about running. In Kennedy's case, dissatisfaction with Carter's leadership (especially the president's "malaise" speech) was important. Paul Kirk, Kennedy's national political director, put it this way:

In 1976, the Senator thought the Democratic party had a chance to reestablish itself and provide certain directions and progress and vision for the country and things he felt needed to be done. Carter's election provided that opportunity. . . . But after two and one-half to three years, it became apparent to the Senator that that kind of vision and leadership really wasn't there, that an opportunity was being missed. It became almost explicit in Carter's own words that he felt his reponsibility in leading the national dialogue was telling people that this is really the best that we can do and that it really doesn't make much of a difference who is in charge of the problems, that they're too complex. Then he gave the speech after Camp David about malaise and in a sense blamed the people for some of the problems that existed in the country.

Meanwhile, Brown had a history of risk-taking. Quinn noted that:

he is more willing to take the risk. The only other person that seemed at all likely to get in was Kennedy. I did not think it was at all likely that Hugh Carey or Pat Moynihan, those I can think of, would be willing to get in and battle it out with a sitting president. . . . They tend to be fairly cautious people. They're just a different personality than Brown. He's willing to take risks where other politicans are not.

And both candidates obviously were encouraged by Carter's "soft" support and personal unpopularity. According to Kirk, "our feeling was that the support for Carter was not and perhaps even today is not all that substantial or deep or deeply-felt." Kennedy speech writer Robert Shrum also said that "there was a perception that it was certainly . . . do-able. I mean, nobody started off thinking it was a kamikaze mission." And Quinn explained that, "Jerry was convinced in his mind, we all were, that Carter was not likely to be reelected," although this was all "pre-Iran and Afghanistan." But despite the various rationales, the open nominating process and the possibility of appealing over the heads of party leaders to the public were major parts of the decision to run.

Once Kennedy and Brown entered the race, weak party discipline (namely, the president's inability to "punish" intraparty challengers) allowed them to stay in the race despite early setbacks. Kennedy stayed in the race until the convention, and Brown persisted even though he garnered only one delegate in the early caucuses and primaries. Their campaign advisors argued that Kennedy and Brown persevered because their political risks were limited. Shrum explained Kennedy's persistence after the June primaries this way:

We weren't losing anything by staying in. I mean, a few people would grumble. We had to deal with the newspaper reporters who would say, "Why are you staying in? I mean, you can't win the nomination." . . . And *that* wasn't even true. I mean, there was some outside chance to win the nomination. . . . There was always the possibility that an event would occur that would damage Carter very severely to the point where the party didn't want to nominate him.

Shrum also argued that Carter's "soft" support made his delegates vulnerable to daily events in Iran or the economy between the primaries and the convention. Similarly, Walter McGuire, Brown's director of scheduling, supported Brown's candidacy after poor early showings:

At the end of New Hampshire, I think, the things that were going through his mind were, one, let's wait. Kennedy's going to fall off. And everybody knew and I think even the Carter people knew that Carter . . . was just rolling off the edge. I mean, no one knew how long he'd hold on and everybody to this day is surprised that he hung on so long, long enough to get the nomination. So you had two people who were in pretty bad shape. We were in worse shape, but we had nowhere to go but up. So it was like, can you hold on and see what happens, even for a month? You'd hate to get out, then see no alternative.

In short, the decline of strong voter attachments unleashed the possibility of "volatility" in the delegate selection process. That prospect, combined with the president's inability to "pressure" challengers, led them to stay in the race.[19]

The unpredictable nature of the new electoral system also encouraged dark horse candidates for the presidency. Although Baker, Connally, Reagan, and, to a lesser extent, Dole had national name recognition, Anderson, Bush, and Crane prided themselves on being the "asterisk" candidates or the "darkest of all possible dark horses." On a national interview show, Bush said, "I don't profess to be a household word, but the enormity of the public attention, it comes from winning or doing better than you think I will do in Iowa. . . . We forget that Carter went in there at one percent . . . and came out of Iowa number 1."[20] And Anderson did not hide his limited resources: "We are still the low-budget candidate of all of those in the race. We don't have $4–1/2 million or $10 million as some of the others do."[21] Despite their limited prospects, these candidates saw opportunities in the open nominating process. By campaigning long and hard, campaign organizers believed that unknown contenders could "break out of the pack." Richard Williamson, Crane's campaign manager, put it this way:

the system is weighed so heavily in the horse race and your first states are small and your first states are much more person-to-person, as opposed to a situation where name ID is that tremendous a help. . . . Any one of those candidates could have been George Bush in Iowa. He was more intelligent, more intelligent in spending, more intelligent in the allocation of his time. But there weren't too many factors inherent that gave him a significant leg up. Yet he emerged at 30 percent, similar to what Jimmy Carter had done four years earlier.

Likewise, David Keene, Bush's national political director, explained that:

With a candidate like George Bush, his name recognition obviously was very low. Not very many people knew him. . . . Given a candidacy of that kind, we felt that what you had to do was pick out some early places and attempt by massing your forces in those places, like the Maine caucuses, the Florida convention, the Iowa caucuses, do something that would generate the kind of activity that would attract national media attention that would allow you to increase your recognition nationwide.

Anderson's strategy also took advantage of the opportunities that the new electoral system provided. William Bradford, one of his early organizers, noted that Anderson could do well in multicandidate primaries: "If there were only two candidates, we wouldn't do so well. But there are more than two. We will have our whole slice of the pie. Others will have to cut theirs."[22] And Dan Swillinger, another early campaign manager, emphasized the small-scale and sequential nature of the early primaries:

You can cut through on issues because you are speaking to a much smaller electorate. You are speaking to it not all at one time, but kind of serially so that when you are in New Hampshire, you can talk about Seabrook, you can talk about gun control, you can talk about heating oil, and things that really are of immediate concern to that electorate,

120,000 to 130,000 people voting in the Republican primary. . . . That's as many people as vote in a healthy congressional race.

In retrospect, these calculations appear to have been reasonable. Bush eventually emerged as the alternative to Reagan in the primaries and ultimately became the Republican vice-presidential nominee (and office-holder), while Anderson enjoyed a flurry of publicity that encouraged him to launch an independent
candidacy in the general election. These "successes" may encourage other long
shots in the future to see opportunities in the contemporary nominating process.

Changes in the campaign process have benefited candidates other than intraparty challengers and dark horses; the new electoral system also contributed to
Reagan's nomination and general election victories. Despite his frontrunner position, Reagan began his campaign with several potential problems: origins in
the right wing of the Republican party, policy positions that were out of the
political mainstream, inexperience in Washington, advanced age, and a background in acting. These weaknesses were serious enough that Carter strategist
Hamilton Jordan uncharitably predicted, "the American people are not going
to elect a seventy-year-old, right-wing, ex-movie actor to be president."[23] Others were no more kind; writing in March, 1980, columnist James Reston argued
that Reagan would turn out to be "Carter's favorite opponent."[24] Fortunately
for Reagan, the new system gave him opportunities to overcome (or divert attention from) these handicaps. The long nominating process gave Reagan the
chance to build support beyond the Republican right wing (see chapter 3); he
used the primaries to expand his solid core of conservative Republican constituencies into a full-fledged electoral coalition. As his chief strategist, Richard
Wirthlin, noted, "the first stipulation of our strategy was that we had to broaden
the base." Even more important, as Reagan defeated Republican opponents, he
brought their campaign organizers into his personal campaign organization: James
Baker (Bush's campaign manager); Richard Williamson (Crane's campaign
manager); Elizabeth Dole (Dole's wife), and James Brady (Connally's press
secretary), among others.[25]

The draining primary sequence also allowed Reagan to demonstrate his phys-
ical fitness. Notwithstanding Bush's incessant jogging and pleas from Crane and
Dole that they represented "younger Ronald Reagans," the sixty-nine-year-old
Reagan proved his endurance on the campaign trail.[26]

Furthermore, Reagan's effective media presence fit nicely with the new electoral system; given the importance of television (and televised debates), the
Californian's background in entertainment became a strength, not a weakness.
During the Illinois debate, Reagan addressed the age question by declaring that
wage and price controls had failed since the time of Roman Emperor Diocletian
and that "I'm the only one here old enough to remember."[27] And few can
forget Reagan's summary question in the general election debate with Carter:
"Are you better off than you were four years ago?"[28] In a media age, Reagan's electronic presence meshed perfectly with the skills required for the new
electoral system.

In addition, President Carter used the new process to his political advantage. As a clear beneficiary of the system in 1976, Carter had shown that the decline of political parties and rise of "candidate-centered" organizations allowed campaigners to appeal over the heads of party regulars directly to voters. According to Les Francis, executive director of the Democratic National Committee, the lesson of Carter's 1976 nomination was this:

the fact is that Jimmy Carter has benefited from the decline of parties. He, in 1975 and 1976, ran outside the system and got the nomination and the presidency precisely because the parties were weak. Where he was able to do well in the early stages, it was because he had his own personally oriented coalition and campaign organization. For example, in the Pennsylvania primary, those of us in the Carter camp beat the entire political establishment of the state, whether it was the party or organized labor or whatever. They just couldn't match us and so Carter is a beneficiary in the decline of the party or was in 1975 and 1976. In fact, I would have to say his candidacy probably had the effect of furthering that erosion of the party's strength because he proved as dramatically as anyone possibly could that you don't need the parties to win the nomination of the Democratic party.

And Tim Kraft, Carter's national campaign chairman, noted that:

The fragmentation of single-interest groups and the proliferation of primaries just opens the whole thing up a lot more. If you had a Jimmy Carter who is two years out of office as a one-term governor of Georgia, he could not have been nominated in 1976 if you had not had the opening up of the party mechanism and the democratization of that process. . . . I'm reluctant to see single-interest politics tear at the fabric of the state party organizations and even at the two major parties. But this sort of opening up of the process has certainly helped somebody like Carter.

Of course, in 1980, because he occupied the presidency, there were other opportunities available to him. With the office of the presidency and the power of television, Carter used the crises in Iran and Afghanistan to justify a "Rose Garden" strategy for the nomination. Like Presidents Nixon and Ford before him,[29] Carter found that "being presidential" at the White House generated as much media coverage as personal campaigning. Rather than taking his "show" on the road, Carter brought representatives of key constituencies to Washington (while also sending numerous "surrogates" on the hustings). At the same time, Carter was not reticent about using the huge increase in federal discretionary grants since the 1960s to reward supporters and punish opponents. In a prenomination memo (January 17, 1979), Carter strategist Hamilton Jordan described a chief weakness of President Ford's 1976 campaign:

President Ford failed to utilize the advantages of incumbency and failed to minimize the disadvantages. He learned a very expensive lesson in the primaries which almost cost him his party's nomination. By the general election, President Ford, the White House staff and his campaign staff had learned to maximize the advantages and minimize the disadvantages, and consequently came very close to beating us.[30]

And the Carter staff also tried to improve their prospects by tinkering with the schedule of primaries and caucuses (an effort that succeeded in several states). According to Jordan:

It is absolutely essential that we win the early contests and establish momentum. If we win the early contests, it is difficult to see how anyone could defeat us for the nomination. Conversely, if we lose the early contest(s), it is difficult to see how we could recoup and win the nomination. . . . The easiest way to establish early momentum and stress the significant role of the south in the party is to win southern delegates by encouraging southern states to hold early caucuses and primaries. . . . It is in our interest to have states that we are likely to win scheduled on the same day with states that we might do poorly in.[31]

So in a variety of ways, Carter used the contemporary process to help him.

Finally, the decline of political parties altered the perceptions of one candidate (Anderson) in the general election. Traditionally (with the exception of Theodore Roosevelt in 1914, Strom Thurmond in 1948, and Eugene McCarthy in 1976), candidates accepted nomination outcomes as final judgments. If candidates did not receive their party's nomination, they accepted the verdict. However, in 1980, Anderson lost the nomination but used his primary support to justify an independent candidacy. His administrative assistant (later campaign manager), Michael McLeod, noted that:

the primary selection process in the Republican party did not accurately represent the mainstream concerns of most of the voters in the country. A very, very small percentage of people select the nominees in either party for that matter. And we felt, that is, what we then saw as the almost inevitable selection of Reagan, did not really reflect the political sentiment of the country, and that there was room this year in the political stew for a centrist-oriented moderate-to-liberal Republican candidate, someone who was basically fiscally conservative and socially liberal.

Perhaps the most interesting feature of Anderson's decision was how the campaign process influenced his judgment. Anderson extended Carter's view, espoused during the 1976 nomination fight, that party regulars were irrelevant to the general election. Although he lacked a major party base, Anderson continued his candidacy because he believed, according to McLeod, that the decline of party made the gamble worthwhile:

elites have failed to recognize the fact that parties are not as important as they used to be and in many respects are like spavine beasts rummaging around for the last few morsels. . . . Our candidacy is somewhat like the Reagan governorship. And that is, just as Reagan in his eight years in California went over the heads of the state legislators to the people, in a sense that's what we're doing too. We are saying to the country . . . that it's time to put country above party. . . . And we are very definitely going over the heads of the two parties.

In addition, Anderson's independent candidacy was even more damning of the major parties because it came from the center, not the extremes, of the political spectrum. Typically, candidates have bolted the major parties over emotional or ideological issues. For example, opposition to busing for purposes of racial desegregation fueled the Wallace campaign of 1968. And, before that, slavery (1860), populism (1892), socialism (1912), and progressivism (1912 and 1924) were instrumental issues. But Anderson bolted his party as a moderate, centrist candidate. While Anderson had deeply held beliefs, he did not emphasize issues at the fringe of the political spectrum. Rather, he discussed "mainstream" versions of fiscal conservatism and social liberalism. With his success (along with that of Libertarian Ed Clark and Citizens' party nominee Barry Commoner) in breaking ballot access barriers, Anderson may have increased the opportunities of future independent candidates.

In conclusion, the new electoral system influenced candidate perceptions of their opportunities (although some of these perceptions may have been inaccurate). The open nominating process played a major role in encouraging Kennedy and Brown to challenge President Carter's renomination and in leading dark horse candidates (Anderson, Bush, and Crane) to seek the presidency. The decline of party discipline allowed Kennedy and Brown to persist in the race after their chances were diminished. The long primary process and existence of mass media gave Reagan the opportunity to build a coalition beyond the Republican right wing. Television and the nominating process molded Carter's reelection strategy. And the weakness of parties encouraged Anderson to launch an independent candidacy in the fall.

CANDIDATES AND POLITICAL RISKS

With the opportunities available to presidential contenders in the new electoral system, it sometimes is easy to overlook the risks that the current situation creates for campaigners. The most obvious feature of the contemporary process is the unprecedented opportunities for young and ambitious leaders: intraparty challenges, dark horse candidacies, persistent challenges, mass media candidacies, Rose Garden strategies, and independent candidacies. But it would be a mistake to ignore the question of risk because the new system has raised a number of dilemmas for candidates (and presidents). The nominating process offers a means of challenging incumbents, increasing the visibility of dark horses, and broadening the base of "narrow" candidates. However, it also imposes huge financial and organizational burdens on candidates. As Richard Maullin, one of Brown's campaign cochairmen, pointed out, "while it is true that the increasing number of primaries offer the opportunities, they also impose a tremendous burden on the challenger to have a very effective organization and a lot of money very early. . . . [You need] some major 'first-blush' ability to capture resources."

Even with federal financial subsidies, presidential campaigns no longer are simple affairs. Campaign "mechanics" in the new system require considerable time and energy. Since organizers must build organizations, recruit consultants, raise money, and meet numerous filing deadlines for caucuses and primaries, candidates have to make their decisions to seek the presidency one to two years before the first delegate is selected.[32] The need for early decisions means that when campaigners make key strategic decisions (i.e., to run, emphasize particular issues, or aim for certain constituencies), they usually know little about campaign dynamics. For example, candidates and advisors may be unsure of their opposition. In 1980, President Ford's delay in rejecting a presidential bid (he announced his decision not to run October 19, 1979 and reaffirmed this position March 15, 1980) undercut the early organizational efforts of the moderate Republicans: Anderson, Baker, and Bush. Likewise, Brown made his decision to run long before it became clear that Kennedy would enter the race. And once the nominating process is underway, its unpredictable nature means that candidates can never be sure which contenders will gain momentum (even if only for limited periods). The unexpected emergence of Bush as the strong Republican moderate doomed Baker's candidacy while Anderson's short-lived success in the Republican primaries complicated the political fortunes of Bush (by attracting moderates) and Kennedy (by appealing to social liberals and Democratic voters).[33]

In addition, election organizers often know little about the campaign's political climate when they make crucial strategic decisions. Kennedy decided to run and emphasize the leadership issue several months before the Iranian hostage takeover and the Soviet invasion of Afghanistan. Obviously, there was no way he (or Brown) could have envisioned the dramatic effects: Carter's sharp rise in popularity; his new image as a strong leader; the change in agenda from domestic to foreign issues, and Carter's decision to stop personal campaigning and withdraw from political debates. Complaining about the way that Iran crowded economic issues off the national agenda, Carl Wagner, Kennedy's field director, argued that:

I have no evidence to suggest that people are not troubled by 20 percent inflation and 20 percent interest rates and 10 percent unemployment. . . . I agree . . . that those issues have not been the primary focus of this primary campaign. But I don't think that's because people don't care about them. I think it's because we've been unable to focus attention on them. And I suggest that we've been unable to focus attention on them largely because of Iran and its implications. . . . Between the third of November and probably the 15th of February, the first seven minutes of all three networks every night was Iran. . . . You want to talk about the ability to influence the national debate?[34]

Similarly, Baker's decision early in 1979 to build his campaign around the second Strategic Arms Limitation Treaty debate (SALT II) was undermined by changing world events. According to Bill Roesing, the political consultant who wrote Baker's strategy, the original reason for the "Senate" strategy was this:

We viewed the SALT debate as . . . turning the corner on our relations and attitudes toward negotiations with the Russians. . . . By being the leader of the movement to turn that corner . . . we were going to, in effect, hit Baker against Carter. And being the principal adversary to an unpopular president in the year before an election [isn't] an all-bad strategy.

Unfortunately for Baker, the long-planned SALT II debate never got underway because of international uncertainties (i.e., Soviet "adventurism") and the success of Senate opponents. In what became the ultimate irony, Baker's success in generating opposition to the treaty undercut his presidential forum. Doug Bailey, Baker's media consultant, noted:

It was delayed and delayed and delayed, partly because of the success of the effort of denying it votes. . . . The absence of the SALT debates and the absence of the issue hurt the Baker campaign because a lot of the decisions, including the time he could get into the race, were shaped by the decision to stay in the Senate long enough to participate in the SALT debate.

Hence, by the time Baker decided to develop campaign organizations in early states, precious time had elapsed. With no national forum and no discernible organization, Baker lost moderate constituencies to Bush.[35]

The need for early decisions in the new electoral system also means that campaigners must allocate their resources among primary and caucus states long before it becomes obvious which contests will be important. In the old electoral system, this problem did not exist; candidates either skipped the primaries (and relied on party leaders to gain nominations) or they entered the New Hampshire primary, which usually was first. However, in 1980, the relative importance of various nominating contests (straw polls at candidate forums and party gatherings, the Florida convention vote, the Maine caucuses, the Iowa caucuses, the Arkansas caucuses, the Puerto Rico primary, and the New Hampshire primary, among others) was not always clear, especially a year before these events began. Looking back at 1980, it is easy to see that Iowa and New Hampshire were *the* crucial early tests. But in studying the original strategies and allocational decisions that candidates were making in 1979 (such as where to develop organizations, which states to emphasize, and where to spend money), it is obvious that no consensus existed at that point among campaign advisors. As examples, in 1979, Connally and Baker were running "national" campaigns. Rather than focusing time, money, and energy on Iowa and New Hampshire (as Bush did), they allocated their travel time and financial expenditures nationwide. Connally's advisors argued that they had to build a national constituency because the "early route" was cut off to them. Lance Tarrance, who was Connally's pollster, said: "We all believed intuitively that if we went through trying to win in New Hampshire and Iowa . . . that we couldn't do it. . . . The Reagan people had gotten control in all the key states more or less since '76

. . . [and] had too many of the chips already called in.'' And Baker failed to develop organizations in Iowa and New Hampshire because his staff felt that with the national prominence the SALT II debate would give him in 1979 and his position as Senate minority leader, he could weather losses in early states. According to Roesing, ''It was not necessarily a cornerstone of our strategy that we had to win Iowa or New Hampshire. The thought was that we had to start winning in March and begin to unravel Reagan after that. . . . We thought that the Minority Leader of the Senate could raise enough money to stay in the race.'' Similarly, two dark horses placed little emphasis on Iowa: Anderson developed a ''four-state'' strategy that focused on New Hampshire, Massachusetts, Illinois, and Wisconsin, while Brown concentrated on early northeastern events. And Reagan himself did not anticipate the transformation of the Iowa caucuses into a major political event. In 1976, with a ''hot'' contest between Reagan and President Ford, the Iowa caucuses had attracted only 25,000 participants (on the Republican side). But by 1980, the explosion of media coverage and the heavy candidate use of media advertising boosted the Republican turnout to 120,000 and brought Iowa extensive national attention. Unfortunately for Reagan and his campaign manager, John Sears, early in 1979 they had decided to de-emphasize Iowa (not knowing that the media would ''hype'' the caucuses). Subsequently, Reagan spent little time or money there; he also was the only major Republican to skip the Iowa debate (as his press secretary Lyn Nofziger humorously put it later, Reagan attempted a Rose Garden strategy without having the Rose Garden). Reflecting on these decisions, Sears explained that the transformation of the Iowa caucuses into a miniature primary (with national consequences) undermined Reagan's original strategy:

We misled ourselves somewhat by failing to anticipate the size of the vote. We had a system and a level of expenditures and a campaign schedule that . . . we knew could deliver a little over 30,000 votes in the caucuses. That gave us 50 percent against the field up to 60,000 people. It was good protection all the way up to '80. Well, you know what—120,000 people voted in the damn things. . . . We didn't think that many people would vote. Therefore, we didn't do any direct mail. . . . As far as the debates were concerned, again if we'd known 120,000 people were going to vote in the thing, there wouldn't have been any problem about going to the debates.

Reagan's initial press secretary, Jim Lake, also argued that Iowa undercut the original emphasis on New Hampshire:

The cornerstone of our primary strategy [was] to win New Hampshire. . . . Everything was dedicated to winning New Hampshire. . . . Once New Hampshire was won, the organization, the work, the politics in all of those subsequent states like South Carolina, Florida, Illinois, and all of those, would be in place and done. . . . Iowa was a phenomena that developed. . . . Iowa has never been any factor in Republican politics. . . . Jimmy Carter made it such in 1976 in the Democratic party and we knew that there was going to be a difference. . . . [But] the strategy for Iowa was predicated on a normal caucus strategy. . . . We didn't spend any money for direct mail. We didn't spend any money for television except one last weekend 30-minute special. . . . Those are not things you do to turn people out to caucuses.

Campaigners face other uncertainties in the new electoral system. Although mass media and modern campaign technologies (polling and direct mail) give them unusual opportunities for communicating with voters, bypassing party leaders, challenging incumbents, and mobilizing popular support, these tools have their problems. First, the new technologies are very expensive. Television costs rose 64 percent from 1972 to 1976 (while the Consumer Price Index went up only 36 percent). And the costs of prime-time television doubled between 1976 and 1980.[36] Meanwhile, candidates can use direct mail to raise large sums of money from small contributors, but the initial investment is high. Richard Viguerie estimated that of the $2.8 million he raised for Crane's presidential effort, $2.3 million was spent to raise it.[37]

Second, the emergence of mass media has undercut the ability of campaigners to control the political agenda and has given rise to new, competing power centers outside the campaign: news reporters, columnists, and network executives. When Connally tried in 1979 to purchase national television time (a crucial requirement for his national campaign strategy), the networks refused to sell him time, saying that in their eyes, the "campaign" did not begin until January 1, 1980. Without strong organizations in early primary states, this decision effectively shut down the Connally campaign.

Third, the use of new technologies by "independent" groups creates problems of "image control" for candidates. According to Frank Donatelli, Reagan's regional political coordinator for Ohio, independent expenditures and media advertising are not always as helpful as they appear: "independent expenditures have the potential to hurt you as much as they help you if the information that is being conveyed by that particular group is not quite what you want, is not quite the image you want to portray, is not quite the issues that you want stressed, and so forth." In fact, polling research in South Dakota by one group, the National Conservative Political Action Committee, showed negative results in the electorate: "among those having seen the ads, twice as many voters were *more* likely than were less likely to vote for McGovern because of the ads."[38] Rather than helping campaigners use modern technologies, these groups sometimes shoot their favored candidates in the foot.

The new campaign process also has increased the risks confronting presidents. With the fluidity of nominations and the breakdown of party discipline, successful candidates cannot rest secure in office. Rather, they continuously must consider the electoral costs of their policies and potential threats to their office. This state of affairs was readily apparent to Carter officials. Writing a year before the first caucus, Hamilton Jordan argued that:

Over the two hundred year history of our country, the myth developed and was sustained by events that incumbent Presidents are always re-elected. . . . The history of

Presidential incumbents seeking re-election in recent history flies in the face of this historical presumption that all Presidential incumbents are re-elected. . . . The fact is that the fragmentation of political power within the party and the tremendous difficulty the modern President faces in finding practical and attractive solutions to this new generation of complex foreign and domestic problems make a serious challenge to an incumbent President much more likely.[39]

Based on the assumption that the most prominent opponent would be Kennedy, Carter decided to lay down the gauntlet. Speaking to a group of congressmen at a White House dinner on June 11, 1979, President Carter told the startled assembly that "if Kennedy runs, I'll whip his ass." Asked later about his response, Kennedy playfully remarked: "I'm sure the president must have been misquoted. I think what he meant to say was that he was going to whip inflation."[40] But whatever the president's intentions, it seems clear that the contemporary campaign environment helps to produce a "permanent campaign" mentality among presidents.[41]

Because of these developments, candidates face a difficult situation in the current period. The need for early organizations forces them to make important strategic decisions about their candidacies, coalitions, and agendas a year before the nominating process starts. Usually, they have limited knowledge about their opponents, the campaign's political climate, and the relative importance of early nominating contests.[42] Modern campaign technologies also offer "double-edged" opportunities; they reach many people but are expensive and subject to the control of others. Finally, the new process produces presidents who govern with one eye looking forward and one looking back.

CONCLUSION

In this chapter, I have explored the effects of the new electoral system on candidates and their advisors. How did they see their political opportunities and risks? Relying on cases from the 1980 presidential campaign, I argued that although campaigners had unprecedented opportunities, they also faced unusual risks. Candidates could challenge incumbents, run as dark horses, and use the campaign process to broaden their popular support. But the need for early strategies and organization also meant that they knew little about the campaign when they made key strategic decisions to run, enter certain nominating contests, and emphasize particular issues.

Reviewing these results, two potential problems stand out. First, one might dismiss the conclusions, saying they are idiosyncratic to 1980. After all, can research on a single election tell us anything about presidential campaigns in general? In part, this question raises a legitimate concern. Analysis of one election (even an interesting one such as that of 1980) limits the scope of the conclusions. Writers can not make definitive judgments about an era based on one contest. However, in comparing the patterns of 1980 with those that scholars have found in other recent elections, it appears that the 1980 presidential campaign represents a continuation of emerging trends in the new electoral system. Rather than being a deviation, the existence of "in-party" challenges and dark horses is consistent with other elections over the past fifteen years (and incongruent with races before 1960). Also, in asking campaign advisors about their rationales for various strategies (such as in-party challenges and dark horse candidacies), they cited key features of the new campaign process. Although Carter's unpopularity was one factor idiosyncratic to 1980 that encouraged renomination challenges, the existence of an open nominating process (especially the large number of primaries) made it possible for dissatisfied and ambitious challengers to capitalize on his unpopularity. Because the new electoral system shaped candidate strategies, it is probable that it represents a force larger than a single election.

Second, in exploring the way that candidates and advisors viewed their political opportunities and risks in the new electoral system, the gap between perceptions and "reality" is striking. With the benefit of hindsight, it is clear that several candidates in 1980 misperceived their political situations. As illustrated by Connally's national campaign, Baker and the SALT II treaty, Reagan and the Iowa caucuses, Brown's persistent candidacy after a miserable start, and Anderson's independent candidacy, expected opportunities sometimes failed to materialize while unexpected risks often arose. Since candidates occasionally are wrong, some writers have jumped to the conclusion that it makes little sense to consider candidates' perceptions of the campaign environment. Why study leaders when their beliefs are faulty? For example, people have used John Kingdon's "congratulation-rationalization effect" to show the foolishness of leader beliefs: winners congratulate themselves by exaggerating the effects of their campaigns while losers rationalize defeat by citing forces beyond their control.[43]

Despite these arguments, candidate perceptions are important (even if based on inaccurate facts or assumptions). Perceptions can be crucial because they influence the choices available to voters. One of the ironies of the new electoral system is that despite the decline of electoral institutions and rise of "mass politics," leaders still play an important role in elections. Voter choices depend heavily on the way that candidates see their opportunities and risks. Presidential aspirants who challenge incumbents, launch independent candidacies, run as dark horses, or propose distinctive policy positions give voters different choices than campaigners who reject these possibilities. If anything, "deinstitutionalization" has heightened the importance of leaders' perceptions.[44]

Leaders' beliefs also are important because their views of the process influence their coalitional strategies. Like those who study elections, many campaign organizers are unsure exactly why people vote the way they do. Bush advisor David Keene gave this honest appraisal: "we don't know, none of us, really what it is that people out there are going to make their decision on. It's a mix. . . . Part of it is the issues, part of it is something else, part of it is something very vague."[45] Yet because of their positions, many professionals have pet theories about "what really decides elections." For Doug Bailey, Baker's media advisor, the key factor is personal trust:

the major reasons why people vote the way they did, either way in 1976 and it would be equally true in 1980, it was a question of personal trust between the voter and their candidate. I don't mean trust just in an integrity sense, but a willingness to trust that person with the safety of the country, with the safety of the family, with the safety of the economy, and making decisions on a whole bunch of complicated issues that the voters are interested in but don't really understand and know they don't understand.

Meanwhile, Bush media advisor Robert Goodman suggested a less cerebral approach: "Voting is emotional. People vote feelings rather than fact. . . . Television is a feeling medium . . . and voting decisions are based more on perceptions and style than substance. . . . In most elections, the issue isn't foreign policy or inflation. The issue is really the human being."[46] In contrast, Sam Hoskinson, Connally's research director, emphasized the role of policy issues:

the voters are probably tired of hearing pious promises of good will and of "I'll try harder" kind of rhetoric from candidates. You know they had that. That's in some respect the lesson that people have learned about Jimmy Carter. There is a realization in the country that the 1980s are going to be a difficult decade, a different kind of decade. People are looking for men who have ideas. So I think probably there's a much greater scope for candidates to be idea candidates or issue candidates and this fits well with Connally because this is what he wants to be.[47]

While this list could go on, the important point is that these assumptions about voting influenced strategies of coalition-building (even though some of the assumptions were questionable). Bailey's television ads for Baker tried to convey trustworthiness. Goodman's views about "style" and "feelings" were reflected in Bush's early media advertising, much of which was not oriented to policy matters. And Connally's controversial speech on Mideast policy (which Hoskinson helped prepare) assumed that voters would respond favorably to a detailed statement on a major foreign policy issue.[48] Therefore, the study of coalition formation must incorporate information about the beliefs and behavior of campaigners.

In the next chapter, I explore coalition-building in the new electoral system. What influenced coalitional strategies? How did the new campaign environment affect these efforts? And what do these things tell observers about the prospects for realignment in the contemporary period?

NOTES

1. See William Crotty, *Political Reform and the American Experiment* (New York: Thomas Crowell, 1977); Stephen Wayne, *The Road to the White House* (New York: St.

Martin's, 1980), and Stephen Hess, *The Presidential Campaign,* rev. ed. (Washington, D.C.: Brookings, 1978).

2. Herbert Asher, *Presidential Elections and American Politics*, rev. ed. (Homewood, Ill.: Dorsey, 1980) and John Kessel, *Presidential Campaign Politics* (Homewood, Ill.: Dorsey, 1980).

3. See Anthony King, ed., *The New American Political System* (Washington, D.C.: American Enterprise Institute, 1978) and Marjorie Hershey and Darrell West, "Single-Issue Groups and Political Campaigns: Six Senatorial Races and the Pro-Life Challenge in 1980," paper presented at the annual meeting of the Midwest Political Science Association, Cincinnati, Ohio, April 16–18, 1981.

4. King, *New American Political System* and Jeff Fishel, ed., *Parties and Elections in an Anti-Party Age*, and James Ceaser, *Presidential Selection* (Princeton, N.J.: Princeton University Press, 1979), pp. 236–259.

5. For a review of campaigns before this period, see Ceaser, *Presidential Selection.*

6. William Keech and Donald Matthews, *The Party's Choice* (Washington, D.C.: Brookings, 1976).

7. See E. E. Schattschneider, *Party Government* (New York: Rinehart, 1942) and V. O. Key, *Politics, Parties and Pressure Groups*, 4th ed. (New York: Thomas Crowell, 1958).

8. Angus Campbell, Philip Converse, Warren Miller, and Donald Stokes, *The American Voter* (New York: John Wiley, 1960).

9. For a critique of this research, see Dan Nimmo, *The Political Persuaders* (Englewood Cliffs, N.J.: Prentice-Hall, 1970), pp. 1–6.

10. Polsby and Wildavsky, *Presidential Elections*, 5th ed., pp. 192–199 and Larry Sabato, *The Rise of Political Consultants.*

11. Figures taken from F. Christopher Arterton, "Campaign Organizations Confront the Media-Political Environment," in James David Barber, ed., *Race for the Presidency* (Englewood Cliffs, N.J.: Prentice-Hall, 1978), p. 7.

12. *Congressional Quarterly Weekly Report,* July 5, 1980, pp. 1870–1873.

13. Recent research suggests that state party organizations have more institutional vitality than usually thought. However, at the presidential level, candidate-centered organizations still outshadow state and national party organizations.

14. Figures cited in William Crotty and Gary Jacobson, *American Parties in Decline* (Boston: Little, Brown, 1980), p. 27.

15. The most prominent advocate of the party "de-alignment" thesis is Walter Dean Burnham. See his *Critical Elections and the Mainsprings of American Politics* (New York: W. W. Norton, 1970), chapter 5.

16. Quoted in Terry Sanford, *A Danger of Democracy* (Boulder, Colo.: Westview Press, 1981), p. 101. The original quote came from Theodore White, "The Making of the President Ain't What It Used to Be," *Life* (February, 1980), p. 67.

17. Of course, as Arterton suggests, the relationship is not completely adversary. Candidates still try to co-opt reporters by giving "scoops." And reporters sometimes tie their "stars" to rising candidates. But in comparing these patterns with the professional norms of "old" journalism, the contemporary situation appears far more contentious. See Arterton's "The Media Politics of Presidential Campaigns," in Barber, *Race for the Presidency*, pp. 26–54.

18. David Broder defends the increased assertiveness of journalists, saying that if reporters did not interpret campaign activities and put them in context, candidates would

mislead and manipulate unsuspecting voters. See his "Reporters in Presidential Politics," in Charles Peters and Timothy Adams, eds., *Inside the System* (New York: Praeger, 1970).

19. It is also possible under the new public finance rules that candidates will persist in the race because the flow of "matching" funds (for debt retirement purposes) requires them to continue to demonstrate electoral support.

20. *Issues and Answers* interview, October 21, 1979.

21. *Face the Nation* interview, February 3, 1980.

22. Quoted in Congressional Quarterly, *Candidates '80* (January, 1980), p. 27.

23. Cited by William Schneider, "The November 4 Vote for President: What Did It Mean?" in Austin Ranney, ed., *The American Elections of 1980* (Washington, D.C.: American Enterprise Institute, 1981), p. 212.

24. Cited by Charles Jones, "Nominating 'Carter's Favorite Opponent': The Republicans in 1980," in Ranney, *The American Elections of 1980*, p. 62. The original quotation came from James Reston, "Carter's Secret Weapon," *New York Times* (March 21, 1980), p. A27. For similar analyses, see James Sundquist and Richard Scammon, "The 1980 Election: Profile and Historical Perspective," in Ellis Sandoz and Cecil Crabb, Jr., eds., *A Tide of Discontent* (Washington, D.C.: Congressional Quarterly Press, 1981), p. 21; William Schneider, "The November 4 Vote for President," p. 244, and Gerald Pomper, *The Election of 1980* (Chatham, N.J.: Chatham Publishers, 1981), p. 115.

25. The Reagan experience suggests that organizational outreach may be more important than staff unity. Reagan won the nomination and general election with an organization that experienced turnover and internal conflict. Meanwhile, Carter lost despite having a staff that was reasonably stable, united, and free of rancor.

26. However, Reagan's age occasionally showed through. In question and answer sessions, he sometimes experienced difficulty hearing questions from audiences. At one appearance in New Hampshire, where a teacher was using sign language to communicate Reagan's message to deaf students, reporters joked among themselves that she should turn around and provide the same service for Reagan.

27. "Reagan: Secret of Success," *Newsweek* (April 7, 1980), p. 27.

28. See the debate text in *Congressional Quarterly Weekly Report* (November 1, 1980), p. 3289.

29. For a discussion of Ford's Rose Garden strategy in 1976, see F. Christopher Arterton, "Campaign Organizations Confront the Media-Political Environment," in James David Barber, ed., *Race for the Presidency* (Englewood Cliffs, N.J.: Prentice-Hall, 1978), pp. 18–19.

30. Reported by Martin Schram, "Carter," in Richard Harwood, ed., *The Pursuit of the Presidency* (New York: Berkley Books, 1980), p. 88.

31. Ibid., p. 92.

32. Because the new electoral system requires early decisions, several candidates (Bush, Connally, Dole, and Reagan) established political action committees soon after the 1976 election. Others made early announcements of their presidential candidacies (such as Crane announcing August 2, 1978).

33. Candidates also can misjudge where potential competitors might harm them in the nominating process. When Carter forces were trying in 1979 to "juggle" the primary dates of key states, they incorrectly predicted that they would lose Illinois. In fact, their landslide victory in Illinois came close to ending the Kennedy challenge. See Harwood, *The Pursuit of the Presidency*, pp. 92–93.

34. To guard against the possibility that changing events in Iran would tilt the general election to Carter, Reagan organizers developed the idea of an "October surprise," which they were prepared to attack if necessary. For details on their contingency plans, see Elizabeth Drew, *Portrait of an Election* (New York: Simon and Schuster, 1981), p. 310 and Jack Germond and Jules Witcover, *Blue Smoke and Mirrors* (New York: Viking Press, 1981), pp. 272–274.

35. By November, 1979, Baker's position had deteriorated so badly that he realized his campaign needed dramatic action to recoup lost time (and lost constituencies among moderate Republicans). Having previously discussed with his staff the need to reform the vice-presidential selection process, Baker decided to combine good policy with good politics. Since he recognized that Robert Ray (R-Iowa) was a popular, moderate Republican governor of the first caucus state, Baker (in early November, 1979) broke with tradition and (in an unpublicized move) asked Ray to be his vice-presidential nominee, so that they could run as a team throughout the nominating process. As explained by several top Baker staffers (who preferred anonymity), Baker on the one hand had a sincere desire to reform the process. Having endured the suspense and personal agony of past selection processes at Republican conventions, Baker not only wanted to spare others that spectacle, but also believed that the convention was not a good selection setting. Of course, on the other hand, he was mindful of the political benefit of a Baker/Ray ticket, particularly in the early Iowa caucuses. With a popular moderate Republican at his side, he could shore up his support with moderate constituencies. Although Ray apparently spent several weeks considering the offer, he finally decided at the Governor's Conference to decline it. For one thing, the political risks would be great. If a Baker/Ray ticket failed to win the Iowa caucuses, it would be a blow to Ray's standing within the state. In addition, he risked splitting his own ranks because several of his supporters worked for candidates other than Baker, notably Bush. While Ray later worked on Baker's behalf, he ignored Baker's pleas to join him on a ticket of moderate Republicanism.

36. Listed in Sabato, *Rise of Political Consultants*, pp. 181–182.

37. Ibid., p. 262 n. 73.

38. Described by Michael Robinson, "The Media in 1980: Was the Message the Message?" in Ranney, *The American Elections of 1980*, p. 188.

39. Quoted by Schram, "Carter," pp. 87–88.

40. Ibid., p. 96.

41. For a more detailed statement of the "permanent campaign" idea, see Sidney Blumenthal, *The Permanent Campaign* (Boston: Beacon Press, 1980).

42. Other scholars have emphasized the uncertainty of campaign processes. For example, Nelson Polsby and Aaron Wildavsky list the ambiguities of nominating conventions (*Presidential Elections*, 5th ed., pp. 104–107). And in her analysis of campaign organizations, Xandra Kayden said, "Uncertainty is perhaps the most important of the environmental factors because it is the most pervasive" (*Campaign Organization*, Lexington, Mass.: D. C. Heath, 1978, p. 63). But the key point that I make is that the early decisions required by the new process accentuate uncertainty.

43. John Kingdon, *Candidates for Office* (New York: Random House, 1966). For a related analysis of "wishful thinking" within campaign organizations, see Kayden, *Campaign Organizations* p. 12.

44. To demonstrate the difficulties of predicting leader behavior without subjective perceptions, see John Aldrich, *Before the Convention* (Chicago: University of Chicago Press, 1980), p. 204. Using various objective indicators described in his second chapter,

Aldrich predicts that Anderson will not be a risk-taker in the 1980 presidential campaign. Yet Anderson's independent candidacy required more risk-taking than any strategy by another candidate.

45. Keene's quote comes from John Foley, Dennis Britton, and Eugene Everett, Jr., eds., *Nominating a President* (New York: Praeger, 1980), p. 124.

46. Cited in Sabato, *Rise of Political Consultants*, pp. 143, 145.

47. These differences in perspective also reflect the differing role orientations of media advisors and research directors. By nature of their jobs, research directors are more enmeshed in policy than are media specialists.

48. Of course, research by Kenneth Shepsle and Benjamin Page shows the value of ambiguous strategies. See Shepsle's "The Strategy of Ambiguity," *American Political Science Review*, 66 (June, 1972), pp. 555–568 and Page's "The Theory of Political Ambiguity," *American Political Science Review*, 70 (September, 1976), pp. 742–752.

3

Candidates and Electoral Coalitions

Campaigns are complicated events. Because the new electoral system requires personal campaigning and the demonstration of popular support, candidates and their advisors have to think carefully about electoral coalitions. Which constituencies should they attempt to rally? Do they want to go with what worked in the past, that is, coalitions that successful candidates of their party put together in previous elections? Or do they want to develop new coalitions?

In making these decisions, candidates usually consider three things. First, as prominent politicians who have sought office before, they are influenced by their own electoral histories. Most candidates, by the time they seek the presidency, have several campaigns under their belts—either for a governorship, the House, the Senate, or perhaps even a presidential race. These campaigns influence candidates' views of electoral coalitions. If campaigners previously won elections with blacks, labor unions, and senior citizens in their coalitions, they are likely in a presidential race to continue those appeals. Similarly, candidates who developed close ties with "big business" are not likely to forget that support when they run for president.

Second, as members of a particular party, they must be aware of their party's electoral history. Despite voter complaints about the indistinguishability of the two major parties, Republicans and Democrats generally have appealed to different constituencies. According to Robert Axelrod, Republicans have aimed at moderate to conservative voting blocs (mainly the better off, white, nonunion families, Protestants, Northerners, and rural and suburban dwellers) while Democrats have appealed to moderate to liberal blocs (generally the poor, blacks, union members, Catholics and Jews, Southerners, central city dwellers, and the young); even though party loyalties have weakened, candidates cannot ignore party histories.[1]

Third, candidates have policy interests. It no longer is fashionable to consider candidates' policy motivations. Much of the work on candidate strategies describes them as "vote maximizers" motivated primarily by electoral incentives.[2] According to this approach, campaigners survey the political landscape and "go hunting where the ducks are." Implicitly, scholars assume that candidates who speak about certain issues or pursue particular constituencies do so to win votes. However, there is evidence that candidates have policy as well as electoral motivations. As Benjamin Page and Richard Fenno have noted, candidates are not merely vote maximizers; rather they are political beings who bring substantive concerns to their positions. This idea is particularly relevant at the presidential level. David Keene, Bush's national political director, provided intuitive support for the notion when he explained the importance of candidate beliefs:

We do not at the presidential level, unless you are dealing with a complete cipher or a total asshole, go out and tell the candidate "here's where you position yourself." By the time a man is ready to run for the presidency of the United States he has presumably developed a worldview and a view of the kind of government he would like to have, the positions he ought to be taking. That's as true of a George Bush as it is of a Barry Goldwater or George McGovern or a Ronald Reagan. . . . The fact is that you do not sit your candidate down and say, "listen Ronald Reagan is for this. Therefore you ought to be against it because that draws a line." You do your line-drawing both within the framework of what your candidate believes and the reality of what he can accomplish within that framework.

Because candidates may build coalitions around issues or constituencies that interest them (even if the political odds look unpromising), it is important to see how the mix of policy and electoral concerns influences presidential coalitions.

Of course, these three factors—electoral histories, party histories, and policy motivations—are not set in concrete. Since Franklin Roosevelt's time, there have been major changes in the "building blocks" of electoral coalitions. During the 1930s, constituencies were identified in demographic terms—income, race, occupation, religion, age, region, and place of residence. Campaigners who wanted to build coalitions generally relied on key "voting blocs"—labor, minorities, Jews, Catholics, Southerners, and so on. However, in the contemporary period, political leaders see constituencies in different ways. While demographic blocs have not disappeared, presidential contenders recognize their diminishing unity and strength. According to John Sears, Reagan's campaign manager:

the building blocks—the coalitions that are available to you today—are really much smaller in number than what used to be the case. When you were talking about organized labor, together with blacks and Jews, those were big groups of people. And when you could get them together . . . you had a lot of muscle going for you. . . . You were very close right there to controlling a national election because of the numbers.

Since demographic categories have weakened, campaign organizers increasingly see their constituencies in "issue" terms.[3] One of the most publicized developments of the new electoral system has been the rise of "single-issue" groups.[4] James Q. Wilson described the phenomenon this way:

These divisions of opinion contribute powerfully to the kind of "one-issue" politics so characteristic of the present era. Pro-abortion versus pro-life; gun control versus the right to bear arms; gay rights versus traditional values; ERA versus anti-ERA; nuclear energy versus solar energy; proponents of affirmative action versus opponents of reverse discrimination—all these causes and more make life miserable for the traditional, coalition-seeking politician. Weakened institutions, individualized politics, and the rise of an educated, idea-oriented public combine to make it highly advantageous for political entrepreneurs to identify and mobilize single-issue constituencies.[5]

While this development is not universally approved, most campaigners understand the need for demographic *and* issue oriented constituencies.

In this chapter, I explore these ideas in greater detail. How did electoral and party histories influence coalition-building? Did policy concerns shape presidential coalitions? And how did the new electoral system (and the new "building blocks") affect these forces?

THE IMPACT OF ELECTORAL HISTORY

Candidates do not begin presidential races with blank slates. Even with the rising number of dark horses, presidential contestants still have political histories. As Figure 3–1 shows, all of the candidates in 1980 had won at least one elective office. Their victories ranged in prominence from a national office (the presidency) and six state-wide contests (three Senators and three governors) to three congressional district races.[6] In addition, their most recent campaigns varied from being just concluded (Anderson, Baker, Brown, and Crane had elections in 1978) to having taken place over a decade ago (Connally's last election was in 1966).

These experiences marked candidates in different ways. For some, electoral histories proved beneficial to presidential efforts; for others, the lessons of previous races were detrimental. The best example in 1980 of a candidate who profited from his political history was Reagan. In many ways, Reagan's constituencies and election activities (such as running media campaigns in California) dovetailed with the opportunities of the new electoral system. While California is no microcosm of the nation, its elections reflect national campaigns better than most political contests (certainly more than the congressional races of Anderson, Bush, and Crane did). Like the presidential level, state-wide races in California feature modern technologies—television, polling, and direct mail—and active news organizations. Party strength also resembles the national pattern: Democrats outnumber Republicans two to one (although the support for both parties has declined over the last two decades).[7] And unlike many states (but like the country), California has a diverse population (including blacks and Hispanics). Hence, to understand Reagan's coalition in 1980, one must trace his political development (both in California and beyond).

Few candidates have been as consistent as Reagan in building core consti-

Figure 3-1
Elective Offices of the Major Candidates

Candidate	Elective Office
Anderson	State's Attorney of Winnebago County, Illinois, 1956–1960
	U.S. House, Illinois, 1961–1981
Baker	U.S. Senate, Tennessee, 1967–present
Brown	Board of Trustees, Los Angeles Community Colleges, 1969–1971
	Secretary of State, California, 1971–1975
	Governor, California, 1975–present
Bush	U.S. House, Texas, 1967–1971
Carter	Chairman, Sumter County, Georgia Board of Education, 1955–1962
	State Senate, Georgia, 1963–1967
	Governor, Georgia, 1971–1975
	U.S. President, 1977–1981
Connally	Governor, Texas, 1963–1969
Crane	U.S. House, Illinois, 1969–present
Dole	State House, Kansas, 1951–1953
	Prosecuting Attorney, Russell County, Kansas, 1953–1960
	U.S. House, Kansas, 1961–1969
	U.S. Senate, Kansas, 1969–present
Kennedy	U.S. Senate, Massachusetts, 1963–present
Reagan	Governor, California, 1967–1975

Source: Congressional Quarterly, *Candidates, '80* (1980).

tuencies.[8] For more than twenty years, the Californian had courted conservative and right-wing support. In his General Electric tours from 1954 to 1962 (to publicize his weekly television series *General Electric Theatre*), Reagan persistently sounded the alarm against big government, high taxes, creeping socialism, and the satanic designs of communism; later he denounced just about every liberal initiative from social security and unemployment insurance ("a prepaid vacation plan for freeloaders") to the Tennessee Valley Authority and the progressive income tax ("a brainchild of Karl Marx").[9] Reagan's nationally televised speech October 27, 1964 on behalf of Barry Goldwater's presidential effort also was a high water mark in his political career. This speech, which David Broder described as "the most successful national political debut since William Jennings Bryan electrified the 1896 Democratic convention with his 'Cross of Gold' speech," enabled Reagan to assume the mantle of conservative leadership after Goldwater's decisive defeat.[10] By arguing that America faced a choice between free enterprise and "the ant heap of totalitarianism," Reagan cemented his ties with conservatives nationwide. In fact, the speech generated such favorable responses (including over a million dollars in campaign contri-

butions) that several California conservatives "drafted" Reagan for the 1966
gubernatorial contest. This race brought him even closer to his core constituencies. Using themes and anecdotes honed during fourteen years on the "rubber
chicken" circuit (for example, jeering redwood conservationists with "how many
do you need to look at?" and telling young demonstrators that if they represented the future, he would sell his bonds), Reagan swept to victory. However,
it would be a mistake to paint Reagan just as a right-wing candidate (as Edmund Brown and Jimmy Carter tried to do). Even in Reagan's earliest campaigns in California, he demonstrated his ability to get Democratic votes. Asked
later by Bill Moyers what people he represented, Reagan said, "I think maybe
the same people that elected me to governor in California, which is a state that
[is] almost two-to-one Democrat. And I won by a million votes. So I must be
able to cross the spectrum."[11] Thus, there were two pillars in Reagan's electoral history—conservative core constituencies and persistent appeals to Democrats.

These experiences served Reagan well in his presidential campaigns. The rise
of television and growing dominance of conservatives in the Republican party
meshed with Reagan's electronic skills and core constituencies. In 1976, Reagan effectively drew on these strengths when his nomination challenge against
Ford began to falter. After losing five straight primaries and running danger-
ously low on cash, Reagan reached out to the medium he knew best (television)
and the constituencies that were most loyal (conservatives). On the eve of the
North Carolina primary, Reagan overruled his advisors (who feared memories
of Reagan's entertainment background) and made a state-wide television address that raised $1.4 million, thereby allowing him to stay in the race.[12] And
in efforts to mobilize his core constituencies (conservatives who increasingly
were dominating the Republican party), Reagan began to speak about foreign
affairs—the Panama Canal, Henry Kissinger, detente, and military strength.
Regarding the Panama Canal, Reagan's rallying cry became, "We built it. We
paid for it. It's ours, and we're going to keep it."

In addition, changes in the campaign setting favored Reagan's coalitional
history. The decline of party attachments among voters helped candidates (such
as Reagan) with histories of "crossover" appeals. As he had done in his gubernatorial races, Reagan's presidential efforts (in 1976 and 1980) made active
efforts to win support from Democrats and independents. During the 1979 announcement speech, Reagan stressed his background in both parties: "I've seen
America from the stadium box as a sportscaster, as an actor, officer of my labor
union, soldier, officeholder, and as both Democrat and Republican."[13] Meanwhile, his advisors also emphasized the opportunities with Democratic voters.
According to Drew Lewis, Reagan's deputy chairman:

Those traditional Democrats who have been voting for Roosevelt the last fifty years and
their families are beginning to realize those programs have not proven overly effective
and I guess in terms of their taxpaying problems, they're tired of seeing the federal gov-

ernment . . . come into a problem and just pour money all over it and not solve the problem.

In reaching out to Democrats, Reagan and his staff saw possibilities with key demographic constituencies—Catholics, blue-collar workers, and ethnic groups. Roger Stone, Reagan's chief political operative in New York, said, "the Catholic blue-collar ethnic vote is up for grabs. They're increasingly conservative on social issues. And I think Ronald Reagan can potentially be very strong among Jewish voters." And Lyn Nofziger, Reagan's press secretary, explained, "you're trying to pick up blue-collar workers who are social conservatives who have been hit hard by the Carter economic policies." However, Reagan's advisors did not limit their vision to demographic blocs; rather they also appealed to newly active issue constituencies, namely right-to-life advocates and religious fundamentalists. Recognizing the value of activists in small primary states, John Sears explained their success with the pro-life movement:

Reagan's position on the right-to-life issue has been in place longer than anyone else's and it actually is more close to the whole loaf of bread than anybody else's. . . . So he started out with very strong cards with that constituency. As soon as he announced his position . . . August of '79, why they just all pretty well fell in line.[14]

According to Frank Donatelli, a regional political director, and Jim Lake, Reagan's first press secretary, Reagan strategists realized that abortion was an effective way of reaching Democratic voters:

Much of the right-to-life leadership is composed of Democrats who would not necessarily, historically, have been attracted to Republican candidates. And to the extent that they're able to help us make inroads with some of the core Democratic groups, your working class Democrats, your ethnic voters, union members, these kinds of groups . . . [they've been] a tremendous plus for us. And they certainly do a much better job to reach those particular voters than certainly any regular Republican apparatus could (Donatelli).

[We] let them [right-to-life activists] know that the only way they had a chance to have a president who felt as they did was to vote for Ronald Reagan and we encouraged party switching. We talked to people who said they could do it. . . . We tried to energize them. We saw to it that they got voter printouts and that sort of stuff that they could have something to work with (Lake).

Similarly, the Reagan camp took advantage of the activism of fundamentalists and their feelings of betrayal by Carter (whom they supported in 1976). Sears put it this way: "Many of the people involved in that institutionally sort of sought Governor Reagan out this time. They were not part of his following in '76. Many of them actually supported Mr. Carter all the way through his nomination and election." In short, issue constituencies (not just demographic blocs) played a major role during Reagan's drive for the presidency.

But one of the most interesting features of Reagan's campaign in 1980 was the consistency of his coalitional activities between the nominating process and general election. Asked about changes in Reagan's coalition after the primaries, Drew Lewis said, "I don't think a great deal has changed. . . . I don't think it's changed significantly at all." Unlike Anderson and Carter, who pursued different constituencies in the fall (Anderson tried to mobilize labor unions, environmentalists, and minorities in the general election but not the primaries, while Carter sought moderate to conservative constituencies in the spring but liberal votes in the fall), Reagan's coalition-building was remarkably similar throughout the year-long campaign (as it had been for twenty years).[15] While he used the nominating process and general election to broaden his support, Reagan's appeals were consistent with his electoral history.

In contrast to Reagan's situation, there were two candidates (Connally and Kennedy) whose previous electoral experiences proved detrimental to their presidential efforts. Connally's campaign was one of the great mysteries of 1980. After raising millions of dollars in 1979 (much of it from corporate boardrooms) and appearing to be Reagan's most serious challenger, Connally's campaign plummeted. In the first five delegate tests, the Texan received 9.2 percent (Iowa), 1.1 percent (Puerto Rico), 1.5 percent (New Hampshire), 1.2 percent (Massachusetts), and 1.3 percent (Vermont). By March, with only one convention delegate from his $10 million in campaign expenditures, Connally withdrew from presidential contention. While there were a number of reasons for Connally's downfall (such as his "national" campaign strategy), no explanation can ignore the way that electoral history handicapped him. Connally operated at a disadvantage because his last campaign had been in 1966 (the most distant electoral history of any major presidential candidate). As discussed in chapter 2, national races have changed dramatically since the mid–1960s (with the dominance of early delegate tests, rise of new technologies, and so on). Despite these changes, Connally conducted his presidential campaign with an "old electoral system" mentality. He did not view Iowa and New Hampshire as any different from later delegate contests (thereby explaining his choice of a national approach); he also did not see the importance of momentum in the new electoral system. And, according to his pollster, Lance Tarrance, Connally did not rely heavily on new campaign technologies:

John Connally had never really campaigned himself since '62 in a hot and heavy way. He was almost twenty years out of sync. . . . He didn't understand some of the new techniques and campaign technologies. . . . He had never been around polls in the '70s; he had only been around them in the '50s and basically didn't understand how much they are used by the new campaign management. . . . Remember back in the early '60s, all you had to do was get enough county chairmen or political machine people behind you and enough money to do some television and you could win about anything. Well, boy have things changed.

Unfortunately for Connally, the lessons that he did learn from past campaigns were not the correct ones for the contemporary era. The best illustration of this occurred in Iowa where a frantic Connally faced prospects of a major defeat in the Republican caucuses. As many candidates do in times of crises, Connally returned to strategies that were successful in past campaigns. In 1962, Connally had been credited with winning the governor's mansion by "barnstorming" Texas for ten straight days. As one of his advisors put it, Connally "raised a ton of money, made a lot of press, and basically went through there like Sherman might have gone through Georgia." In 1980, confronted with dismal Iowa prospects, Connally "returned to his roots" (as Reagan had done in 1976 with his North Carolina television address). Hoping to rally Iowa voters, Connally barnstormed the state: "Connally went up there with a barnstorming tour, forty straight hours flying around the state in Iowa. It was a fair resemblance of what he did in 1962 in the governor's race. There's a man that went back to old history of what worked well twenty years ago" (Tarrance). However, unlike Reagan, whose return to his television roots meshed with the opportunities of the new electoral system, barnstorming Iowa did not turn the trick for Connally.[16]

In addition, Connally's previous elections handicapped him because his "learning" took place in the Democratic party. A lifelong Democrat who had switched parties only in 1973, Connally's presidential campaign in 1980 marked the Texan's *first* race as a Republican. Not only did this put his electoral base into question, it also meant that his learning was limited. Unlike Reagan, who effectively used earlier campaigns and constituencies, Connally's electoral history did not help him. Of course, Connally could have reduced this problem by having campaign advisors who were experienced Republicans (which he did to a certain extent with his campaign manager, Eddie Mahe, Jr., the former executive director of the Republican National Committee from 1974 to 1977). But Connally minimized this learning opportunity by surrounding himself with "loyalists," those who had been with him for thirty years (many of whom were Democrats and equally limited in Republican politics). Connally further complicated his plight by wanting to run his own campaign. More so than other candidates, Connally refused to concede the limits of his past experiences; in the end, he paid a heavy price for his refusal to trust professional managers.[17]

Kennedy's presidential effort also suffered from his electoral history. While his races were recent and state-wide, they were not hotly contested. In 1964, with the legacy of a slain brother and a plane crash that put the senatorial candidate in the hospital, Kennedy received 74 percent of the general election vote. In 1970, despite Kennedy's personal tragedy at Chappaquidick, his margin dropped only to 62 percent. And in 1976, with a weak challenger, Kennedy received 69 percent of the vote.[18] Because his previous contests did not involve strong opponents, Kennedy failed to adapt well in 1980. Presidential races in the new electoral system require the effective use of campaign technologies— namely, polling and television. But Kennedy and his advisors never fully appreciated the value of these tools. Consultant David Garth, whom Kennedy approached about a campaign position, said this: "Their approach is from twenty years ago, when reporters didn't ask questions. The Kennedy campaign just opened their doors and said we're doing business. You've got to have a strategy and a vision. They didn't understand media. And what's really shocking to me is that they didn't understand the modern use of polls. . . . They still think in terms of getting Teddy moving around. But you don't have to stage a barnstorming tour. You [should] have one press conference and one media event a day.''[19] And Kennedy advisor, Richard Stearns, noted that his candidate's attitudes about polls infused the entire campaign organization: "Kennedy does not like polls, even those that we have taken. We have had some very competent polls done by Peter Hart and others. [But] Kennedy never asked to see them. He cared little for the result. . . . The campaign didn't like polls because the candidate wasn't really enamored with them. If Ted Kennedy said from the beginning that I have to have a poll every three days, the campaign would have provided a poll every three days.''[20] In part, Kennedy's negative feelings about polls were shaped by his electoral history. According to his pollster, Peter Hart: "here is a person who has never needed a poll. I mean in 1962 or 1964 or 1970 or 1976, basically his opposition has been fairly limited and while he's always had polls, I don't think that they've ever been an integral part of the conduct of his campaign. . . . If you are in a one-sided situation, polls are obviously less important. And Edward Kennedy in Massachusetts was more of a one-sided situation." But these beliefs about polls also reflected attitudes about the vagaries of public opinion polls.[21] Stearns attributed Carter's lack of leadership and his inability to follow policies consistently to an overreliance on polls: "The polls do not seem in the final analysis to have served Carter all that well. If anything, they left a sense of inconstancy to the public perception of his presidency.''[22] Meanwhile, Kennedy's media campaign was in no better shape. Since there was extensive turnover on the media staff, the organization never defined a clear theme or message. Tony Podesta, a Kennedy scheduler, said that, "I don't think there was an adequate effort made to kind of define the magic description and magic words. In part, that was a function of the fact that there were 1100 people on the media committee and a rotating chairmanship everyday. . . . The Kennedy campaign was much more anarchic . . . and as a consequence the committee never came up with a slogan." So like Connally, Kennedy's campaign did not master the technologies of the new electoral system.

Kennedy's early coalition-building also ran aground because of uncertainty about his constituencies. Similar to Reagan, Kennedy had developed throughout his career consistent core constituencies (namely, liberals). But with media claims about a rightward drift in the country and Kennedy's early popularity, Kennedy chose not to stress his core constituencies at the beginning of the race. Instead of entering the race as a lifelong liberal (which he was), Kennedy deemphasized his liberal background and stressed "leadership" against Carter. Robert Shrum, one of Kennedy's speech writers, said: "His strategy was to run on the theme of leadership. I think the notion was that if you got 60 or 70 percent in the polls, you don't screw around by alienating parts of your constituency by taking very hard-line positions." But Kennedy quickly ran into difficulties. When asked why he was challenging an incumbent president, Kennedy appeared uncertain and inarticulate because he could not give (or chose not to give) the "liberal" answers that he had been giving for two decades. The problem was not (as some journalists claimed) that he did not know the answers. Rather, Kennedy's dilemma was that he was consciously downplaying his twenty-year-old core constituencies but had not yet developed the "new" message. It was not until after Iowa, when Kennedy dropped the bland leadership message and returned to his liberal roots (see chapter 4), that he began to campaign effectively.

To summarize, electoral histories played an important role in the coalitional efforts of major candidates. Because they had successfully sought political offices before, presidential contenders drew on their experiences when they moved up the political ladder.[23] Constituencies that politicians cultivated throughout their careers were vital parts of candidates' coalitions. And electoral tactics that served campaigners well before often were revived for presidential efforts (especially during times of electoral crises). However, prior experiences did not benefit candidates equally well. Some candidates (such as Reagan) benefited because their previous experiences and constituencies dovetailed with the opportunities of the new electoral system. In contrast, candidates (like Connally) who relied too heavily on their prior electoral experiences (which were in the 1960s) were unable to take advantage of their coalitional opportunities. And presidential contenders (such as Kennedy) whose earlier contests did not involve strong opponents failed to adapt to national races requiring effective use of polling and television. For better or worse, political histories molded the electoral strategies of presidential candidates.

THE IMPACT OF PARTY HISTORY

Campaigners were also influenced by their party's electoral history. Despite the decline of partisan attachments in the electorate, parties are far from dead. More than 60 percent of voters still identify with one of the major parties. Robert Axelrod and John Petrocik also point out that historically party coalitions have rested on different constituencies. And the nominating process continues to be built around parties; with differences in party setting and the differing policy views of Republican and Democratic activists, candidates cannot ignore parties completely. According to Connally manager, Eddie Mahe, Jr.:

there is absolutely no relation between the Republican and Democratic election process. . . . Can you imagine Kennedy winning a Republican primary with the positions he takes on the issues? Can you imagine Connally winning a Democratic primary favoring nuclear power, decontrol of oil and gas, and capital punishment and opposing gun control? Can you really see him winning the Democratic nomination? I mean, who votes in the Democratic primaries? It's liberals, labor unions, and minorities. Now that's your Democratic primary electorate. Who votes in a Republican primary? Conservatives, by and large.

However, while party history is important, it does not affect candidates in the same ways. Some candidates (whom one can call the "innovators") actively tried to remake party coalitions. For example, in 1980 Anderson and Brown most clearly followed this approach. Both were party "mavericks" who wanted to reshape their parties. Interviewed on national news shows, Anderson said:

The Republicans have finally discovered that they are a minority party, that if they want to win they have got to build a coalition. . . . If we want to become the majority party we have got to appeal to blacks, 91 percent of whom went for Carter in 1976. We have got to appeal to the 51.3 percent of the constituency in this country that are women. . . . That is the kind of coalition that I am trying to build in my campaign. It can restructure and reshape and remake this minority Republican Party into a majority political force in this country.[24]

The issues are so important today that we ought to build a new coalition of voters and we ought to do it in the nominating process. Every one of these other candidates that are running against me claim they can get Democratic votes in the fall if they are nominated. I am proving right now in the primaries in the nominating process that I can do that. I think we need a new coalition in this country of Democrats, Independents, and Republicans who think that the issues are too important to just confine the nominating process to the same old narrow political aspect that it has had before.[25]

Similarly, Brown stated the need for fundamental change:

My effort is a major insurgent effort to disestablish the present people in charge of the Democratic party. . . . Through the next several months I [intend to] create a mandate and a governing coalition to reshape both the assumptions that this country has operated on over the last decade and its future of vision. I am presenting to the Democrats an option, an alternative, a fundamental choice.[26]

Other presidential contenders also sought changes in their parties' traditional bases. Connally experimented with an "attitudinal" constituency that crossed party and demographic lines (see note 17). Crane and Reagan targeted demographic groups (blue-collar workers and ethnic voters) and issue constituencies (right-to-life supporters and fundamentalists), many of whom previously had identified with the Democratic party.[27] Dole, because of his policy interests and personal history, sought votes from "needy" constituencies (for example, veterans, the handicapped, and the elderly) that were not major components of the Republican coalition (see next section). And Carter tried to push the Democratic party in a more moderate (some would say conservative) direction (described later in this section).

These candidates had a variety of incentives for coalitional change. First, the nominating process encouraged them to use "open primaries" (those that allow Republicans to vote in Democratic primaries and vice versa) to win crossover votes. Combined with the decay of party allegiances and rising number of independents, these primaries led several Republican candidates (notably Anderson and Reagan) to seek support from independents and Democrats. According to Anderson's unpublished strategy memos: "The growing number of independent voters will be a factor in the 1980 primary election. (About 15 states allow independent or unaffiliated voters to vote in either party's primary). This list includes Illinois, Wisconsin, Indiana, Michigan, New Jersey and Ohio." In addition, Reagan strategist Drew Lewis noted the importance of crossover states: "[In] a number of primaries we already had the outreach because we're running in primaries where you can cross over. So part of our program consistently has been to run a campaign that deals not only with Republicans but Democrats."

Second, the growing number of nonvoters has not been lost on presidential aspirants. With the large pool of citizens (roughly half the electorate) who do not participate in national elections, candidates have a large group of unattached citizens whom they can attempt to mobilize.[28] Both Anderson and Brown made active efforts to attract these people. Richard Maullin, Brown's campaign cochairman, explained it this way:

Large numbers of people haven't really participated in a national election . . . [since] 1960 or 1964. And as a result there is always this thought that, "Gee, there's this untapped number of people who, if you could ever turn them on, you could walk away with something." . . . Brown was trying to reach a lot of these people. A lot of his involvement with the anti-nuclear movements . . . had some basis in that.

And Anderson's strategy memos suggested that "an effort be made to expand the Republican electorate . . . to appeal to new groups (young, labor, Blacks, Jews) and to previously disaffected individuals who have not voted." Because of their interests in mobilization, both candidates spent substantial amounts of time on college campuses. While this emphasis reflected the levels of enthusiasm and need for volunteers that Anderson and Brown found in colleges, it also fit with their coalitional strategies. Owing to the limited political histories of young people, students generally have weak party allegiances. Consequently, Anderson and Brown saw students as crucial and unaffiliated sources of support from which to create new coalitions. Third, many candidates (Crane, Reagan, Anderson, and Brown) saw newly active issue constituencies as a device for changing party coalitions (either tearing down the Democratic coalition or building new coalitions). For example, Crane and Reagan saw opportunities with anti-gun control groups, right-to-life supporters, fundamentalists, and opponents to the Equal Rights Amendment (ERA), among others. Meanwhile, Anderson wooed pro-choice groups, supporters of the ERA, gun control advocates, and the like. And Brown built his campaigns in Maine and New Hampshire around groups opposed to nuclear energy and the military draft (of all the presidential contestants, Brown was the only one whose campaign posters in New Hampshire advertised a particular policy position, Brown's opposition to nuclear energy). Brown advisor Walter McGuire explained how his candidate wanted to use newly emerging issue groups to build momentum and gain media attention:

We weren't trying to win New Hampshire, but rather score well enough that it would give us the momentum to move into the later primaries. . . . If you're only trying to get a segment of the vote, I guess the thought was . . . to try to grab certain pockets of people and put them together into 20 or 25 percent. . . . If we could capture what seemed to be a fairly good chunk of people who were strongly anti-nuclear and get the message that that was a vote as much anti-nuclear as anything that you might be able to get that percentage of the vote.

Similarly, in the Maine caucuses, Tom Quinn (Brown's campaign manager) argued:

When you get in a caucus situation, special interest people and pleaders can have a disproportionate influence. It's not like it's an election. So you can go out to individual groups that can mean something, that can add up to real numbers. . . . It did seem to me that the anti-nuclear approach, also Jerry's opposition to the draft . . . might be successful in Maine.[29]

Of course, not all of Brown's advisors were optimistic about this strategy. Brown's New England coordinator, Joe Beeman, was much more critical (he eventually left the campaign):

I think a great flaw in Jerry Brown's thinking is his notion . . . that you go to a group which no one else has paid much attention to, you identify yourself with the issues that they are promoting, and that they therefore will become adherents of your candidacy. . . . Jerry Brown would start with groups like the followers of the swami . . . organic farmers in New England . . . people interested in holistic health . . . the no-nuke movement. . . . Brown believed that a collection of single issues, a little piece here and there [could be] patched together to form a presidential coalition. It was like a house built of cardboard. . . . The first gust of wind that came blew the house over.

Finally, modern campaign technologies helped candidates (from an organizational point of view) reshuffle coalitions. Anderson's advisors noted that direct mail fundraising played a major role in convincing him to launch his independent candidacy. In reviewing the factors surrounding that decision, campaign manager Michael McLeod said, "An analysis of our donor base, which had gone from roughly 4 or 5 thousand at the end of January to 88 thousand at the end of April, indicated that there was a great deal of support out there for John Anderson." Tom Mathews, Anderson's direct mail specialist, confirmed this:

John Anderson was at the center of a real political phenomenon and it was a big one in terms of being able to raise money and be an independent political voice. . . . He gradually came to see . . . what his real constituency was, that his constituency did not lie in the Republican party nor did it in the Democratic party. It lay within what you call the alienated middle which is the independent group of people who are turned off both parties.[30]

Because of these forces—open primaries, the large number of nonvoters, issue constituencies, and modern technologies—candidates in both parties made major efforts to reshuffle party coalitions.

But not all candidates followed this approach. Several of them chose to work within existing party coalitions. Rather than pursuing "mobilization" (appeals to nonvoters and unaffiliated citizens) or "conversion" strategies (appeals to disenchanted voters from the other party), these men tried to hold the constituencies their parties already had. The best examples of this approach were Baker and Bush in the nominating process and Carter in the general election. Baker and Bush were competing for the moderate to conservative Republican vote. Baker's campaign chairman, Senator Richard Lugar, saw Baker's constituencies this way: "in the nomination stage, Howard Baker's best opportunities are literally with Republicans across the board. I'm not certain he can identify any particular Republicans." And Bush's demographer, John Morgan, said, "The ideal thing about George Bush was that he was conservative enough to appeal to most of the conservatives, but he still was out of the moderate Eastern wing of the party. . . . He was the eastern establishment candidate." These descriptions contrast with those of the other candidates. While Anderson, Brown, and Reagan worked to change their parties, Baker and Bush consciously stayed within existing coalitional boundaries. Morgan made this explicit when he explained that Bush targeted geographic areas that had voted for Ford during the 1976 primary contests with Reagan:

We want to target for the areas that we feel will yield us the best results. . . . Like these maps [aggregate election returns by county], we did it for every one of these primary states. We tore apart the state. We looked at what the Ford-Reagan thing was, where we could get support and where we couldn't. . . . Like Oregon, the orange and pink areas are the Ford areas and the other parts of the state are the Reagan areas. Obviously, we are going to target . . . where the Republican vote is. That's where the Bush vote is and it's obviously the Ford vote.

In addition, their approach to single-issue groups differed considerably from that of the innovators. Using abortion as an example, Crane and Reagan saw opportunities with pro-life groups; Anderson capitalized with pro-choice supporters, but Bush chose to ignore them (as did Baker, who supported the Supreme Court decisions liberalizing abortion laws). When asked about the pro-life lobby, Bush responded, "I'm one who finds these contentious single issues to be a trend in politics that I would rather not enhance by elaborating on."[31] And his press secretary, Pete Teeley, echoed this perspective by explaining, "I don't know of any candidate in the Democratic or Republican party who runs around and builds a campaign speech around the issue of abortion. . . . I don't think anybody is advising the candidate to make abortion the issue." Finally, neither Baker nor Bush tried to mobilize student voters, as Anderson and Brown did. According to Lugar, "student voters are difficult to identify because they are not registered or students are away at the time of the primary." But it was no accident that neither candidate saw students as crucial for the Republican nomination; their interests in coalitional maintenance made students irrelevant to the race.[32]

President Carter also worked within his party's boundaries (at least in the general election). As a candidate for the Democratic nomination in 1980, Carter had *not* campaigned as a traditional New Deal candidate. Rather he had followed his 1976 nominating strategy and appealed to moderate, rural, and southern constituencies.[33] In part, Carter's strategy was influenced by Kennedy's challenge. While the president was able to retain parts of labor, most elected officials, and part of the black vote, Kennedy successfully appealed to the liberal factions of these groups. But Carter's strategy also rested on the advice of pollster Pat Caddell, who earlier had told him to "co-opt many of their [GOP] issue positions . . . to take away large chunks of their normal presidential coalition."[34] Carter believed that Democrats had to remake their coalition because of the country's drift to the right. According to Gerald Rafshoon, his media advisor, "unless the Democratic party can be perceived as being the moderate party, it cannot survive. . . . It's just a small percentage of the electorate that's liberal." Hence, to save the future of the Democratic party, Carter wanted to alter the party's image.[35] However, in the general election, having disposed of Kennedy and facing a campaign contest where Democrats outnumbered Republicans two to one in the electorate, Carter became a traditional Democrat. Robert Keefe, a Carter political operative, described the general election coalition this way:

The constituency that we tried to build was based on the old Democratic coalition. . . . [Carter was trying] to bring in those elements that had supported Senator Kennedy through the spring. . . . The inability to end the nominating process by late spring cost them dearly in achieving good bridges to the more liberal constituencies and caused them not to be able to build that coalition. . . . In the ideal world, he should not have had to appeal so overly to the left-wing elements within the coalition.

And Malcolm Dade, his deputy campaign chairman, said:

I don't think President Carter is any different than any other Democrat. I think the story of Democrats and Republicans is that Democrats try to hold together what is their broad-based, often competing, constituency . . . and Republicans basically try to make inroads into these groups.

So unlike his nomination coalition, where he tried to recast the party, Carter returned to the fold in the fall.[36]

In short, party histories influenced the coalitional strategies of presidential contestants. With party activists having different policy concerns and parties historically appealing to different constituencies, campaigners ignored parties at their own peril. But candidates also realized that changes in the campaign environment and in coalitional building blocks created unusual opportunities for coalitional change. In investigating these efforts, I found that they were present in both parties. Since Democratic identifiers outnumber Republicans, one might expect simply in terms of electoral incentives that Democratic candidates will stick with existing party alignments while Republicans pursue coalitional change. Or to state the idea more generally, coalitional "innovators" will most likely be minority party candidates. However, there is little support for this proposition in the nominating process. A number of candidates in both parties tried to use the primaries to remake party coalitions. Apparently, something other than minority party status fueled candidate efforts at coalitional change. While there needs to be further exploration of this subject, it appears that key features of the new electoral system encouraged candidates to try to remold their parties— open primaries, the large number of nonvoters, the decline of party allegiances, newly emerging issue constituencies, and modern campaign technologies.[37] In these ways, the new electoral system helped some candidates overcome the dictates of party histories.[38]

THE IMPACT OF POLICY INTERESTS

It was fitting that the decade which trumpeted the irrelevance of candidates' policy interests closed with the election of the most ideological president (Reagan) the country has had in several terms. If Carter's administration goes down in history as the "passionless presidency" (one without distinctive policy interests or an overarching political vision),[39] his successor's may become known as the "impassioned presidency." Reagan brought numerous policy concerns to political life (many of which he had been emphasizing *before* they became politically acceptable). In domestic affairs, the Californian has well-known views about the limits of government. Rather than accepting governmental activism, Reagan persistently has challenged this approach. His acceptance speech at the Republican convention made this clear:

our federal government is overgrown and overweight. Indeed, it is time for our government to go on a diet. . . . Everything that can be run more effectively by state and local government we shall turn over to state and local government, along with the funding sources to pay for it. We are going to put an end to the money merry-go-round where our money becomes Washington's money, to be spent by the states and cities exactly the way the federal bureaucrats tell them to.[40]

And for twenty years, Reagan has warned about "godless totalitarians" and the spreading threat of communism. These positions represent more than casual rhetoric. Reagan's actions as president illustrate the consistency of his beliefs. To limit domestic spending, Reagan not only wanted to cut monies for social programs, he tried to make this policy more permanent by cutting taxes over three years (thereby restricting the financial capacity of leaders to rescind this decision in the future). In fact, one might explain Reagan's persistence in supporting tax cuts (despite unprecedented deficits in 1982) by referring to his policy concerns. For someone with Reagan's philosophy, these tax cuts represented more than an economic recovery program. Indeed, if that was all they stood for, Reagan's intransigence would have been nonsensical (given the political damage from budgetary deficits and the poor performance by the economy). Instead, one must realize that Reagan stood by his economic program (especially his tax cuts) because they were intimately linked to his longstanding policy beliefs. If he sacrificed the tax cuts, he was throwing overboard the means of reducing government growth. Since this concern was one of the primary things that propelled him into politics, he could change course only as a last resort.

Reagan's policy beliefs also influenced his actions in foreign affairs. For many years, Reagan has viewed regional conflicts as power struggles between East and West. This pattern was not changed when he assumed the presidency. Problems in the Middle East and Central America were not seen as regional issues having complex power configurations. Rather they were defined as part of the strategic battle against communism. This worldview encouraged Reagan to see the sale of sophisticated radar equipment (the AWACs) to Saudi Arabia not as a threat to Israel but as a buffer against the Soviet Union (an interpretation the Israeli government rejected). And battles between rebels and right-wing forces in El Salvador and Guatemala were seen not as internal power struggles but as part of a Soviet conspiracy to take over the Caribbean (despite conflicting interpretations from Congress and across the country). Hence, in both domestic and foreign affairs, Reagan's beliefs molded his public policies, even sometimes at the cost of popular support.

Of course, it is easy to dismiss Reagan as the exception. One could argue (with some validity) that few presidents have come to office with the consistent policy views of Reagan and even fewer have tried to remold public policies in their own images.[41] Instead, the more common view is that of politicians (such as Carter) who check the electoral winds before choosing constituencies and issues.

But this objection is not wholly accurate. Policy motivations are not limited to ideologues. Several candidates in 1980 were influenced by their policy beliefs (at times making decisions that looked stupid electorally). For example, the policy concerns of some candidates played a role in their decisions to run. Dan Swillinger (Anderson's manager) emphasized the role of policy interests in Anderson's candidacy:

His principal motivation really was to be the guy talking about issues. Issues are what interest him. Politics does not interest him. It is very difficult to get him to focus on political and strategic kinds of things. He can talk about energy policy for hours. Try to get him to talk about an electoral vote strategy.

Meanwhile, aides to Brown (the candidate most ridiculed for political expediency) explained Brown's personal philosophy this way:

He has always won elective office by being somewhat on the . . . fringe of the party. . . . Obviously [with] the concerns of the anti-nuclear group and some of the groups that believe in holistic medicine, some of the people who have his view on health, you get together a collection of people that a lot of people in the press [and] a lot of politicians see as everything from curious to threatening. But he believes that sometime in the future . . . we will be having a different way of life and that participants in that different way of life and people that understand that could become a strong political force (Richard Silberman, Brown's campaign co-chairman).

And Kennedy advisors argued that part of the reason for Kennedy's candidacy was unhappiness over Carter's conservative policies.

In addition, policy concerns influenced the choices of constituencies. Most candidates did not ignore electoral forces when they built coalitions. Rather they considered what had been successful in the past—either for themselves or their parties. But sometimes (especially among coalitional innovators) candidates who felt strongly about particular issues tried to build coalitions around those things, even when politically the prospects looked poor. One example in 1980 was Anderson's efforts to rally "social liberals." With the dominant role of conservative activists in the Republican nominating process, Anderson's support of abortion, busing, and gun control (among other policies) seemed foolish. However, these positions make sense when one recognizes Anderson's strong personal interests in these areas. Through a long period of personal reflection, Anderson had evolved from a doctrinaire conservative (in the early 1960s) to a social liberal (although his views on foreign and fiscal issues remained moderate to conservative). By the time he chose to seek the presidency (on the heels of a bitter primary battle in 1978 against a right-wing fundamentalist), Anderson had definite views on public policies. Given his strong opinions, it was natural for him to build a coalition around constituencies and issues that interested him. Similarly, Dole's coalitional strategy reflected his personal beliefs. While Dole had a reputation as a right-wing conservative (which his performance as the Republican vice-presidential nominee in 1976 did nothing to deter), he also believed that it was time in 1980 for the Republican party to drop its "country club" image. Rather than protecting only the nonpoor, Dole argued that it was time for Republicans to show a compassionate side: "Republicans . . . fall into the trap of saying, 'Well, I want to reduce all these social programs that are there for poor people and we don't represent poor people.' That may be a perception but it's wrong about our party."[42] In keeping with these beliefs, Dole tried to build support with veterans, the handicapped, and the elderly during his presidential effort. According to Anne McLaughlin, his campaign treasurer:

What Dole says is . . . the Republicans have compassion, have a record to stand on, have made life worth living to certain of these groups by the governmental action they have taken. . . . He saw himself able to build some very unique constituencies, veterans, handicapped, farmers, . . . the elderly. So I think he more than the others . . . [tried to] identify these constituencies with the issues that he had a record on.[43]

And Mari Maseng, his staff director, argued that "nobody had more of a legitimacy in doing that than Dole. . . . He was hoping to be able to mobilize that to affect a general election." These appeals to veterans and the handicapped arose less from their electoral clout in Republican primaries than from Dole's personal history of war wounds and partial paralysis. McLaughlin said that Dole's experiences gave him enduring policy interests in this area and that these interests shaped his coalitional strategy:

The Dole campaign actively did that [appeal to veterans and the handicapped] more because he had a record that was personal and he had experience for many years that was personal. That allowed him to be very credible with that approach.

Thus, Dole's personal beliefs contributed to his efforts at coalitional innovation.

Finally, policy motivations were important for campaign rhetoric. As I discuss in chapter 4, candidates chose issues for a variety of different reasons (including electoral considerations). But no discussion of rhetoric can ignore the candidates' personal beliefs. Kennedy's early decision to de-emphasize his liberal policy views showed the limits of rhetoric that was *not* tied to personal beliefs. Since Kennedy (up until his Georgetown speech when he returned to the liberal fold) gave up the liberal message he felt comfortable with and which he had been delivering for twenty years, it was not surprising that his rhetoric and presentational style suffered in the early days of the campaign. After all, he was delivering a message that was new to him. His presentational style did not improve until he returned (in the Georgetown speech on January 28, 1980) to the liberal message with which he felt comfortable. Robert Shrum, one of Kennedy's speech writers, explained the Georgetown speech this way:

The Georgetown speech . . . represented a decision on Kennedy's part that if he was going to go forward, he was going to go forward on the terms he wanted to go forward on . . . doing what he wanted to do and what he believed in, rather than putting together a convenient political strategy. . . . I remember at one point, we had all agreed on the wage and price controls and gas rationing, somebody said about gas rationing, "this will be really tough in New England. Maybe we shouldn't do it. It might cost us 10 points in New Hampshire and Maine." He said, "I don't want to hear it. . . . We've done it that way so far [and] it hasn't worked. . . . We're going to do what I want to do and what I believe in."

By the time Kennedy reached the Democratic convention (August, 1980), where he delivered perhaps the best speech of the campaign, Kennedy had a message that was not just convenient electorally (as his staff conceded the leadership message had been) but was near to his heart and compatible with his policy interests. Brown's rhetoric also illustrated the impact of personal beliefs. At the beginning of the campaign, the Californian emphasized two diverse issues—support for a balanced budget (generally endorsed by conservatives) and op-

position to nuclear energy (a liberal issue). While many observers cited these
issues as evidence of Brown's political expediency, confusion, or incompe-
tence, his advisors pointed to an explanation rooted in Brown's policy interests.
Walter McGuire, Brown's scheduler, said this:

That one discussion is probably the most crucial one to understand Jerry Brown. . . .
That he is perceived as inconsistent is his biggest dilemma. He sees those [balanced
budget and nuclear energy] as totally consistent viewpoints. . . . [It's a view of] always looking forward. . . . We didn't balance the budget at the beginning of the Vietnam War. . . . What we did is we continued to print money to try to pay for things.
We borrowed against the future. . . . When you run deficits, you're borrowing against
future generations to pay for something you're not willing to pay for yourself. . . . He
says the same thing applies to nuclear power. . . . Future generations have no choice
but to live with the problems of nuclear waste which we still don't know how to get rid
of. We don't know what the real effects of it are. . . . Why do we have the right to
lay this on our future generations just because we're not willing to bite the bullet?

In their eyes, Brown's issue choices did not rest just on electoral considerations. Rather they made sense only in reference to the candidate's policy interests (and his efforts at building a new coalition).

To summarize, campaign advisors did not paint their candidates as statesmen
who ignored electoral considerations. As Anthony Downs, David Mayhew, and
others have pointed out, the electoral connection is a realistic part of the political world. But participants also argued that campaigners were not (to use one
advisor's description) complete ciphers or total assholes having no policy interests. Unlike House elections (which were the foci of Mayhew's work), presidential races attract contestants who have political histories. They have run for
office before and they have dealt with policy matters. Because of their experiences, presidential contenders often hold strong personal beliefs, and these positions influence their campaign strategies. In 1980, candidates who felt strongly
about particular issues (such as Anderson on abortion, Brown on nuclear energy, and Dole on the handicapped) tried to build innovative coalitions around
these issues and constituencies, even when politically the prospects were not
strong. Campaigners (such as Kennedy and Reagan) having close identifications with political philosophies were influenced by these beliefs (for example,
to run, emphasize certain issues, or target various constituencies). And contenders (Reagan) who went on to capture the highest office pursued policies
that reflected their personal views. It may be no accident that a number of candidates in 1980 tried to turn their policy views into electoral strengths. There
are a number of ways in which the new electoral system attracts and rewards
candidates having strong policy concerns—the rise of issue constituencies, changes
in the political agenda (i.e., the increase in cross-cutting issues), dominance of
issue activists in the Republican and Democratic nominating processes, low
turnout in primary elections, small scale of early delegate tests, need to attract
financial contributors, and rise of new technologies (such as direct mail) which

help candidates identify and mobilize issue constituencies. These features of the contemporary process give candidates electoral incentives to emphasize issue constituencies. For these reasons, scholars need to revise models of candidate behavior to include policy motivations as well as electoral considerations.

THE ROLE OF LEADERSHIP IN COALITION-BUILDING

In this chapter, I have investigated the coalitions that presidential aspirants in 1980 tried to put together. Which constituencies did they attempt to rally and why did campaigners emphasize these people? Candidates generally considered four things when they made these decisions: their personal electoral histories, the party's electoral histories, their policy interests, and changes in the campaign process. These forces did not affect all candidates in the same ways. Some candidates benefited from their electoral histories and the new electoral system while others did not. In addition, some (the coalitional innovators) actively tried to remake party coalitions even though their rivals did not.

But more basically, leaders played a major role in coalition-building. Contrary to the impressions that we got on election day, presidential coalitions did not arise full-blown or by accident. Candidates and their advisors spent months and years rallying support. They made conscious decisions to target some constituencies and ignore others. In Reagan's case, his electoral success with Democrats did not arise by itself (although the poor state of the economy did not hurt); Reagan made active efforts throughout the nominating and general election campaigns (as he had done earlier in his political career) to appeal to disenchanted Democrats. Since candidates are at the center of coalition-building, we need to see what the 1980 campaign tells us about their behavior in general.

First, there was a high level of coalitional consistency among candidates. Since several of them (notably Baker, Brown, Connally, Crane, and Dole) fell on hard times early in the nomination campaign, one might guess that they would have altered courses and pursued different constituencies as their campaigns nosedived (especially when they made major adjustments in campaign personnel and resource allocations as the campaign developed). Certainly the classic view of campaign organizers as ad hoc strategists would suggest that electoral failure might lead to changing coalitional strategies. However, analysis of the ten major candidates showed only three major changes: Carter's coalitional switch between campaign stages from an innovator to traditional Democrat; Kennedy's switch to liberal Democrats following his Georgetown speech; and Anderson's switch from Republican to independent candidacies. In all other cases, candidates more or less stayed with the voting blocs that they originally attempted to activate. Even the celebrated case of Reagan's staff changes (he fired his campaign manager, national political director, and press secretary on the day of the New Hampshire primary) did not substantially change Reagan's pursuit of conservative core constituencies and disenchanted Democrats.

Because candidates apparently find it easier to fire staff members and reallocate resources than to remold their coalitional strategies, one can argue that there is something fundamental about coalitional efforts (and candidates' perceptions of their constituencies). Candidates appear to have limits on their coalition-building activities. While some scholars (such as Anthony Downs) argued that candidates can slide along the political spectrum from conservative to liberal constituencies and back again, this research suggests otherwise. The process by which national leaders build popular support is so long and requires so much effort that politicians guard the constituencies they have cultivated throughout their careers as one would guard the national treasury. Once candidates have built support with particular people, they generally are loathe to alienate that support. As Fenno has suggested for House members, candidates' perceptions of their constituencies are not the result of expedient political calculations. Rather they are a basic part of the candidates' political being.

Second, this research has implications for the realignment-de-alignment controversy. Observers have argued for a long time whether the contemporary period is ripe for realignment (strengthening of party coalitions) or de-alignment (decline of party coalitions). On the one side, writers such as Kevin Phillips, Richard Scammon, Ben Wattenberg, Adam Clymer, and Kathleen Frankovic have argued that the opportunities for realignment are available (if not overdue) in the modern period.[44] And on the other side, Walter Dean Burnham, the foremost advocate of the de-alignment thesis, points to the persistent decline in party identification among voters.[45]

Although this research does not explicitly address the question of whether the 1980 election will produce realignment or de-alignment (since realignment is a process that takes place over several elections), it is related to those processes. Perhaps the primary finding that has relevance for this debate is the idea that the actions of political leaders play a crucial role in shaping the coalitional options of the public. Through their strategic decisions—the choices of issues and constituencies—presidential aspirants either expand or reduce the voters' opportunities for realignment. To illustrate this point, the large number of coalitional innovators in 1980 expanded voter choices. Since so many campaigners wanted to remake party coalitions, voters could choose among a variety of conventional and unconventional candidates. Unlike elections in the old electoral system (when voters could select more conventional Republicans or Democrats), voters in 1980 were less restricted in their decisions.

This idea is important for the debate over realignment or de-alignment because many writers ignore the role that leaders play in party alignments. Too many times, they discuss the future of political parties without considering the actions of candidates. Essentially, they assume that parties will be invigorated (or weakened) irrespective of coalitional strategies. However, since citizens vote within the confines of the coalitional options that presidential contenders make available, one can argue that the future of party coalitions depends in part on candidates. Do they offer voters realistic choices for realignment, that is, the opportunity to vote for serious candidates who want to remake party coalitions or put together unconventional constituencies? Or do candidates inhibit realignment by pursuing strategies that destabilize party coalitions?

While there are no simple answers to these questions, a variety of signs suggest that leaders have not given up hope of party realignment. With the popularization of the realignment concept (through Kevin Phillips and others), many candidates want to do more than win a single election; they want to leave a legacy for their parties. Republican campaign advisors have visions of restoring the party to majority status. And despite their plurality of party identifiers, Democratic organizers seek coalitional change out of fears that "the times" may be passing them by. In part, these visions of new party alignments rest on personal ambitions; many candidates want to secure their place in history beside Franklin Roosevelt and other prominent realigners. Other candidates sought party change to bring their policy concerns to the forefront of a new coalition. And there were some farsighted campaign organizers (even a few in the Reagan campaign) who were interested in realignment because they realized after Carter's governing difficulties that strong electoral coalitions help presidents govern effectively. In this case, we heard Reagan asking voters not only to put him in office but to give him a Republican Congress that would enact his programs.

There is also evidence from the 1980 campaign (and the early days of the Reagan Administration) that some candidates take party organizations (and implicitly party-building) more seriously than others. Unlike past presidents (such as Carter) who subordinated party goals to their own political fortunes, Reagan apparently believes that a strong Republican party is in his political interests. In light of his efforts at fundraising and grass-roots development, Reagan seems intent on long-term coalition-building (which should strengthen party prospects for realignment).[46]

In addition, in terms of campaign organization, the need to allocate scarce resources among a large number of primaries and cope with an uncertain and rapidly changing environment in the general election has increased the importance of campaign planning. It no longer is uncommon for top advisors to prepare lengthy planning documents a year before the primaries.[47] Increasingly, campaign organizers believe that the length and expense of presidential campaigns require careful and systematic planning. Although campaigns still have their share of crises, ad hoc strategies, and incremental decision-making (the traditional staple of campaign organizations), strategists attempt to minimize these fragmenting tendencies by imposing as much order as possible on campaigns.

Finally, modern campaign technologies help candidates "cement" permanent change. Realignments always have been a two-stage process involving elections and governance. Elections provide presidents with opportunities for realignment while the governing process enables them to take advantage of (or lose) these opportunities. In 1980, Reagan's ten-percentage-point margin over Carter (along with the Republican sweep of the Senate) and his successful pursuit of crossover votes gave him unusual opportunities to produce enduring partisan change.[48] But as with any potential realigner, Reagan entered office with only an opportunity; he needed to translate his electoral "landslide" into an enduring improvement in Republican party fortunes. In comparing Reagan's plight with presidents from the 1850s, 1890s, and 1930s, it is clear that Reagan has more sophisticated methods for aligning government programs with popular sentiments. The rise of public opinion polls makes it possible for potential re-aligners to gauge the political consequences of various policy options. While presidents may choose to ignore polling results (as Reagan did in 1982), they have sophisticated tools for monitoring the process of realignment throughout their administrations.

However, all is not positive for party realignment. The new electoral system also encourages (and rewards) candidates who pursue strategies that destabilize party coalitions. With its emphasis on candidate-centered (not party-centered) coalitions, candidates sometimes end up with coalitions that are idiosyncratic and personalistic. And the new electoral system gives campaigners incentives to adopt "anti-system" behavior. One of the sad commentaries on the contemporary situation is that campaigners follow strategies that they realize harm the political system. Several campaign organizers tried to mobilize single-issue groups even though privately they worried about the dangers these movements posed for the political system. In discussing this problem, advisors noted that single-issue groups fragment public opinion, weaken political parties, and impose heavy demands on candidates. These groups also lead to fragile coalitions. According to one manager (whose candidate made active efforts to appeal to issue constituencies), coalitions based on single-issue groups inherently are instable: "as you begin to become popular with a-group, b-group, and c-group, and then you get up to about d or e, . . . you're going to become internally inconsistent and then the whole thing will fall apart." Yet campaigners felt compelled to rely on these groups for political advancement despite the systemic dangers. These trends do not portend good news for stable political parties. But whatever the long-run prospects for the party system, it is clear that leaders play an important role. By their decisions to offer coalitional "choices" and "echoes," leaders structure the coalitional options of the public.

NOTES

1. Robert Axelrod, "Where the Votes Come From," in Jeff Fishel, ed., *Parties and Elections in an Anti-Party Age*, pp. 86–99. Also see John Petrocik, *Party Coalitions* (Chicago: University of Chicago Press, 1981).

2. The best statements of this position can be found in Anthony Downs, *An Economic Theory of Democracy* (New York: Harper, 1957) and David Mayhew, *Congress: The Electoral Connection* (New Haven, Conn.: Yale University Press, 1974).

3. For a similar analysis of this development, see Kessel, *Presidential Campaign Politics*, chapter 3.

4. For a detailed discussion of the rise of single-issue groups (in particular, the emergence of right-to-life groups), see Marjorie Hershey and Darrell West, "Single-Issue Politics: Pro-Life Groups and Senate Campaigning in 1980," in Allan Cigler and

Burdett Loomis, eds., *Interest Group Politics* (Washington, D.C.: Congressional Quarterly Press, 1983).

5. James Q. Wilson, "American Politics, Then and Now," *Commentary* (February, 1979), p. 45.

6. If 1980 is any indication, the Senate may be losing its grip on presidential "incubations" (because national prominence is not the only route to the White House in the new electoral system). For the conventional view of the Senate's primacy in supplying presidential contenders, see Robert Peabody, Norman Ornstein, and David Rohde, "The United States Senate as a Presidential Incubator," *Political Science Quarterly*, 91, no. 2 (Summer, 1976), pp. 237–258.

7. For a detailed description of California politics, see Michael Barone, Grant Ujifusa, and Douglas Matthews, *The Almanac of American Politics 1980* (New York: E. P. Dutton, 1979), pp. 49–55.

8. By core constituencies, I mean the candidate's most loyal supporters. For related ideas, see Richard Fenno's discussion (*Home Style*, chapter one) of personal constituencies (the intimates) and primary constituencies (the strongest supporters) and Kessel's analysis (*Presidential Campaign Politics*, pp. 57–58) of "core groups" and "strategy groups" at the leadership level.

9. See "Ronald Reagan Up Close," *Newsweek* (July 21, 1980), pp. 36–38.

10. Broder was quoted by Cannon in Harwood, *The Pursuit of the Presidency*, p. 262.

11. *Bill Moyers' Journal* interview, July 10, 1980.

12. Jules Witcover reported that Reagan "had been pushing to go on television in his old style for weeks. 'All along,' an insider said later, 'Reagan was saying, God damn it, you guys, I ought to go on national TV. I can raise a lot of money. But we all would put him down. We thought it was old stuff, that it wouldn't work. You know, you did it in 1964 but this is 1976.' " See Witcover's *Marathon* (New York: Viking Press, 1977), p. 441.

13. See Reagan's announcement speech in New York City on November 13, 1979 (text made available by the Reagan for President Committee).

14. On July 27, 1979, Reagan sent the following letter to Representative Henry Hyde, one of the pro-life movement's strongest supporters in the House (Hyde forwarded this letter to the National Right-to-Life Committee, which distributed it nationwide):

Dear Henry:

I want you to know that I have long admired your courage, determination and articulate championship of the vital cause of the unborn child in America today. I realize there is a great difference of opinion regarding the subject of abortion. People on both sides of this issue have very sincere, strongly held views.

I personally believe that interrupting a pregnancy is the taking of a human life and can only be justified in self-defense—that is, if the mother's own life is in danger. In 1976 the Republican Party platform protested the January 22, 1973 Supreme Court decision which overruled the historic role of the states in legislating in the areas concerning abortion and took away virtually every protection previously accorded the unborn. Later decisions have intruded into the family structure through their denial of the parents' obligations and right to guide their minor children. The platform called for a continuance of the public dialogue on abortion, and expressed support of the efforts of those who seek enactment of a constitutional amendment to restore protection of the right to life for unborn children.

I fully concur with our platform.

But the process of amending the Constitution is lengthy and difficult. As in other cases where I favor additions to our Constitution—to limit federal spending, and to balance the federal budget—my preference would be to first use the legislative process. If that fails, I would hope that Congress itself would propose the amendment and send it to the states for ratification. As a last resort I support the right of the people of the United States to call a constitutional convention for the specific purpose of proposing an amendment.

In the meantime, I am opposed to using federal tax money to pay for abortions in cases where the life of the mother is in no danger.

Sincerely,
Ronald Reagan

In response, the political action committee of the National Right-to-Life Committee endorsed Reagan January 20, 1980 and sent the following letter to its membership March 31, 1980:

An open letter on the endorsement of Ronald Reagan

It is with profound sorrow that I must inform the members of the National Right to Life Committee of Ellen McCormack's attack on Governor Ronald Reagan through letters to pro-life voters in New Hampshire, Massachusetts, Vermont, and Florida—as well as full-page ads in newspapers in New Hampshire and Illinois.

Mrs. McCormack had earned the gratitude of the pro-life movement for her 1976 presidential candidacy which increased public awareness of the tragedy of the U.S. Supreme Court abortion decision through spot television announcements.

The impressive political growth of our movement during the past four years has, however, resulted in our ability to significantly influence the election of a pro-life president.

Mrs. McCormack chose to run in 1980 as an independent candidate despite a personal appeal by Congressman Henry Hyde that she not divide the pro-life vote in the general election.

On January 20th the Board of Directors of National Right to Life Political Action Committee, after careful consideration, endorsed Governor Ronald Reagan for President of the United States.

The attack on Governor Reagan, the day before the crucial New Hampshire primary, can only be described as divisive and destructive.

The critique singled out Ronald Reagan, the only electable pro-life presidential candidate. There was no mention of John Anderson's or Howard Baker's outspoken endorsement of the Supreme Court's abortion decision nor of George Bush's refusal to support any but a states' rights amendment with an additional rape-and-incest exception clause.

Governor Reagan's public support of the Human Life Amendment has been clearly articulated and consistent since 1975. His position was recently reaffirmed in an open letter to Congressman Henry Hyde which expressed in addition, his willingness to pursue, if necessary, the constitutional convention route of amendment.

As president of the National Right to Life Committee and chairman of National Right-to-Life Political Action Committee, I am convinced, both through Ronald Reagan's statements and from my private interview with him on January 17th, of the Governor's deep commitment to the protection of the unborn and the incapacitated through the enactment of a Human Life Amendment.

Governor Reagan is thus far the only presidential candidate endorsed by National Right to Life PAC.

Ronald Reagan deserves the support of every pro-life voter.

Carolyn F. Gerster, M.D.

15. As he had done in 1976, Carter targeted moderate, rural, and southern voters during the 1980 nominating process but became a conventional New Deal Democrat for the general election. While candidate strategies alone do not explain election results, one can suggest that his coalitional inconsistencies in 1980 put him in a precarious position. First, Carter's coalitional shifts may have contributed to his history of "soft" support (which one Carter advisor described as "a mile wide but an inch deep"). Unlike Reagan, who consistently pursued certain core constituencies (and thereby developed emotional followings), Carter never developed dedicated, loyal, and enthusiastic supporters. Second, in terms of general election strategies, Carter's coalitional gymnastics strained his relations with liberal Democrats. Having been "spurned" in the primaries by a president who favored moderate to conservative constituencies (and governed with conservative fiscal policies), Democratic liberals were slow to join Carter's fall efforts with any intensity. Finally, the coalitional changes (combined with soft support) may have left Carter unusually vulnerable to last-minute campaign events (such as his debate with Reagan and the Iranian hostage negotiations). While pollsters debate the sources of Carter's electoral plummet during the last week of the campaign, they often ignore the point that if Carter had been consistent in his coalition-building and had developed loyal supporters, these last-minute developments might have been less important.

16. Right after announcing his presidential candidacy in 1979, Connally revived his barnstorming technique in Texas. Visiting twenty cities around the state, he literally stole the opening show from Reagan and Bush, according to his advisors. The success of this tour apparently encouraged him to use the technique in Iowa. For another description of Connally's Iowa tour, see Harwood, *The Pursuit of the Presidency*, p. 121.

17. Unlike Reagan and others, Connally did not take advantage of newly emerging issue constituencies, such as right-to-lifers and fundamentalists. This decision is odd given the fact that his advisors understood the limits of demographic constituencies and pursued what they called an "attitudinal" constituency. Tarrance explained, "Connally, his campaign manager, and his staff were trying to do something different. . . . We challenged the more traditional classic demographic ways, meaning old people, young people, union people, nonunion people, etc." And Eddie Mahe, Jr., said, "We're not going for a demographic constituency. We're going for an attitudinal constituency that crosses demographic lines. . . . We are interested in reaching people who have a conception of the presidency as wanting someone who is strong and forceful and commanding and knowledgeable." But Connally's attitudinal constituency (which was based on a 1979 Tarrance survey project that investigated role orientations toward the American presidency) had no room for these issue constituencies.

18. See "The 1982 Elections," *Congressional Quarterly Weekly Report* (February 27, 1982), p. 390.

19. Quoted in Sidney Blumenthal, *The Permanent Campaign*, pp. 262–263. This point also is discussed in Harwood, *The Pursuit of the Presidency*, pp. 29–30.

20. As an example of the strategic costs of Kennedy's failure to use polling, Carter pollster, Pat Caddell, argued that Kennedy often made moves at the wrong times. Right

after Carter's hawkish State of the Union address, Caddell's polls showed the development of a dovish backlash in the upcoming New Hampshire primary:

Kennedy at that moment made one of the real strategic errors that I don't even think they realized, I don't know that they know it today, when they attacked Carter that week. Instead of going at Carter on that issue [the hawkish backlash] or even on the economy where he had been playing around, he chose that week to attack Carter again over Iran, which was, in fact, Carter's strongest grounds with these voters who were in the process of making movement.

Caddell and his staff also developed a "second vote" question that enabled them to predict primary results in a fairly accurate manner (in contrast to polls published by news organizations, which consistently were wrong).

21. Of the major candidates, Bush, Carter, and Reagan were most committed to polling; Brown, Connally, and Kennedy were most skeptical, and Anderson, Baker, Crane, and Dole lacked money for polling.

22. With the volatility of polls in the 1980 nominating process (caused partly by the Iranian hostage takeover), some candidates became even more skeptical of poll results.

23. Other scholars have emphasized early political experiences. For example, James David Barber has discussed the importance of the "first independent political success." See his *The Presidential Character* (Englewood Cliffs, N.J.: Prentice-Hall, 1972), p. 10. And Marjorie Hershey and Darrell West also have discussed the impact of previous races on Senate campaigners. See their "Single-Issue Groups and Political Campaigns."

24. *Issues and Answers* interview, December 9, 1979.

25. *Face the Nation* interview, February 3, 1980.

26. *Issues and Answers* interview, October 14, 1979.

27. According to Richard Williamson, Crane's campaign manager:

Phil Crane was trying to put a coalition together that composed elements of what's now referred to commonly as "the new right" . . . some of the Catholic, ethnic votes that Ronald Reagan is now going after, who are increasingly disillusioned with the Democratic party, and therefore are up for grabs and we've seen that ever since '72. Also, some of the fundamentalist religious groups. Also, some of the social conservative groups, right-to-life, and others. . . . We had a sense then and it's a sense now shared within the Reagan campaign that those people no longer have as deep an alignment to the Democratic party.

28. In fact, research on Roosevelt's realignment suggests that "mobilization" strategies (appeals to nonvoters or newly enfranchised citizens, such as immigrants) played a stronger role than "conversion" strategies (appeals to the other party's supporters). See Kristi Andersen, *The Creation of a Democratic Majority* (Chicago: University of Chicago Press, 1979).

29. Brown's approach to coalition-building was influenced by his electoral experiences. In California, with the large "in-migration," demographic blocs are fluid and the class structure is diverse. Brown advisor Richard Maullin argued that, "group cohesiveness is just not as strong—if it is strong, it tends to be strong within very small groups." These patterns mean, according to Maullin, that to build coalitions in the traditional, demographic sense, a candidate has "got to be an incredibly agile sociologist." Because of the difficulties in doing that, it often is easier to rely on issue constituencies than demographic groups.

30. Since Anderson recognized the prevailing force of habitual party loyalties in the

general election, he tried to sell his independent candidacy as a temporary deviation, not a permanent party realignment: "There is this traditional allegiance to two parties. . . . That's why I didn't form a third party. I was afraid that it would be an unsettling thing as far as many people were concerned. And I wasn't trying to institutionalize this effort." See his *Face the Nation* interview, October 12, 1980.

31. Quoted by Robert Scheer in "Bush Assails Carter Defense Strategy," *Los Angeles Times* (January 24, 1980), p. 30.

32. Ironically, both Baker and Bush talked about their abilities to get independent and Democratic votes in the general election. Yet neither undertook the efforts that Anderson and Reagan did to attract crossovers in the primaries.

33. According to Tim Kraft (national campaign manager), Carter's 1980 strategy was similar to that of 1976 (the president had fought liberals during the nominating process but tried to bring them back into his coalition in the fall). Kraft described the 1976 experience this way:

Jimmy Carter, having won the nomination in a series of commando actions in different primary and caucus states, often at odds or certainly not in alliance with say the state party and the major office-holders and Democratic governors and whatever, had to appeal [in the general election] to traditional Democratic constituencies to try to forge an alliance to build up enough votes and enough electoral states to win the election.

34. Quoted by Blumenthal, *The Permanent Campaign*, p. 40.

35. Of course, in choosing to change the Democratic party, Carter sowed seeds of dissatisfaction among those who feared he was abandoning the party. Stephen Smith, Kennedy's campaign chairman, argued that Carter's move away from the party's traditional policies (notably fiscal policies) sparked Kennedy's challenge: "He was moving away from more or less traditional Democratic concerns. . . . It was a situation that . . . the president was going to continue to move . . . to more or less traditional Republican approaches."

36. The ultimate irony of the Carter campaign came when post-election observers interpreted his defeat as the triumph of conservatism and repudiation of liberalism. For a candidate who tried to move his party in a more conservative direction during the primaries, it must have been a surprising interpretation.

37. In the next section, I also show that candidates' policy interests stimulated some efforts at coalitional change.

38. Since political attachments have grown weaker over the past two decades and the electoral process has opened up, one would expect that there are more innovators now than in the old electoral system.

39. James Fallows, "The Passionless Presidency," *Atlantic* (May, 1979), pp. 43–46.

40. See text of his convention acceptance speech, *Congressional Quarterly Weekly Report* (July 19, 1980), p. 2064.

41. However, A. James Reichley found in tracing the ideological roots of the Nixon and Ford administrations that ideological motivations were more common than generally assumed. See his *Conservatives in an Age of Change* (Washington, D.C.: Brookings, 1981), and "The Conservative Roots of the Nixon, Ford, and Reagan Administrations," *Political Science Quarterly* (Winter 1981–82), pp. 537–550. For a similar view, see Paul Light, *The President's Agenda* (Baltimore, Md.: Johns Hopkins Press, 1982).

42. Dole made this comment during the Republican debate in Manchester, New Hampshire, February 20, 1980.

43. As a farm-state senator, Dole has backed liberal social legislation (such as food stamps and subsidized school lunches) that benefits agriculture. These actions led George McGovern to describe Dole this way: "Bob Dole is a mellower individual these days. . . . Of all the people I know in the Senate, he has grown the most." See McGovern's description in Congressional Quarterly, *Candidates '80* (January, 1980), p. 51.

44. See Kevin Phillips, *The Emerging Republican Majority* (New Rochelle, N.Y.: Arlington House, 1969); Richard Scammon and Ben Wattenberg, *The Real Majority* (New York: Coward, McCann and Geoghegan, 1970); and Adam Clymer and Kathleen Frankovic, "The Realities of Realignment," *Public Opinion*, 4, no. 3 (June/July, 1981), pp. 42–47.

45. Burnham, *Critical Elections and the Mainsprings of Electoral Politics*.

46. See Jones, "Nominating 'Carter's Favorite Opponent' " and David Broder, "Introduction," in Seymour Martin Lipset, ed., *Party Coalitions in the 1980s* (San Francisco: Institute for Contemporary Studies, 1981) for similar interpretations.

47. For examples of these memos, see reprints of Caddell's and Wirthlin's planning documents in Drew, *Portrait of an Election*, pp. 349–439.

48. If 1980 becomes a realignment (its prospects are looking bleaker all the time), it would have taken place under very different conditions than realignments in the 1850s, 1890s, and 1930s. First, it would not have taken place in an emotionally charged atmosphere (a usual precondition) but under conditions of widespread public apathy, cynicism, and mistrust. Second, it would have occurred at a time of declining, not increasing, voter turnout. Third, it would not have involved sharp and uncompromising issue discussions by the candidates.

4

Campaign Rhetoric and the Political Agenda

Rhetoric has a bad name. According to Webster, rhetoric is the "insincere" use of language. William Safire, one of the more colorful observers of language, is no more kind; in his *Political Dictionary*, he defines the term as "high-flying oratory" (although it originally meant the "persuasive presentation of argument").[1] Scholars also take offense at rhetoric, telling us not to take campaign promises seriously; instead we should "watch what they do, not what they say." As the old joke goes, when leaders proclaim the need for trust and understanding, voters should keep firm grips on their wallets and purses because the deft hand of the federal government will not be far behind.

Of course, this skepticism is partially justified. Everyone can cite examples of political leaders who changed their minds or broke campaign promises. In 1964, Johnson campaigned as the peace candidate, yet escalated the skirmish in Vietnam to a major war. Meanwhile, Carter's top advisor (Hamilton Jordan) predicted that voters would not find "a Cy Vance as Secretary of State and Zbigniew Brzezinski as head of National Security"; but these men were appointed anyway.[2] And even though Reagan promised to select justices who were pro-family, for the first vacancy on the Supreme Court, he nominated Sandra Day O'Connor, who previously supported pro-choice positions on abortion.

But despite these policy reversals, it would be a mistake to ignore campaign rhetoric. Few choices are more fundamental for presidential candidates than rhetorical content (what they discuss) and style of communications (how they discuss it). By emphasizing some topics more than others, campaigners bring issues to the political forefront. For example, Reagan's entrepreneurial activities in 1980 on behalf of supply-side economics brought an idea to public attention that previously had not been at centerstage. Conversely, there were several important issues (such as disarmament, world poverty, and child care) that received little attention from the major candidates. Clearly, issues do not always arise full-blown on the political agenda; rather leaders play a crucial role in defining the terms of debate (especially during campaigns when they have the nation's attention).

Rhetoric also plays an important role in coalition formation. By emphasizing topics of interest to people they want to rally, campaigners signal their coalitional strategies. As an example, .it should be clear that candidates who take anti-abortion, anti-busing, and anti-gun control positions have different coalitions in mind than those who advocate environmental protection and the Equal Rights Amendment. Of course, campaigners sometimes take positions that do not appear to go together. One of the many problems of Brown's campaign was his support for a balanced budget (often seen as a conservative issue) and his opposition to nuclear energy (usually an issue of liberals). In this case, Brown's rhetoric confused voters and the media because it made him look inconsistent or "weird" in his coalition-building. But these are the risks when candidates use rhetoric in unusual ways.

Finally, rhetoric is important for communications style—how campaigners present their subject matters to the public. Candidates can say the same thing in a variety of different ways. Sometimes they can be serious; at other times their speeches resemble comedy monologues. Robert Dole (whose biting wit is well known among political professionals) started one appearance at a New Hampshire candidate forum with a series of jokes, political barbs, and humorous complaints that would rival a Johnny Carson performance:

As I look at the three Democratic candidates, I hear a voice from the past, a drawl from the present, and a beep-beep-beep from outer space (laughter). Is Howard Baker here? I wondered where he'd been. I hadn't seen him in Congress (laughter). But he hasn't seen me there either the last week (laughter). Let me say in the five minutes I have that I know all the candidates and, as someone said, they've been referred to as the "Magnificent Seven." I think any one of the seven should provide the leadership for the 80s. I have said many times that I don't know a single one of these men who I can't use in my administration (laughter and applause). And I've even suggested where I might use one or two of them (laughter). Having said that and having walked into this crowded room—I thought I was going to a Secret Service convention for a minute (laughter)—I wondered where all the press had been.[3]

Humor may appear to be inconsequential in presidential campaigns, evidence more of frivolity than seriousness. But this conclusion would be mistaken. Candidates often use humor to communicate political messages. Dole's lines were funny; yet, they delivered a succession of serious thoughts: an attack on the three Democratic candidates; Dole's personal doubts about a nominating process that takes leaders away from the Senate; his support for most but not all of the potential Republican nominees, and unhappiness over his infrequent press coverage. Judging from audience reactions, these messages came through loud and clear. So communications style is not limited to policy discussions; relevant political commentary also may take other forms.

In this chapter, I explore rhetoric in the 1980 campaign. What did candidates talk about on the campaign trail? How did they present themselves and their positions to voters? What role did issues play? Did Republicans and Democrats talk about the same things? And did their appeals change between the nominating process and general election?

THE NATURE OF CAMPAIGN RHETORIC

Political observers persistently have found that candidates do not discuss "the issues" in detail. Because politics is not a high priority in the daily lives of many citizens, specific policy statements are not prevalent. In his analysis of the 1960 general election, Page discovered that Kennedy spoke about public policy in 23 percent of his campaign appeals while Nixon did in 16 percent. More commonly, these nominees emphasized goals, problems, and past performance (49 percent for Kennedy and 43 percent by Nixon).[4]

Of course, since 1960 there have been major changes in election processes (see chapters 2 and 3). Issue constituencies have arisen. The nominating period has become longer and more strongly contested. News reporters are more vigilant in pursuing and challenging candidates. And some scholars argue that voters have become more likely (than in the 1950s) to vote on the basis of policy issues.[5]

Because of these developments, one must ask whether candidates use rhetoric in the same way as before. Are policy discussions more frequent in the new than the old electoral system? To see how 1980 compares with 1960, I tabulated campaign appeals in the 1980 nominating and general election stages.[6] Following Page's work and the standard categories of voting research (party, issues, and candidate qualities), I used seven categories of rhetoric:

1. specific policy statements—policy discussions involving dollar figures, particular legislative remedies, or promises of concrete policy actions,
2. general problems or performance—discussion of general policy areas without specific recommendations,
3. general goals—references to abstract concepts such as freedom or liberty,
4. personal qualities—the candidates' personal backgrounds or characteristics, such as honesty, competence, or principles,
5. campaign activities—references to strategies, organizations, or the "horse race,"
6. party appeals—specific references to one of the parties, and
7. other—statements of greeting, expressions of thanks, or requests for support.

Table 4–1 lists the nomination appeals of the major contenders (or, in the case of President Carter who did not campaign in the spring, his two major surrogates: Walter Mondale and Rosalyn Carter).[7] This table shows a number of patterns. In terms of overall appeals, press coverage of campaign rhetoric was skewed toward "visible" candidates. The *New York Times* reported 957 statements by Kennedy, compared to 396 for Reagan and 315 for Bush. At the other end of the scale, the newspaper included only 2 appeals by Crane and 44 statements

Table 4-1
The Nature of Campaign Appeals During Nominations

Campaign Appeal	Anderson	Baker	Bush	Connally	Crane	Dole
Specific Policy	20.3	16.0	15.5	10.0	0.0	2.3
General Problems	28.4	27.5	37.6	56.7	0.0	0.0
Goals	3.8	9.5	7.0	1.9	0.0	0.0
Personal Qualities	8.5	16.0	10.4	6.5	0.0	15.9
Campaign	28.6	26.1	24.8	16.8	0.0	68.2
Political Party	8.6	2.9	2.2	5.8	100.0	6.9
Other	1.6	1.4	3.4	1.8	0.0	6.8
Total	99.8	99.4	100.9	99.5	100.0	100.1
N	186	137	315	107	2	44

Campaign Appeal	Reagan	Brown	R. Carter	Mondale	Kennedy
Specific Policy	13.4	15.0	10.8	13.3	16.4
General Problems	58.4	42.1	26.9	28.3	55.9
Goals	11.1	2.4	1.6	4.0	1.9
Personal Qualities	4.1	11.9	38.3	23.0	7.4
Campaign	9.5	19.5	10.0	11.0	12.9
Political Party	1.0	7.8	4.6	11.8	3.7
Other	1.7	0.8	8.4	9.3	2.1
Total	99.2	99.5	100.6	100.7	100.3
N	396	128	131	128	957

Note: The figure refers to the percentage of total campaign statements (N) reported in the *New York Times* that fall within each category.

by Dole. Clearly, as other researchers have found, some candidates were advantaged in communicating their messages to the public via the media. While it is beyond the scope of this research to explain these discrepancies, the unusual nature of Kennedy's candidacy (including the Camelot legacy, challenge to a sitting president, and assassination threats) certainly contributed to the disproportionate coverage of his campaign appearances.

Looking at the substance of campaign rhetoric, specific policy appeals were not frequent (and fell within a range similar to 1960). In keeping with his image as an outspoken candidate, Anderson made the most policy statements (20.3 percent), followed by Kennedy (16.4 percent), Baker (16.0 percent), Bush (15.5 percent), and Brown (15.0 percent). Relative to these candidates, Rosalyn Carter (10.8 percent), Mondale (13.3 percent), and Reagan (13.4 percent) were less specific. Despite the higher specificity of Bush and Brown (and Reagan's lower level), it was Bush and Brown whom the media criticized for vagueness.[8] In contrast, Reagan received little criticism for ambiguity. Apparently, his well-known conservatism and "track record" insulated him from criticism on these grounds. And Rosalyn Carter was not criticized because, as a family surrogate, she was "allowed" to be less substantive and more personal in her rhetoric.[9] Surprisingly, there were no issues on which all candidates took specific positions. On government spending, everyone except Mondale made policy commitments. Defense generated specificity only from Anderson, Baker, Bush, Reagan, and Kennedy, while the grain embargo emerged as an issue for Baker, Connally, Reagan, Brown, Mondale, and Kennedy. In addition, there were several important issues (such as disarmament, the Third World, child care, and poverty) on which no candidates took specific positions (although some contenders discussed them in general terms). As Page found for earlier campaigns, strategies of ambiguity (either fuzzy rhetoric or no discussions) were prevalent in 1980.

Perhaps befitting an era of "de-alignment," party appeals were even more rare than issue discussions in the nominating process. Excluding Crane, who had infrequent press coverage, most candidates discussed political parties less than 10 percent of the time. Among the "high" party mentioners were Mondale (11.8 percent), Anderson (8.6 percent), Brown (7.8 percent), Dole (6.9 percent), and Connally (5.8 percent). At the low end were Reagan (1.0 percent), Bush (2.2 percent), Baker (2.9 percent), Kennedy (3.7 percent), and Rosalyn Carter (4.6 percent). Mondale discussed party the most because his role was to rally party regulars against the Kennedy challenge. In the cases of Anderson and Brown (who were interested in changing party coalitions), their references were not flattering to parties; they often called on parties to become more relevant institutions. As one would expect in a period of declining voter identification with parties (and when many candidates wanted to remake parties), campaigners did not base their appeals on political parties.

If candidates did not emphasize specific issues or parties, what did they discuss? While there were differences among candidates, presidential aspirants predominantly discussed general problems. For many campaigners, discussion of substantive problems *without* specific policy recommendations was their most common topic. Reagan discussed general problems 58.4 percent of the time while Connally did so 56.7 percent of the time, and Kennedy followed with 55.9 percent. Both Kennedy and Reagan harped on the general failures of the Carter Administration without developing elaborate sets of counterpolicies (although Kennedy's Georgetown speech eventually provided more of an alternative framework than Reagan ever did). Even candidates at the low end of the scale devoted substantial time to general problems: Rosalyn Carter (26.9 percent), Mondale (28.3 percent), and Anderson (28.4 percent). In contrast, few candidates discussed goals (such as national confidence) at length. Kennedy spoke about goals 1.9 percent of the time, while Anderson discussed them 3.8 percent. However, the notable exception to this pattern was Reagan who devoted more attention (11.1 percent) to goals than any other candidate. Among other goals, Reagan spoke of the need for national confidence, national strength, and spiritual renewal. By emphasizing broad goals of concern to various segments of the electorate (without going into complex substantive discussions), Reagan presented voters with simple and easily grasped messages.[10] In these ways, the content of Reagan's rhetoric (as well as a well-honed style) contributed to his image as a "great communicator." Other campaigners emphasized personal qualities. Rosalyn Carter discussed personal qualities (38.3 percent) much more than her competitors (which fits with a description of family surrogates as not oriented to policy issues). Meanwhile, Anderson (28.6 percent), Baker (26.1 percent), Bush (24.8 percent), and Brown (19.5 percent) devoted their attention to campaign phenomena, such as strategy, organization, or the horse race. These figures are interesting because they are far higher than the 3.0 (Kennedy) and 6.0 (Nixon) percent that Page cited for campaign discussions in 1960 (see p. 156). Perhaps the growth of media coverage, importance of momentum, and expansion of the nominating process encouraged candidates to discuss campaign phenomena more frequently in 1980.

Table 4–2 lists comparable breakdowns in rhetoric for the general election. Several differences stand out. Some candidates were much less specific about policy in the fall than in the spring. Owing to his role as vice-presidential nominee on a ticket headed by his chief rival, Bush apparently decided to play it safe; he devoted only 3.7 percent of his rhetoric to specific policy statements, compared to his earlier figure of 15.5 percent. And Anderson dropped from 20.3 to 10.3 percent as he was more cautious about political controversies in the general election. In contrast, Reagan (12.8 percent) and Mondale (14.3 percent) maintained their levels of specificity, and Jimmy Carter devoted 15.3 percent of his statements to specific policy.

Table 4-2
The Nature of Campaign Appeals During General Election

Campaign Appeal	Reagan	Bush	J. Carter	Mondale	Anderson	Lucey
Specific Policy	12.8	3.7	15.3	14.3	10.3	0.0
General Problems	58.6	40.0	44.1	50.2	50.9	36.9
Goals	5.0	8.9	3.3	4.0	7.1	0.0
Personal Qualities	10.5	12.2	8.7	4.6	10.3	0.0
Campaign	8.1	27.3	14.2	16.1	14.9	52.6
Political Party	3.1	5.6	6.5	8.6	3.3	10.5
Other	2.4	2.8	7.6	2.9	3.3	0.0
Total	100.5	100.5	99.7	100.7	100.1	100.0
N	549	216	574	175	392	19

Note: The figure refers to the percentage of total campaign statements (N) reported in the *New York Times* that fall within each category.

Different issues also emerged on the fall political agenda. Reagan took specific positions on civil rights and urban policy, issues on which he had not taken
positions in the primaries. And both Carter and Reagan made commitments on
environmental policies in the fall, even though neither had done so in the spring
(nor had Anderson). Of course, this is not to say that there were no issues on
the political agenda that were common in both stages. Issues that the major
candidates discussed in both periods included unemployment, government
spending, defense, and the grain embargo. But the limited number of common
issues suggests that the differing settings of nominations and the general election encourage candidates to raise different issues on the political agenda. In
particular, the broader nature of the fall electorate and the need of Republicans
to attract Democratic and independent votes require GOP nominees to broaden
their rhetoric.

In terms of similarities, party appeals again were not common in the general
election. Given the head-to-head competition of candidates from different parties, one might have expected more attention to political parties. But this was
not the case. Although the Democratic nominee (Carter, 6.5 percent) discussed
parties twice as frequently as the Republican (Reagan, 3.1 percent), owing to
the greater number of Democratic identifiers, neither spent much time on this
subject.[11] Instead, candidates mixed a variety of general substantive discussions, personal qualities, and campaign topics. As in the nominating process,
the largest category of rhetoric was discussion of general problems: Reagan devoted 58.6 percent to that topic; Carter spent 44.1 percent, and Anderson 50.9
percent of the time. Several campaigners also emphasized personal qualities and
campaign phenomena.[12]

THE DIRECTION OF CAMPAIGN RHETORIC

Not only did candidates make decisions about the content of their rhetoric,
they chose the direction of their appeals. In the 1980 campaign, media observers sometimes bemoaned "negative attacks" and questioned whether candidates gave voters positive reasons for support. But despite media criticism, these
appeals had several features that were attractive to presidential contestants. For
minority party candidates, their prime virtue was that they sharpened candidate
differences without necessarily drawing attention to the attacker's party status.
For "in" party challengers (such as Kennedy), attacks were useful for a related
reason: they pinpointed differences without requiring detailed policy alternatives. Campaigners could criticize the incumbent's policies for being out of tune
with the party or the nation, but they did not have to show how their programs
filled the void. Finally, attacks were useful for coalitional innovators. Since several
presidential aspirants wanted to remake party coalitions, attacks may have helped
them mobilize unconventional or disenchanted constituencies.

To investigate the proportion of appeals in which candidates attacked the policies, personal qualities, goals, campaign tactics, or party appeals of other contestants, I compiled the percentage of attacks in the nominating and general

Table 4-3
The Direction of Campaign Appeals During Nominations

Direction	Anderson	Baker	Bush	Connally	Crane	Dole
Attack	28.4	22.1	38.0	40.2	100.0	3.6
Nonattack	71.6	77.9	62.0	59.8	0.0	86.4
Total	100.0	100.0	100.0	100.0	100.0	100.0
N	190	136	316	107	2	44

Direction	Reagan	Brown	R. Carter	Mondale	Kennedy
Attack	24.1	35.2	2.3	16.4	59.3
Nonattack	75.9	64.8	97.7	83.6	40.7
Total	100.0	100.0	100.0	100.0	100.0
N	396	128	132	128	956

Note: The figure refers to the percentage of total campaign statements (N) reported in the *New York Times* that fall within each category.

election processes. Looking first at nominations, Table 4–3 shows the importance of strategic considerations in negative rhetoric. Exluding Crane, whom the press covered sporadically, Kennedy had the highest percentage of attacks (59.3 percent). Kennedy also was the only candidate whose negative appeals outnumbered positive ones. Given his challenge to Carter and need to clarify differences between them, this was not surprising. In contrast, both Rosalyn Carter and Mondale generally refrained from attacks (although in the latter stage of the primary season, Carter's media advertising was very negative). On the Republican side, two challengers (Bush and Connally) to frontrunner Reagan launched the most attacks (38.0 and 40.2 percent, respectively), followed by Anderson (28.4 percent). Perhaps in an effort to hold the party together, Reagan's attacks (24.1 percent) were less frequent (and generally were aimed at Carter, not his Republican challengers). However, during the general election, as Table 4–4 shows, there were sharp increases in attacks by all candidates. Reagan's total jumped from 24.1 percent in the spring to 49.4 percent in the fall (Carter was not far behind with 44.1 percent). Meanwhile, Bush, Mondale, and Anderson also increased the negative thrust of their rhetoric (the latter two doubled their attacks in the fall). In short, negative rhetoric was a dominant feature of the 1980 general election.

RHETORIC AND AGENDA-BUILDING

The limited policy specificity and prevalent use of negative attacks has led some people to conclude that rhetoric is irrelevant in modern campaigns. After

Table 4-4
The Direction of Campaign Appeals During General Election

Direction	Reagan	Bush	J. Carter	Mondale	Anderson	Lucey
Attack	49.4	48.1	44.1	36.6	54.6	36.8
Nonattack	50.6	51.9	55.9	63.4	45.4	63.2
Total	100.0	100.0	100.0	100.0	100.0	100.0
N	549	216	574	175	372	19

Note: The figure refers to the percentage of total campaign statements (N) reported in the *New York Times* that fall within each category.

all, they argue, why study communications that are broad, vague, and person-alistic? While this skepticism is partially justified, it misses the subtle role that candidate rhetoric plays in agenda formation. One of the paradoxical features of contemporary elections is that even though presidential aspirants do not talk very specifically about policy matters, their rhetoric still influences (and limits) the policy alternatives deemed worthy of public debate.

Leaders exercise influence over the agenda in different ways. On some issues (what one can call the "top-down" agenda), presidential contenders bring to public attention issues and policy alternatives that previously have not received extensive national discussion. In 1980, there were several examples of agenda leadership. Reagan's economic package of tax cuts and budget reductions gave legitimacy to an economic theory (supply-side economics) that was untested and scorned by leading economists.[13] Anderson's espousal of a fifty-cent-a-gallon gasoline tax (plus a cut in social security taxes) did not result in legislation. But it focused attention on policy alternatives that otherwise would have been ignored. And Kennedy's support (in his Georgetown speech) of wage and price controls and gasoline rationing gave voters additional policy choices.[14]

Of course, all agenda items do not arise because of leadership. Some topics (what one can call the "bottom-up" agenda) bubble up irrespective of candi-date behavior. For example, the taking of hostages in Iran would have become a national issue no matter how President Carter responded. Economic disrup-tions also do not need leadership to take their place in national political debates (because of their widespread visibility and carryover effects in other policy areas). And abortion became part of the campaign agenda despite the beliefs of some participants that it did not belong there. According to one advisor whose can-didate actively attempted to mobilize pro-life constituencies:

the issue of abortion certainly in my mind doesn't even belong in the presidential elec-tion. It has nothing to do with the presidency. It has been thrust at presidential candi-dates just because under this system, which depends on primary voters, there are votes in it. That's why. I mean if we went back to the old system where the local party leaders picked the delegates, it wouldn't be at the presidential level. They wouldn't let it. They'd keep it down below where it wouldn't hurt anybody, and the same to a certain degree is true with gun control.

However, even with the "bottom-up" agenda, where issues rest on social and political forces larger than campaigns, candidates exercise leadership by the way they funnel pressures into various policy alternatives. In the case of the Iranian hostages, Carter could have funneled national anger in different directions: military, diplomatic, or economic reprisals. He also had the option of making the crisis a *personal* issue requiring him to put his political capital on the line (which he did) or a *government-to-government* issue requiring less personal intervention. By taking visible actions, Carter highlighted his personal responsibility and mortgaged his political future to the hostage issue.[15]

Leaders also exercise influence in economic areas. Because economic disorders have been intractable over the last decade, candidates have some discretion about how they respond. Looking at the broad range of policy alternatives proposed in 1980—reindustrialization, targeted tax cuts, across-the-board tax cuts, social security tax cuts, gasoline tax increases, windfall profits taxes, and wage and price controls, among others—it seems clear that public frustration over the economy (as well as voter tendencies to penalize the party controlling the presidency) has given candidates flexibility to consider a variety of economic policies.[16] In a situation like this (i.e., "try anything as long as it works"), presidential aspirants mold the policy alternatives available to the country and then accept responsibility for economic outcomes.

Finally, the abortion controversy leaves some room for leadership maneuver. While the right-to-life movement is firmly opposed to abortions, its leaders and legislative supporters disagree about tactics: legislation defining life at conception, a constitutional amendment allowing states the right to legislate restrictive abortion rules, or a constitutional amendment prohibiting abortion across the board. These differences (which often arise in any social movement) mean that leaders favorable to pro-life goals have control over the way that anti-abortion sentiments are expressed in the political system.

THE LIMITS OF AGENDA LEADERSHIP

Although candidates' policy alternatives influence the national political agenda, their efforts at agenda leadership sometimes fall flat. In 1980, Iran and its aftermath dampened Kennedy's efforts to discuss domestic issues and criticize past support of the shah. Originally, Kennedy's presidential challenge rested on Carter's lack of leadership. But the seizure of hostages in Iran transformed the campaign. With the hostages in danger and Americans rallying behind the president, attempts by Kennedy as well as other candidates to question Carter's leadership, policies toward Iran, and overall foreign policy were short-circuited. Rather than stimulating debate of policy options, the Iranian developments paralyzed national discussion and provided Carter with a rationale for his Rose Garden strategy.[17] According to Carl Wagner, Kennedy's national political director, the hostage seizure (which came three days before Kennedy's candidacy announcement) "made an enormous difference in the first three months of this campaign. It dominated debate. It provided the president with the rationale not to debate. It submerged many of the economic issues that propelled Senator Kennedy into the race." And Robert Shrum (Kennedy's speech writer) noted the impact on foreign policy rhetoric:

We didn't talk much about foreign policy after New Hampshire for about a month or two months. . . . We were getting killed everytime we'd do it. We'd say the right thing and we'd still get killed. I mean, we'd give a speech at the Kennedy school and we'd say, "we really ought to try to use the U.N. to get the hostages out." And we had said it in the Georgetown speech as well. And suddenly you have Jody Powell all over you for revealing a secret government plan which had been leaked. It was garbage. I mean, it was absolute garbage. But people would say, I mean voters would say, gee, maybe you shouldn't be screwing around with that. It's too delicate. So you stopped. I mean, we tried our best.

Meanwhile, Connally's attempt to place a Mideast policy proposal (which called for Israeli withdrawal from occupied territories, Palestinian self-determination, and an American treaty alliance in the region) on the campaign agenda produced waves of controversy from which Connally never recovered. In presenting his plan, Connally and his advisors realized (and hoped to benefit from) the unconventional act they were undertaking. Every national politician realizes the critical role of the Middle East in world stability. Connally himself noted this when he began his speech announcing the plan:

I know full well that the issues presented by the Middle East are as sensitive and delicate as any that can be raised. I realize that there are no simple and easy solutions which will fully satisfy either the Arabs or the Israelis. But peace in the Middle East is too important—too important to our friends there, too important to ourselves and too important to the world—for full and frank discussion to be evaded or avoided.[18]

But despite the importance of this area, presidential aspirants commonly have ignored the subject or refused to make specific commitments. According to Sam Hoskinson, Connally's research director: "That's been a topic that's been kind of ruled out from presidential politics. Academics can write about it, journalists can write about it, speak about it. Even governments can talk about it. But presidential politicians haven't been allowed to write about it." Alternatively, candidates have dealt with the issue by promising Israel everything during the campaign and then pressuring Israel after the election for concessions. Connally explicitly rejected these approaches saying:

The Office of the American Presidency . . . imposes special obligations upon all who offer themselves for that high office. It imposes an obligation to be forthcoming, to speak clearly and without concern for political consequences about the great issues of peace. It imposes an obligation for candor, to share one's views and thoughts and plans with the American public before—rather than after—they make their decisions about their national leadership.

While Connally's forthrightness was remarkable (and deserves the applause of all who value policy specificity, no matter what their substantive preferences), the stormy reaction from American Jews, the Israeli government, and other presidential candidates showed the high costs of leadership in this area. Connally lost part of his campaign staff (several of whom quit in protest over the speech). Financial contributions began to dry up. And most important, the speech put Connally on the defensive; he had to spend valuable time explaining why he made a speech that appeared stupid (rather than courageous). Two months after the speech, Hoskinson reflected on the long-term lessons of Connally's Mideast initiative and said that "if it is perceived that one of the major reasons for his defeat was the speech, then I think it will remain out of the political scene for a long time." Given the dismal fate of Connally's campaign, future presidents probably will come to office uninformed by campaign debate over the Middle East.

These cases illustrate the factors that limit agenda leadership. The fact that both "failures" lay in foreign policy suggest the dangers of agenda leadership in this domain. Although occasionally candidates (such as Reagan and the Panama Canal treaty) may benefit from leadership in international affairs, the risks are great. International events are controversial (as Connally discovered with his Mideast proposal). They also are unpredictable (as Baker found out when he unsuccessfully tried to duplicate Reagan's Panama Canal leadership on the SALT II treaty; see chapter 2). And as Kennedy learned with Iran, foreign policies are more subject than domestic concerns to presidential control and manipulation. Aaron Wildavsky's "two presidencies" thesis (which posited greater presidential autonomy in foreign than domestic affairs) may have weakened in the last two decades.[19] But presidential candidates must recognize the different opportunities for agenda leadership in each policy arena.

RHETORIC AND ELECTORAL COALITIONS

Candidates used rhetoric for more than agenda formation; as campaigners interested in building popular support, their rhetoric also reflected their coalitional strategies. For example, the coalitional innovators used rhetoric that communicated their interests in mobilizing new constituencies and attracting support from the other party. Alone among Republicans in the nominating process, Anderson discussed issues usually of concern to Democrats: health, housing, urban affairs, equal rights, tax reform, and the elderly. Similarly, Brown started the campaign "out front" on two crosscutting issues (nuclear energy and the balanced budget).[20] Reagan also emphasized a variety of cleavage issues (abortion, busing, and gun control) of interest to constituencies he sought to take away from Democrats.

However, unlike the rhetoric of realigning eras, there was no dominant issue around which candidates tried to reshuffle party coalitions. In the 1850s, realignment centered on slavery; the silver issue formed the basis of realignment in the 1890s, and the Great Depression was instrumental in Roosevelt's victories in the 1930s.[21] But in 1980, candidates used a variety of issues to attract disenchanted constituencies. The multiple issues in Reagan's rhetorical repertoire may have complicated his task of realignment. The diversity of issues probably undercut Reagan's abilities to turn his electoral landslide into a realignment. Without consistent (or reconcilable) issues, candidates are unable to cement diverse constituencies into enduring party coalitions. In addition, strategies of coalitional change did not rest completely on policy appeals. Candidates also relied on personal style. Since many voters are not policy-oriented or do not agree on policy proposals, campaigners used stylistic messages (such as boldness, unconventionality, a "fresh face," innovativeness, and so forth) to gain new supporters. While this approach may produce voters (or even landslides), it again complicates the task of realignment. Unless candidates draw coalitional lines on substantive matters (as Roosevelt did with New Deal programs in the 1930s), presidents with opportunities for realignment are unlikely to galvanize voters and effect enduring partisan change. In short, rhetoric can facilitate or hinder party realignment.

The link between rhetoric and coalitional strategies was not limited to innovators. Kennedy's Georgetown speech (where he endorsed gas rationing and wage and price controls) explicitly was designed to rally his core constituencies—liberal activists. According to Paul Kirk, Kennedy's campaign manager: "It was apparent that there was more [needed] than just talking about leadership. . . . [He] needed to rally the forces politically, and I think also he was comfortable with the issues that he spoke to." Similarly, delegate director Richard Stearns described the rhetorical shifts this way:

The campaign, I think, [for] two months had been [focusing] simply on dissatisfaction with the quality of leadership that Carter had provided. I don't think there is anything particularly wrong with that theme, but in the midst of the rally for Carter because of the hostage and Iranian/Afghani crises, it wasn't that satisfying an answer. . . . The Georgetown speech was meant to explain and spell out the actual content. . . . It supplied the intellectual capital that basically sustained the campaign for the rest of the primary season. . . . [It] had the effect of putting . . . Kennedy to the left of Carter.

For the remainder of the nominating period, Kennedy's rhetoric bore a close relation to his coalitional strategy.[22] Of course, there were examples of rhetoric that appeared to have weak ties to constituencies. The two candidates who received the most media criticism for vagueness and ambiguity were Bush and Brown. Although frequency counts of policy appeals (see Table 4–1) do *not* show lower levels for these candidates (in fact, Reagan was less specific than Bush or Brown), there were definite reasons for media concern. First, in terms of specificity, journalists applied different standards to the candidates. Campaigners (such as Reagan, Mondale, and Kennedy) who were well known and had compiled track records on issues over time were insulated from media criticism about ambiguity. Reagan gave a goal-oriented speech that was not very specific. Yet, based on his history and well-known conservatism, Reagan did not come across as shallow and ambiguous on the issues. In contrast, other candidates (such as Bush and Brown) were not afforded this luxury.[23] Since they were less widely known, the media needed more information about their policy positions to feel comfortable that these candidates were discussing issues in adequate detail. Reflecting on this problem, Bush advisor David Keene said:

When you get known very quickly, all the voter has is a perception and an outline. It's not filled in. But it takes time to fill it in. By the time a Hubert Humphrey runs for president or the time a Barry Goldwater or a McGovern runs for president, guys who have been around and in a position speaking to the issues for some years, people have a shorthand for them. If he's on the ideological extremes of the two parties, it's easy because they can say, "he's a left-winger or he's a right-winger," and that automatically fills in the profile. If he does not fit into that category and he hasn't been around for very long, you don't know what to think of him. You don't know what his views are. . . . Hubert Humphrey didn't have to go out and talk about the issues. Hubert Humphrey had developed over the years an issues persona in the minds of the voter that was there. But if you are a candidate who gets well known [quickly], that's not there.

Second, Bush compounded this "issues" problem by his rhetoric after the surprise win in Iowa. During 1979, Bush had publicized his policy positions. But because he was a dark horse, the media paid little attention. According to Keene:

During the summer months, we put out an issue-based press release every day for ninety days, which received virtually no coverage, the reason being that virtually no one cares what somebody they'd never heard of and who they don't think has a chance of winning anything thinks about anything. There's no reason for them to care and there's no reason for reporters to report it. Issues become important outside your own narrow base only when people begin to think of you as a potential nominee. Earlier than that, issues are not important.

However, with his Iowa victory, Bush's policy positions became more important to reporters. Unfortunately, Bush and his advisors made a strategic mistake (which they later conceded). Rather than using the Iowa publicity to fill in Bush's policy profile for the public, his speeches and media advertising focused on momentum. Bush's campaign manager, James Baker, explained the consequences of this move: "We began to get vibes that people wanted to know what he was. After Iowa, we made a decision not to tamper with what was working. In retrospect, we should have answered the question as to what he was. . . .

Immediately after Iowa, we should have gone straight from George Who to George What."[24] And Keene argued, "what we should have done, something which we both acknowledge, is that we should have pulled all our advertising post-Iowa, made two or three very heavy direct issue ads, and thrown them on for the rest of that period to try to color that in and give an issues component to the knowledge about Bush. We didn't do that and that was the substantive mistake that we made." In explaining how the campaign arrived at this decision, Keene explained:

we were riding on the momentum at that point. . . . The [issues] speeches were not delivered because they were scheduled at a time that the press was not going to cover them. They were just covering the momentum story. The momentum story runs out after about ten days. But by that time, we didn't make the reversal until New Hampshire had taken place. So we should have made that change at that time. We still would have lost New Hampshire, but it would have been much closer and it would have been a horse race to the wire.[25]

Brown complicated his "issues" problem by the way he discussed substantive matters. More so than other candidates, Brown did not use rhetoric in conventional ways. Generally, campaigners gave speeches discussing their views on four or five issues. And while these positions did not always fall neatly in one spot along the ideological spectrum, presidential contenders usually could be described as left or right of center. However, Brown broke these conventions. His rhetoric was substantive, but he discussed policy in different ways. Rather than giving his positions issue by issue, Brown debated policies at philosophical levels. For example, his analyses of nuclear energy and budgetary deficits were given in terms of justice and concern for future generations (since they would bear the burdens of nuclear waste and financial mismanagement). Also, his rhetoric did not fit standard ideological patterns. As his advisor, Walter McGuire, described it:

That was the dilemma of Jerry Brown. He was giving what was a very complicated message. He was not neatly labeled right or left, which automatically brings with it people who also think that. It was a whole new thing and there is no coalition for that. . . . People have not gone through that paradigm shift.

Unfortunately for Brown, by breaking rhetorical conventions, he made it difficult for reporters to translate his message to voters. Since they were used to issue-by-issue discussions, Brown's philosophical (but nonideological) approach came across as vague, ambiguous, and nonsubstantive. Ironically, Brown's broad-based rhetoric (which served him well in California) was not that different from Reagan's goal-oriented, but nonspecific, approach. But Reagan escaped criticism because of his track record and ideological background. Without these shields, Brown's rhetoric sounded "weird" and expedient (which did nothing for his presidential chances).[26]

RHETORIC AND COMMUNICATIONS STYLE

Presidential aspirants must make choices about rhetorical content, but they also must think about style of communications. How do they present their messages to the public? Communications style is important because the manner of delivery influences the way audiences (including the media) interpret the campaign. No case illustrates the relevance of style more than Kennedy. As the perennially reluctant candidate of American politics, Kennedy's decision to run created great excitement among political activists. In fact, while Brown, Crane, and Dole struggled for media coverage, Kennedy began his campaign swings with dozens of reporters. But optimistic expectations were quickly dashed. His early forays showed a candidate who sounded inarticulate, bumbling ("fam far-milies"), and politically unsure of himself. According to Robert Shrum, Kennedy's speech writer, the Senator's early performance (including the infamous interview with Roger Mudd) gave voters negative impressions:

You cannot run on the basis of leadership against an incumbent president and then look incoherent or not very sure of what you are saying. I think the public was getting a general impression of disappointment, that this guy wasn't Jack and he wasn't Bobby. . . . I think that's how it hurt. I mean, the sense of here was this omniconfident, inspiring, charismatic figure coming to the rescue and suddenly you don't quite understand what he's saying, at least in the thirty second television clips. I could begin to sense audiences out there watching to see whether he would make a mistake. And that all went away after time, but not really till after Iowa.[27]

And one Republican advisor (Robert Mosbacher, Jr., of Baker's campaign) argued that Kennedy's bumbling style cast doubts on his personal competence:

His manner tells voters he's not very bright or only of average intelligence. Some people can pause at great length between statements and pull it off because it makes them look like they're collecting their thoughts. If they say something reasonably intelligent, they've overcome that pause. But Kennedy's pauses are followed by "uh's" and "er's" and I don't think people are persuaded that he knows what he's saying or what he wants to say. I noticed after the Roger Mudd interview he went on one of the weekly news programs and I think he had been so whipsawed by people telling him not to pause because it made him look stupid that, when asked a question, he would go flying off into an answer that rambled and rambled without a point. It was hard to follow and hard to understand.

In short, communications style was relevant to Kennedy's political fortunes. By poor performances, he created uncertainties that endured even when his speaking manner improved considerably (after the Georgetown speech, where he returned to his liberal roots). It was not until the Democratic convention that Kennedy was able to show his rhetorical skills to a national audience, and by then it was too late for 1980.

Meanwhile, communications style contributed to Reagan's success. Every generation has politicians who conquer the medium of the era. In the heyday of radio, Franklin Roosevelt was the undisputed king. With press conferences, John Kennedy developed a reputation for excellence. But in the age of television, few will dispute Reagan's mastery of the electronic eye. Reagan's video skills and relaxed speaking style have earned him the reputation as a "great communicator." Whether deserved or not, this image gave him political resources that were unavailable to other leaders (such as Carter, whose communications style even offended those within his inner circle). During the campaign, Reagan used rhetorical skills to defuse perceptions (spurred by his opponents) that he was dangerous, extremist, and uncaring. Peter Dailey, Reagan's media advisor, summarized the debate against Carter this way:

The debates were important, not that they be won but that they took the horns off the governor. They were the final absolution in that phrase, "I can't stand Carter, but I am not sure about Reagan." And all Governor Reagan had to do was stand up there and show that . . . he was a calm and reasonable man. . . . He wasn't going to bomb the world. And I think that was a great strength in the debates for us.

And Anderson Carter, Reagan's field director, argued that:

The only thing he had to achieve in the debates . . . [was to come] through as an intelligent generalist, compassionate person, a caring person. He destroyed the image as being trigger happy and shoot from the hip type. People didn't perceive him that way. They've been told that's what he was, but once they saw him for ninety minutes, they didn't feel that way about him, and I think that's what turned them around. It wasn't a specific issue that turned them at all. The same position statements had been made by both candidates for months, but Carter had done a reasonably good job up to that point of creating this image of Reagan being a threat to war and peace and all that bit, but once they listened to him and heard him, it wiped out that perception that Carter had built up.

Reagan's style also enabled him to communicate simple and easily grasped messages. Lyn Nofziger (Reagan's press secretary) said this about the Californian's manner: "Every politician usually winds up with a style that's comfortable to him. Clearly, Reagan has a low-key style in which he depends heavily on anecdotes and a goodly number of illustrative facts." However, the source of Reagan's rhetorical success creates an Achilles' heel as well. Since much of his reputation as a great communicator is derived from encapsulizing skills, Reagan is especially vulnerable to charges that he oversimplifies and distorts the facts. For better or worse, Reagan's political fortunes are tied directly to his style of communications.

Despite the variety of communications styles, no discussion of rhetoric can end without considering the role of humor in campaigns.[28] Candidates use jokes and barbs for different reasons. Sometimes, they add humor to relax audiences. According to Peter Teeley, Bush's speech writer, "most audiences enjoy a candidate getting up and telling two, three, or four jokes or light stories. . . . It kind of breaks up the tension."[29] At other times, politicians joke around to show that they are "ordinary people." Kennedy advisor Richard Stearns noted that humor "makes the candidate appear a little less glacial, stuffy, or remote."[30] But campaigners often rely on humor to make political points. In an era when politics ranks low on voter priorities and issues require complicated or controversial solutions, leaders need communications styles that hold audiences' attention. Since policy discussions do not always serve this purpose, presidential contenders incorporate humor into their presentations as a "nonpolitical" way of communicating political messages.[31] Figure 4–1 lists jokes that were used commonly in the 1980 presidential campaign. Three points stand out. First, humor serves as a form of political commentary. Unlike jokes delivered on situation comedies (which lack political undertones), campaign barbs are innately political. For example, Dole's joke about "taxing memories" incorporated a clever attack on Kennedy's liberalism. And Mondale's story about Reagan having as much in common with working people as Colonel Sanders had with American chickens challenged Reagan's political sensitivities. Second, these jokes have partisan (or ideological) components, especially in the general election. Voters often complain that candidates talk about the same things. Yet analysis of political humor shows that there are discernible differences in Republican and Democratic jokes. Republicans usually joke about Democratic liberalism, excessive spending, and big government. In contrast, Democrats make fun of Republican sympathies for the well-to-do and excessive military zeal. Because of these patterns, it is apparent that interparty (and intraparty) competition takes place not just in voting booths but at the level of humor as well. Third, jokes often attack the opposition. As Stearns suggested:

you can use humor . . . as an aggressive weapon. You can in a joking way say things without inspiring the offense your target might take if you actually said them seriously. When Kennedy appeared in a fundraiser to benefit the ERA, that was a point that there had been a great deal of difficulty trying to reach any sense of compromise with Carter's people on platform issues and they were beginning to take the line that Kennedy was purposefully trying to divide the party. At that fundraiser, Carter waited to make sure that he got his speech in and out five minutes before Kennedy arrived to make sure that the two of them would not meet to find themselves on the platform at the same time. That was also the period when Kennedy was pressing Carter for some type of joint debate. Kennedy was able to say that the Democratic party wasn't as divided as everyone thought because tonight proved that they were only five minutes apart. . . . If Kennedy actually got up there and said, "Tonight illustrates just what's wrong with Jimmy Carter, that he is so afraid of encountering me that he deliberately got out of this building five minutes before," that would have been taken as a little bit boorish or at least antagonistic.

In this way, humor allows candidates to say things about their opponents that otherwise would sound too harsh; unfortunately, because of this quality, humor also contributes to the high level of negative rhetoric in modern campaigns.

Figure 4-1
Partisan Differences in the Uses of Humor

Republican Jokes

Dole on Kennedy's liberalism—I was on the Senate floor a couple of weeks ago when one of my liberal friends was making a speech and he was all wound up. He was about ready to conclude and he said, "now gentlemen, let me tax your memories." And Ted Kennedy jumped up and said, "why haven't we thought of that before?" (speech to the Federation of Republican Women, Portsmouth, New Hampshire, February 18, 1980).

Anderson—How many Anderson supporters does it take to screw in a light bulb? Four. One to hold the light bulb and three to hold the fundraiser (quoted in *New York Times,* October 21, 1980, p. B6).

Connally on Japanese trade—I'd tell the Japanese that unless they're prepared to open markets for more American products, they'd better be prepared to sit on the docks of Yokohama in their Toyotas watching their Sony televisions because they aren't going to ship them here (quoted in *New York Times Magazine,* November 18, 1979, p. 181).

Dole on Kennedy's Roger Mudd interview—Seventy-five percent of the country watched *Jaws,* twenty-five percent watched Roger Mudd, and half of them couldn't tell the difference (quoted by Germond and Witcover, *Blue Smoke and Mirrors,* p. 75).

Reagan's controversial "duck" joke—How do you tell the Polish guy at a cockfight? He brings a duck. How do you tell the Italian guy? He bets on the duck. How do you tell the Mafia is there? The duck wins (quoted in ibid., p. 120).

Connally on Kennedy and nuclear power—More people died at Chappaquidick than at Three Mile Island (quoted in *New York Times Magazine,* November 18, 1979, p. 38).

Bush on Carter and inflation—When he came to office, he said he was going to do something about it. He did. He made it a lot worse (quoted by Drew, *Portrait of an Election,* p. 91).

Reagan—Balancing the budget is like protecting your virtue. All you have to do is learn to say no (quoted in ibid., p. 113).

Reagan—A conservative is a fellow that if he sees someone drowning, will throw him a rope that's too short and tell him that it would be good for his character to swim for it. A liberal will throw him a rope that's long enough but when he gets hold of it he'll drop his end and go away to look for someone else to help (quoted in *New York Times,* July 15, 1980, p. B6).

Connally on Bush's Texan credentials—He's all hat and no cattle (quoted in *New York Times,* July 20, 1980, p. E21).

Figure 4-1 (continued)

Reagan on Carter—We have a president who promised he would never lie to us. That reminds me of the quote from Ralph Waldo Emerson: "The more he talked of his honor, the faster we counted our spoons" (quoted in *New York Times,* September 21, 1980, p. E3).

Bush on Billy Carter—I saw a poll recently showing that beer was more popular than Billy Carter. The American people much prefer something with a head on it (quoted in *New York Times,* September 28, 1980, p. 4E).

Reagan on Billy Carter's brother—It is embarrassing to have a brother that is kind of a buffoon and everyone's criticizing and talking about. You know, I haven't heard Billy complain once (quoted in *New York Times,* October 3, 1980, p. A19).

Reagan on Carter's campaign attacks—I'll confess to being irresponsible if he'll admit to being responsible [for the nation's problems] (quoted by Pomper, *Elections in America,* p. 74).

Reagan on economic depression—A recession is when your neighbor loses his job. A depression is when you lose your job. Recovery is when Jimmy Carter loses his job (quoted by Germond and Witcover, *Blue Smoke and Mirrors,* p. 218).

Bush on Mondale—Fritz is taking such a low road that he has to breathe through a snorkel (quoted in *New York Times,* September 13, 1980, p. 10).

Bush on Carter—I would bring up Mr. Carter's economic policies, but I hate to see grown men and women cry (quoted in *New York Times,* October 12, 1980, p. 32).

Anderson—President Carter is like the man who shot his mother and father and then asked the jury at his murder trial for leniency on the grounds that he was an orphan (quoted in *New York Times,* October 17, 1980, p. A22).

Anderson—President Carter's favorite hymn is "Amazing Grace" because the American people are going to have to show amazing grace to forgive him for what he's done the last four years (quoted in *New York Times,* November 3, 1980, p. D13).

Democratic Jokes

Kennedy on Carter's Rose Garden strategy after Carter avoided a joint appearance— Who was that man who just rushed out of here? He had to get back to the White House to read a critical national security document—the Portland, Maine telephone book (quoted in *Newsweek,* February 18, 1980, p. 45).

Mondale on Brown—If Jerry Brown becomes president, he'll sell Air Force One and get a glider. Then, if the American people want to know where he is coming from, they can just check the prevailing winds (quoted in *New York Times,* November 11, 1979, p. E5).

Figure 4-1 (continued)

Carter on Brown after watching a science fiction movie—It sounds like Jerry Brown's agenda for the next constitutional convention (quoted in *New York Times,* April 3, 1980, p. B10).

Kennedy on surrogate speakers—I tried to figure out who could act as my surrogate. I thought of someone who in the Senate had supported national health insurance and a man who had opposed grain embargoes. But then I was reminded by Fritz that he was already representing someone else (quoted by Drew, *Portrait of an Election,* p. 84).

Kennedy's debate negotiations with Brown over sitting or standing—Brown would be more at home in a lotus position (quoted in *Newsweek,* December 24, 1979, p. 19).

Kennedy, surprised by his campaign workers at airport—I thought it was the right-to-lifers (quoted by Drew, *Portrait of an Election,* p. 87).

Kennedy on Carter's ''surprise'' foreign policy—They were surprised when the hostages were taken; they were surprised in Afghanistan; they were surprised at the U.N., and we're going to give them a surprise here in Pennsylvania (Robert Shrum interview).

Kennedy speaking to a group of state legislators—Neil Goldschmidt [the Secretary of Transportation] is outside taking down your license numbers (quoted by Drew, *Portrait of an Election,* p. 63).

Kennedy to Mondale—I have something to give my good friend Fritz Mondale—a New England Patriots football shirt. I present it as one good patriot to another (quoted in ibid., p. 83).

Mondale on Illinois primary—Illinois is going to be one of the great battlegrounds of this campaign. Let's get this family together. Let's unite and keep a good president . . . and by the way a marvellous vice president (quoted in ibid., p. 236).

Mondale on Reagan—Mr. Reagan has about as much in common with the working people of this country as Colonel Sanders has with the American chicken (quoted in *New York Times,* October 10, 1980, p. D15).

Mondale on Reagan's inexperience in foreign policy—We'll have to have international summit conferences with name tags: ''Hello, I'm Helmut Schmidt, Germany'' (quoted in *New York Times,* August 15, 1980, p. B3).

Mondale on Republicans—Don't be too rough on the Republicans. They've had a tough month. They sent my opponent to China to start the campaign, and they almost ended it there (quoted in *New York Times,* September 25, 1980, p. B10).

Figure 4-1 (continued)

Carter on Reagan—When you're sitting across the negotiating table with President Brezhnev trying to guarantee the future of our nation and the peace of the world, you can't rely on 3-by-5 cards and you can't read from a teleprompter (quoted in *New York Times,* October 22, 1980, p. A25).

Mondale—There is a difference between Ronald Reagan in the movies and Ronald Reagan in the White House. At least when Ronald Reagan rode off in the movies into the fiery sunset, he didn't take us with him (quoted in *New York Times,* November 2, 1980, p. 38).

Carter—Have you ever heard a Republican candidate quoting a Republican president? You haven't heard Ronald Reagan quote Herbert Hoover, have you? Have you heard Ronald Reagan quoting Richard Nixon? (quoted in *New York Times,* November 2, 1980, p. 40).

RHETORIC AND LEADERSHIP

In this chapter, I have argued that the way candidates use rhetoric has important consequences for the political system. Campaign rhetoric influences the agenda. By the way presidential aspirants speak about public policies, they broaden (or restrict) the range of policy alternatives under consideration. Campaigns are one of the few times when leaders have the attention of ordinary people. For governmental actions that require popular approval (or at least tacit acceptance), campaigns provide opportunities to redirect public opinion. In an era when many policy solutions are complex and controversial, candidate rhetoric can move the electorate to higher (or lower) planes of understanding.[32] Campaign appeals also shape voter choices. By emphasizing some topics (and excluding others), presidential contestants establish the broad boundaries in which elections are fought. Candidates can use their rhetoric to give voters positive reasons for supporting them. Or, as is more commonly the case, they can provide negative ones through attacks on the opponent's candidacy. In either case, it should be clear that voter choices depend on candidate decisions.

But speaking more generally, this review suggests that rhetoric is relevant to presidential performance. Critics of American politics (such as Murray Edelman) argue that campaign discussions are misleading and manipulative.[33] Since leaders distort facts and hide their policy intentions, Edelman concludes that campaign appeals tell us little about prospective presidents. However, I found in many cases that rhetoric was consistent with the constituencies candidates wanted to rally and that it provided significant clues about the policy intentions of presidential contenders.[34] While the returns are not complete for the Reagan Administration, his presidential agenda has been remarkably similar to the issues and themes he raised in 1980 (and had been raising for several years).[35]

Some observers were surprised at the ideological tenor of his presidency. But Reagan's legislative proposals (cutting social programs and upgrading military capabilities) and budget policies (supply-side economics) were consistent with his campaign agenda (see chapter 3). In addition, his administrative appointments matched his campaign statements; he selected a person with ties to the right-to-life movement to head the Office of Family Planning (the federal agency that oversees national policy on birth control and sex education) and people from pro-development organizations to head the Department of Interior and Environmental Protection Agency. Perhaps the reason observers were surprised at Reagan's presidency was that he did stick with his campaign appeals. Since the popular view of rhetoric denigrates its sincerity (despite evidence showing definite links between campaign statements and executive actions), presidents who do what they say they are going to do are seen as mysterious beings. Of course, Reagan's campaign discussions did not always provide perfect clues about his policy intentions. In some cases (notably that of the Professional Air Traffic Controllers Organization—PATCO), his campaign promises were broken (although Reagan's actions against PATCO were consistent with his general hostility to labor organizations).

In other cases, Reagan's campaign rhetoric was internally inconsistent. But these rhetorical failures came back to haunt his administration. In 1980 Reagan had knit together diverse policy blocs: traditional Republican adherents of balanced budgets, those favoring supply-side budget cuts, and hawks wanting major increases in military spending. However, the onset of huge deficits in 1982 caused this marriage of disparate policy views to come apart (and perhaps undo his presidency). The lesson seems clear—presidents who fail to resolve agenda inconsistencies during the campaign may suffer dreadful consequences.

In addition, this research has implications for party realignment. Scholars generally have ignored the rhetorical roots of realignment. This omission is unfortunate, since rhetoric can hinder or facilitate party change. Looking at the early days of the Reagan Administration, it seems clear that the conduct of the campaign (particularly agenda development) molded and sometimes limited Reagan's efforts at realignment. Like many other candidates, Reagan developed few innovative policy proposals during the campaign. On foreign policy, he offered little but general statements ("stop the Russians"). Consequently, it came as little surprise that once in office, Reagan showed a great deal of caution in this area as he searched for a foreign policy. However, in other areas that were more fully developed during the campaign (namely economic affairs), President Reagan showed a great deal of policy boldness. Taking advantage of supply-side economics (an idea that several Republicans developed during the campaign), Reagan devised an economic program that leading economists disavowed. Not only did he push through Congress massive budget cuts in social programs, Reagan also successfully proposed a three-year package of tax cuts to stimulate the economy.

These patterns suggest that the level of policy discussions and agenda devel-

opment in presidential campaigns influences the conduct of coalitional innovators once they are in office. In Reagan's case, the campaign agenda created
some options for realignment but foreclosed others. Specifically, his greater
preparation on economic issues (compared to other policy areas) molded his
strategy for cementing a realignment. Essentially, he had little choice (at least
in the short run of his presidency) but to try to forge a realignment on economic
issues.[36] Speaking more broadly, one can argue that candidates who disregard
agenda development in campaigns may be handicapped once they are in office.
Since many innovators do not use campaigns to develop policy agendas or formulate innovative policy proposals, they come to office ill-equipped to execute
realignments. Even if election victories have given them opportunities for realignment, they may lack the policy ideas to take advantage of their opportunities. Basically, candidates want coalitional innovations without policy innovativeness. While it may not be necessary to be innovative on policy matters
to win electoral landslides, issues are very important in the second stage of realignment when presidents try to cement new party coalitions. Without some
way of drawing substantive lines, potential realigners are unlikely to produce
long-term coalitional changes.

NOTES

1. William Safire, *Safire's Political Dictionary* (New York: Random House, 1978),
p. 611.
2. Quoted by Robert Scheer in "Jimmy, We Hardly Know Y'All," *Playboy* (October, 1976), p. 192.
3. Dole delivered these lines February 18, 1980 at a candidate forum that the Federation of Republican Women organized in Portsmouth, New Hampshire.
4. Page, *Choices and Echoes in Presidential Elections*, p. 156.
5. The most prominent proponents of this view are Norman Nie, Sidney Verba, and
John Petrocik, *The Changing American Voter* (Cambridge, Mass.: Harvard University
Press, 1976). For critiques of their conclusions, see John Sullivan, James Piereson, and
George Marcus, "Ideological Constraint in the Mass Public," *American Journal of Political Science* (May, 1978), pp. 233–249 and (in the same issue) George Bishop, Alfred
Tuchfarber, and Robert Oldendick, "Change in the Structure of American Political Attitudes," pp. 250–269.
6. My data consist of campaign speeches by the major Republican and Democratic
contenders as reported in the *New York Times*. I included only those accounts that dealt
with public speeches and rallies and excluded editorial or opinion page pieces as well
as interpretative campaign stories (because they did not represent candidate rhetoric). In
addition, I considered only direct and indirect quotes from the candidates; since my major interest was *candidate* rhetoric, I did not analyze what reporters were saying about
candidates, only what candidates themselves were saying in public. I chose press accounts (rather than speech texts) because candidates often did not speak from formal
texts, particularly in the primaries. While it would have been preferable to study speeches
directly, there is no complete or even nearly complete record of campaign speeches for
all the candidates. One is left with news reports as the most complete alternative.

7. I included speeches from November 1, 1979 (when all were campaigning actively) to the end of primaries on June 3, 1980 (or the withdrawal date of unsuccessful candidates).

8. A discussion of why this happened appears later in this chapter.

9. The lack of policy specificity by surrogates suggests that the widespread use of family members on the campaign trail (such as the Carter family, the Bush family, and the Kennedy family) robs audiences of substantive information. As one Kennedy advisor put it, many of the Kennedy cousins simply "told anecdotes about their early lives with Uncle Ted." However interesting this may be for those of us with *People* magazine mentalities, it undermines the campaign's capacity for educating voters.

10. According to Bush advisor David Keene, Reagan's typical speech can be described this way: "Reagan gives his philosophical talk, which is good; it's a goal-oriented philosophical talk. He doesn't get bogged down on how he's going to get there. He says here's where we ought to go. He doesn't deal with a lot of minor issues. He deals with one or two major issues and that's really all you can get through in a campaign."

11. The fact that Bush and Mondale used party appeals more than their respective running mates suggests the differing rhetorical roles that vice-presidential nominees played. Because they were low men on the totem pole, one of their primary jobs was to rally the party troops.

12. It is important to remember that candidates communicated through a number of channels: speeches (which I describe here), press conferences, television ads, radio ads, newspaper ads, and direct mail, among other means. Of these, direct mail tended to be the most issue-oriented while television advertising was the least. Candidate rhetoric generally fell in the middle.

13. For a brief history of supply-side economics and its differences from traditional Republican thought, see "GOP's Detroit Convention Marked the Coronation of Supply Side Economics," *Congressional Quarterly Weekly Report* (July 19, 1980), pp. 2002–2003.

14. For the text of this speech, see the *New York Times* (January 29, 1980), p. 12.

15. This decision had great ramifications for his campaign. In the nominating process, the hostage issue sparked Carter's resurgence in popular support, deflected Kennedy's leadership criticisms, and turned attention away from the failing economy. But in the general election (which marked the one-year anniversary of the hostage takeover), the hostages served as a remainder of national humiliation and may have fueled speculation about Carter's manipulation of the Iranian affair for personal benefit.

16. For reviews of the economic voting thesis, see James Kuklinski and Darrell West, "Economic Expectations and Voting Behavior in United States House and Senate Elections," *American Political Science Review* (June, 1981), pp. 436–447 and Morris Fiorina, *Retrospective Voting in American National Elections* (New Haven, Conn.: Yale University Press, 1981).

17. Although it is difficult to prove that Carter manipulated the Iranian and Afghanistan situations for political benefit, the circumstantial evidence is bothersome. Before the Iowa caucuses, Mondale challenged Kennedy's patriotism for opposing the grain embargo. The morning of the Wisconsin primary, Carter called a news conference and personally announced that a breakthrough in the hostage negotiations was imminent (a move that one Kennedy hand described as Carter's equivalent of "peace is at hand"). And shortly before the Michigan delegate test, Carter ordered an unsuccessful military raid on Iran. Of course, Carter also used these foreign crises to stop personal campaign-

ing in the nominating process and pull out of scheduled debates with Kennedy and Brown. Finally, two days before the general election, Carter returned to Washington to resume high-level discussions about Iran.

18. This quote comes from the text that the Connally campaign distributed after the speech; Connally delivered this address October 11, 1979 to the Washington Press Club.

19. For an argument that the two presidencies thesis has declined, see Lee Sigelman, "A Reassessment of the Two Presidencies Thesis," *Journal of Politics* (November, 1979), pp. 1195–1205. Wildavsky's original statement can be found in "The Two Presidencies," *Trans-Action* (December, 1966).

20. Brown's leadership on nuclear energy eventually pushed Kennedy to strong positions against nuclear power, an issue on which Kennedy originally had not been specific.

21. With the exception of James Sundquist, Lance Bennett, and William Haltom, scholars have paid little attention to the rhetorical roots of realignment. See Sundquist's *Dynamics of the Party System* (Washington, D.C.: Brookings, 1973) and Bennett and Haltom's "Issues, Voter Choice, and Critical Elections," *Social Science History*, 4, no. 4 (Fall, 1980), pp. 379–418.

22. Carter's "malaise" speech also reflected coalitional disputes within the inner circle. For a discussion of disagreements between Caddell and Mondale over this speech, see Germond and Witcover, *Blue Smoke and Mirrors*, chapter two.

23. Anderson also fell within this category. But because he spoke with the greatest specificity among candidates in the nominating process, he protected himself from criticism about his rhetoric.

24. Quoted by Douglas Kneeland in "Bush and Aides Seek Ways to Steady a Faltering Drive," *New York Times* (March 21, 1980), p. A17.

25. Ultimately, media criticism of Bush's rhetoric became so strenuous that in March, 1980 (around the Illinois primary), Bush refused to discuss campaign strategy, organization, and momentum in press conferences. Instead, he said he would discuss only his policy positions.

26. For a candidate who has strongly held policy beliefs and has thought more about new directions in political life than most of his colleagues, media criticisms about Brown's "shallowness" seem shortsighted in retrospect.

27. Shrum noted how the new electoral system requires different rhetorical performances by candidates. News clips of John and Robert Kennedy show that pauses and "uhs" were parts of their speaking style as well. But media reporters in the 1960s did not call attention to these imperfections.

28. Political figures continually have been the object of ridicule by comedians. Of Jerry Brown, Johnny Carson said, "Do you realize that Jerry Brown is the only governor whose parents are trying to deprogram him?" (quoted in *Newsweek*, April 14, 1980, p. 29). Similarly, Mark Russell (the comic sage of Washington, D.C.) said that Nancy Reagan would not make it to the inaugural ball because "she fell down and broke her hair" (cited by Harry Rosenthal in "He'd Had His Last Laugh in Washington," *Philadelphia Inquirer*, January 13, 1982, p. 7–F). Russell also reported that if elected, Gerald Ford had promised to pardon President Carter (quoted in *New York Times*, December 5, 1979, p. C1).

29. Fundraisers sometimes use humorous film spots to relax audiences at party gatherings. Larry Sabato (*The Rise of Political Consultants*, p. 158) reports that Bailey, Deardourff, and Associates used the following spot in Michigan: "Visual: Two gargan-

tuan rhinos, mating. Announcer: Do you know what is being done to us by the Democratically controlled legislature in this state? Do you have any idea how it hurts taxpayers to have the Democrats behind things in Lansing? Why would anyone want to be in this position for ten years? Isn't it about time we get the Democrats off our back?''

30. Occasionally, rhetoric can backfire and reveal speakers' weaknesses. At one 1980 candidate forum in Massachusetts, Harold Stassen, the perennial Republican challenger, was discussing poor presidential performance and inadvertently named President Eisenhower instead of Carter.

31. In repressive nations, humor also can provide ''nonpolitical'' ways of belittling authorities. After the martial law crackdown in Poland, reporters noted that the army had become the object of Polish humor. One joke making the rounds asked, ''What is the lowest rank in the Polish army?'' The answer was, ''television newsreader,'' referring to army seizures of news programming. See Brian Mooney, ''Army is Butt of New Round of Polish Jokes,'' *Philadelphia Inquirer*, January 25, 1982, p. 4–A.

32. For an interesting analysis of the implications of presidential rhetoric for public policy, see Jeffrey Tulis, ''Public Policy and the Rhetorical Presidency'' (paper presented at the annual meeting of the American Political Science Association, New York, September 3–6, 1981).

33. The work that most directly expresses Edelman's views on elections is his ''The Politics of Persuasion,'' in James David Barber, ed., *Choosing the President* (Englewood Cliffs, N.J.: Prentice-Hall, 1974), pp. 149–174. For a more general statement of ''leader manipulation,'' see Edelman's *The Symbolic Uses of Politics* (Urbana: University of Illinois Press, 1964).

34. Some people also have argued that ''selective audience appeals'' (talking about different subjects to various audiences) are evidence of leader deceit and dishonest coalition-building. However, a less cynical interpretation would say that candidates vary their policy emphases because they realize that every audience is not interested in the same topics.

35. This argument is similar to those that other scholars have made about past presidents. Generally, research on campaign promises (as expressed in speeches and party platforms) and executive enactments has shown moderately strong relationships. For example, see Pomper, *Elections in America*, and Fishel, *From Presidential Promise to Performance*, as well as John Kessel, ''The Seasons of Presidential Politics,'' *Social Science Quarterly*, 58 (December, 1977), pp. 418–435 and Benjamin Ginsberg, *The Consequences of Consent* (Reading, Mass.: Addison-Wesley Publishing Co., 1982). Paul Light challenges these conclusions in *The President's Agenda* (Baltimore, Md.: Johns Hopkins Press, 1982). Yet he concedes that campaigns set agendas on important issues and sensitize presidents to ideas outside their previous experiences.

36. Fortunately for Reagan, economic affairs historically have been a fertile ground for party realignment.

5

Constituencies and the Allocation of Travel Time

Perhaps no feature of presidential selection personifies the modern era more than the extensive campaigning that accompanies office-seeking. Traditionally (in the 1800s), presidential contenders followed George Washington's "aloof candidacy" and did not publicly campaign. Rather, like William McKinley, who campaigned in 1896 from his front porch, they stayed home and left the "stumping" to surrogate speakers and party organizers.[1] Occasionally, there were exceptions to this pattern. As the Democratic nominee in 1860, Stephen Douglas conducted an extensive personal campaign. Similarly, in 1896, William Jennings Bryan traveled 18,000 miles on whistle-stop tours. But since presidential selection was an "elite game" with limited public participation in the nominating process and significant control by party regulars, these efforts at active personal campaigning were rare.

However, in the new electoral system, lengthy campaigning is the rule. With the exception of Rose Garden strategies by incumbents, candidates spend months and sometimes years on the campaign trail. In the 1980 contest, Crane announced his presidential intentions (the traditional kickoff for active campaigning) in August, 1978, more than two years before the general election. And in 1979 alone, Bush logged 246,174 miles, considerably above Bryan's total in 1896.[2] Because candidates spend so much time campaigning, it is important to understand what they hope to accomplish with their campaign visits. Fenno argues that campaigning by House members is crucial to the relation between leaders and the public. Not only do candidates learn what is on the minds of voters, but campaigns also require that leaders allocate their time among various constituencies. Since campaigns shape leaders' perceptions of constituency, they have an important impact on public policy. Given these findings, one might expect similar processes among presidential candidates. In this chapter, I investigate one component of campaign visits: how presidential contenders allocated their travel time among particular audiences. Specifically, what did their travel allocations reveal about the electoral coalitions they wanted to put together? Did Republicans and Democrats emphasize different constituencies? Did their coalitional strategies influence the choice of constituencies? And did these relations vary between the nominating process and general election?

CAMPAIGN VISITS AND ELECTORAL COALITIONS

Research on travel allocations generally has emphasized how candidates allocate their time among different states. For example, in their analysis of campaign appearances during the general election from 1960 to 1972, Stephen Brams and Morton Davis argue that candidates allocated their travel time roughly in proportion to the electoral college vote distribution in each state.[3] Generally, this means that candidates traveled predominantly in states with large votes. Stanley Kelley, and Claude Colantoni and his associates reached similar conclusions although they argued that it was not just the electoral college vote distribution, but the doubtfulness or competitiveness of states that influenced travel allocations.[4] And Aldrich, Brams, and Davis have suggested that resource allocation is equally important to candidate strategies in the nominating process.[5]

While it is useful to investigate *state* travel allocations (since primary and general elections take place at the state level), researchers have not devoted much study to the allocation of travel time among various *constituencies*. Constituency allocations are important because they reflect substantive priorities better than states do. State allocations represent strategic priorities, but it is difficult to evaluate their substantive value because they are aggregate and heterogeneous units of geography. In contrast, allocation of travel time among particular constituencies (such as blacks, Hispanics, Jews, Catholics, and farmers, among others) can be interpreted more easily in substantive terms. For example, by studying the constituency allocations of Republican and Democratic contenders, one can see which audiences were common to both parties and which ones were unique to individual parties. One also can study the relation between strategic allocations and coalitional strategies to see if innovators visited different audiences than their counterparts did. Given the expressed interest of Anderson and Brown in mobilizing unaffiliated voters and remaking their parties' coalitions, one might expect distinctive campaign visits from them. Finally, to see if these relations varied between the nominating process and general election, one can compare the campaign audiences of different candidates in each campaign stage.

Constituency allocations also deserve attention because of the candidates' need to symbolize concern with particular audiences. In the new electoral system, contenders face a dilemma. The campaign system requires that they establish popular support in a variety of settings. Yet their time is limited and the public is disinterested in politics.[6] Because of this situation, presidential aspirants use campaign visits with key constituencies to communicate their "identifications" and sympathies with voters. Even though candidates do not always make specific policy commitments (see chapter 4), campaign organizers hope that the candidate's physical presence as well as media accounts of the visit will generate popular support. In fact, candidates who ignore the symbolic value of campaign visits often provoke the fury of constituencies. Witness this reaction by Benjamin Hooks, executive director of the National Association for Colored People (NAACP), to Reagan's failure as the Republican nominee to visit the NAACP convention: "We will not attempt to speculate on why Mr. Reagan found it unimportant to come to Miami. It is sufficient just to note that he found a week of play and recreation of higher priority. One can only wonder whether their decision means he has written off the black vote. It would be tragic if this is the case."[7] For this reason, candidates and their advisors must think carefully about constituency allocations.

Finally, constituency allocations provide information about campaigners' perceptions of constituency. As Fenno noted in his study of House members, few things are more crucial than the way in which candidates define their supporters. Candidate perceptions influence "home styles," which in turn shape how members represent their districts and carry out their policy interests. But despite the centrality of candidate perceptions, there are few easy or direct ways of investigating those perceptions (short of Fenno's style of intensive analysis). Because of this difficulty, scholars usually have relied on indirect approaches. For example, Axelrod presents a demographic breakdown of the vote. Basically, he studied the constituencies to which candidates successfully appealed (that is, their electoral coalitions). While that approach is useful for certain questions, one also can suggest the need to explore the constituencies that presidential campaigners *tried* to mobilize in their electoral travels. In fact, intended coalitions may be more important than actual coalitions because they reflect the constituencies that candidates valued enough to visit during periods of heavy demands on their time. Since campaign travels provide a list of desired constituencies (analogous, perhaps, to Fenno's notion of "reelection" constituencies), candidate itineraries deserve more attention than they previously have been given.

TRAVEL SCHEDULES AND CONSTITUENCY ALLOCATIONS

In recent campaigns, new information has made possible more complete analysis of candidate travels. Previously, travel schedules were not very detailed. For example, the most commonly cited sourcebook of campaign itineraries lists only the dates, cities, and states of public appearances.[8] But as the new electoral system has become longer, grown more public (because of primaries), been covered more extensively by news media, and seen security threats to candidates, campaign organizers have formalized the scheduling process. In particular, the large press contingent and the need to coordinate the candidates' security with the Secret Service have forced campaign organizations to prepare minute-by-minute accounts of how candidates will spend their time. Not only do these itineraries list the state of campaign appearances (the dominant topic of previous research), they also show the city of the appearance, nature of the audience addressed, type of event, and length of event. Hence, it is now possible to study allocations other than state allocations.[9]

Relying on daily itineraries that campaign organizations made available, I investigated constituency allocations by the ten Republican and Democratic candidates.[10] My analysis is distinctive in two ways. Scholars usually have relied on newspaper reports of campaign activities to study travel allocations. For reasons that I will explain shortly, it is preferable to rely instead on travel itineraries. In addition, researchers generally have used the number of days that candidates spent in each state as their measure of allocation. This measure is misleading (when applied either to state or constituency allocations) because it equates half-hour visits with day-long appearances. Aldrich justifies this approach by saying that a single campaign appearance receives the same coverage in state media as a series of events would.[11] However, this procedure minimizes the variety of campaign appearances (and press coverage) that candidates use to build support. If one studies travel to analyze the coalitions that candidates tried to put together, this measure underestimates the range and variety of campaign visits. Instead of counting the number of days that candidates devoted to various constituencies (a measure that is analogous to the "days per state" calculation), I devised an alternative approach. Using candidate itineraries, I counted the total number of campaign events (fundraisers, rallies, media interviews, press conferences, and receptions) for each candidate in the nominating process and general election. Then, relying on information that these travel schedules provided about the audience (such as the "Polk County Republican dinner," "United Auto Workers Local Number 29," or "NAACP convention"), I categorized the audience of each campaign event into the following constituencies: Blacks, Hispanics, Indian, Asian, Italian, Irish, Polish, Women, College students, Elementary and High School students, Union, Business, Service Club, Republican, Democratic, Republican Women, Democratic Women, Senior Citizens, Catholic, Jewish, Protestant, Fundamentalist, Sportsmen, Veterans, Medical, Agricultural, Public Affairs, Municipal, Media Association, Lodges, Other ethnic, Child Care, Environmental, Community activists, Legal, Unemployed, Energy, Humanitarian, Reform, Handicapped, Military, or Gay.[12] For audiences where there was no obvious classification or no information about audience composition (such as "rally in downtown"), I listed the audience as a "general" constituency. After cross-tabulating campaign events and constituencies for each candidate, I developed a measure of the total campaign events that candidates devoted to various constituencies in each campaign stage. To simplify comparisons, I converted "campaign events per constituency" into a percentage so that the tables list the percentage of total campaign events that candidates spent on particular constituencies, such as (hypothetically) 7.2 percent to blacks, 15.5 percent to college students, 0.0 percent to Republicans, 3.2 percent to unions, and so on. Thus, like analysis of state travel allocations, this measure permits study of candidates' travel allocations among different constituencies.[13]

AN EMPIRICAL ASSESSMENT OF NEWS REPORTS AND ITINERARIES

Before studying the link between campaign events and constituencies, it is important to determine whether the data (news reports versus daily itineraries) influence conclusions about travel allocations. Previously, scholars have debated the completeness of newspaper accounts of campaign travel. But despite the uncertainty, no one has systematically collected evidence on this point. To turn what usually has been a speculative argument into an empirical debate, I compared allocations as determined from news reports *and* daily travel schedules.

Candidates spent their time in a variety of campaign activities: fundraising, public speeches and rallies, leadership meetings, print media, radio, and television interviews, press conferences, and coffees, receptions, and walking tours. Table 5–1, which lists candidates' activities in the nominating process, shows that these allocations varied between the two sources. Looking at overall coverage, press reports of candidate travels fluctuated considerably. In terms of number of events covered, the *New York Times* reported 170 campaign events for Kennedy, 138 for Reagan, 124 for Bush, 56 for Anderson, and 40 for Mondale; those receiving less coverage included Crane (4 events) and Dole (11 events). Of course, one might argue that variations in press reporting arose because candidates campaigned at different paces. Itineraries show that Bush scheduled the most appearances (1,019), followed by Kennedy (992), Anderson (744), and Reagan (636); befitting the "controlled" exposure of incumbents, Mondale made fewer appearances (340), as of course did those candidates who ceased campaigning before the end of primaries.[14] But differences

Table 5-1
Candidate Activities in the Nominating Process

Function	Anderson		Baker	
	NY Times	Schedules	NY Times	Schedules
Fundraiser	7.1	0.3	0.0	8.9
Public Speech, Rally	50.0	33.6	40.0	24.7
Leadership Mtg.	0.0	3.9	0.0	9.1
Print Media Intvw.	5.4	9.5	6.7	3.1
Radio Interview	0.0	6.7	0.0	1.7
TV Interview	7.1	8.6	13.3	5.8
Press Av. or Conf.	23.2	7.9	13.3	18.0
Coffee, Recptn., Wlk. Tour	7.1	29.4	26.7	28.6
Total	100.0	100.0	100.0	100.0
N	56	744	30	482

Table 5-1 (continued)

Function	Bush		Connally	
	NY Times	*Schedules*	*NY Times*	*Schedules*
Fundraiser	3.2	6.7	10.3	1.2
Public Speech, Rally	50.8	25.1	44.8	89.5
Leadership Mtg.	1.6	7.0	3.4	0.0
Print Media Intvw.	3.2	6.8	10.3	0.0
Radio Interview	0.8	3.2	0.0	0.0
TV Interview	4.8	10.5	10.3	1.2
Press Av. or Conf.	16.1	13.9	20.7	1.2
Coffee, Recptn., Wlk. Tour	19.4	26.8	0.0	7.0
Total	100.0	100.0	100.0	100.0
N	124	1,019	29	86

Function	Crane		Dole	
	NY Times	*Schedules*	*NY Times*	*Schedules*
Fundraiser	0.0	2.3	9.1	0.4
Public Speech, Rally	0.0	47.3	27.3	32.4
Leadership Mtg.	0.0	3.1	0.0	4.2
Print Media Intvw.	0.0	4.7	18.2	6.7
Radio Interview	0.0	3.9	9.1	11.3
TV Interview	75.0	8.5	27.3	5.5
Press Av. or Conf.	25.0	8.5	9.1	8.0
Coffee, Recptn., Wlk. Tour	0.0	21.7	0.0	31.5
Total	100.0	100.0	100.0	100.0
N	4	129	11	238

Function	Reagan		Brown	
	NY Times	*Schedules*	*NY Times*	*Schedules*
Fundraiser	3.6	11.0	9.1	2.0
Public Speech, Rally	47.8	35.1	54.5	77.5
Leadership Mtg.	2.2	9.3	3.0	2.0
Print Media Intvw.	5.8	4.2	12.1	0.7
Radio Interview	0.0	2.2	0.0	0.7
TV Interview	5.1	6.0	3.0	3.3

Table 5-1 (continued)

Function	Reagan		Brown	
	NY Times	*Schedules*	*NY Times*	*Schedules*
Press Av. or Conf.	24.6	16.0	12.1	7.3
Coffee, Recptn., Wlk. Tour	10.9	16.2	6.1	6.6
Total	100.0	100.0	100.0	100.0
N	138	636	33	151

Function	R. Carter		Mondale	
	NY Times	*Schedules*	*NY Times*	*Schedules*
Fundraiser	10.0	5.2	10.0	2.1
Public Speech, Rally	55.0	11.6	62.5	21.8
Leadership Mtg.	0.0	2.4	2.5	5.3
Print Media Intvw.	0.0	0.8	0.0	6.5
Radio Interview	0.0	1.2	0.0	0.9
TV Interview	2.5	2.8	0.0	0.9
Press Av. or Conf.	0.0	22.4	12.5	26.5
Coffee, Recptn., Wlk. Tour	32.5	53.6	12.5	36.2
Total	100.0	100.0	100.0	100.0
N	40	250	40	340

Function	Kennedy	
	NY Times	*Schedules*
Fundraiser	4.7	8.4
Public Speech, Rally	54.1	23.4
Leadership Mtg.	4.7	4.9
Print Media Intvw.	1.8	7.2
Radio Interview	0.6	5.7
TV Interview	4.7	23.6
Press Av. or Conf.	12.4	4.4
Coffee, Recptn., Wlk. Tour	17.1	22.4
Total	100.0	100.0
N	170	992

Note: The figure refers to the percentage of total campaign events (N) reported in the *New York Times* and listed in daily schedules that candidates spent in different activities. Since President Carter did not campaign actively in the primaries, on this and following tables I report the travel allocations of his vice-president, Walter Mondale, and his wife, Rosalyn Carter.

in the scope of campaigning did not explain all of the inequalities. If one calculates the percentage of campaign events listed on travel schedules that the press reported, it is obvious that coverage varied significantly. While the *New York Times* reported 138 of Reagan's 636 events (21.7 percent), it covered only 17.1 of Kennedy's activities, 12.2 percent for Bush, 11.8 percent for Mondale, and 7.5 percent for Anderson. As one would expect given the nature of media reporting, press coverage was incomplete for some candidates.

These variations were not limited to overall coverage. The portrait painted by the *New York Times* suggests that presidential aspirants spent half their time in public speeches and rallies. For example, newspaper accounts show that Mondale spent 62.5 percent of his time at public rallies, similar to Bush (50.8 percent), Anderson (50.0 percent), and Reagan (47.8 percent). But actually schedules reveal that most campaigners spent only one-quarter of their time in these appearances (instead using a variety of other campaign appearances—coffees, receptions, walking tours, and press opportunities).[15] In addition, the *New York Times* overreported media activities (interviews and press conferences) of the candidates. According to the newspaper, Anderson devoted 23.2 percent of his time to press conferences; his schedules reveal that he spent 7.9 percent. The media also show that Kennedy spent 12.4 percent of his time in news conferences, while itineraries show that the actual figure was 4.4 percent. Finally (in analyses not reported in the table), press coverage exaggerated visits to some parts of the country. Comparing state allocations as the *New York Times* and daily itineraries reported them, the press overreported visits to New York by two or three times the actual percentage. As an example, press accounts suggest Anderson spent 12.5 percent of his time in New York, while his schedules show that he spent 5.1 percent. Likewise, for other candidates, there was substantial overreporting: Reagan (9.4 and 3.9 percent), Brown (15.2 and 3.3 percent), Rosalyn Carter (25.0 and 8.0 percent), Mondale (26.8 and 10.7 percent), and Kennedy (17.4 and 5.4 percent). Since "visible" (i.e., well-covered) states tend to be large, industrial areas (which were also overreported in many cases), past research about the tendency of presidential candidates to emphasize large states may be an artifact of data bases developed from newspaper accounts.

These problems were not unique to the nominating process. Table 5–2, which lists candidate activities in the general election, shows that press coverage was

Table 5-2
Candidate Activities in the General Election

Function	Reagan		Bush	
	NY Times	*Schedules*	*NY Times*	*Schedules*
Fundraiser	3.8	7.9	7.3	7.7
Public Speech, Rally	64.4	51.0	63.6	29.9
Leadership Mtg.	2.9	15.2	1.8	3.7

Table 5-2 (continued)

Function	Reagan		Bush	
	NY Times	*Schedules*	*NY Times*	*Schedules*
Print Media Intvw.	2.9	1.3	1.8	9.1
Radio Interview	0.0	0.0	0.0	1.1
TV Interview	6.7	0.0	5.5	9.9
Press Av. or Conf.	3.8	1.3	7.3	17.9
Coffee, Recptn., Wlk. Tour	15.4	23.2	12.7	20.5
Total	100.0	100.0	100.0	99.7
N	104	151	55	374

Function	J. Carter		Mondale	
	NY Times	*Schedules*	*NY Times*	*Schedules*
Fundraiser	2.2	12.6	2.4	0.0
Public Speech, Rally	64.0	62.2	65.9	35.9
Leadership Mtg.	2.2	7.2	0.0	5.3
Print Media Intvw.	2.2	0.0	9.8	2.9
Radio Interview	1.1	0.0	0.0	0.0
TV Interview	5.6	0.9	2.4	0.0
Press Av. or Conf.	0.0	0.0	4.9	29.4
Coffee, Recptn., Wlk. Tour	22.5	17.1	14.6	26.5
Total	100.0	100.0	100.0	100.0
N	89	111	41	170

Function	Anderson		Lucey	
	NY Times	*Schedules*	*NY Times*	*Schedules*
Fundraiser	3.6	3.7	0.0	0.4
Public Speech, Rally	54.8	30.7	0.0	33.7
Leadership Mtg.	0.0	6.4	0.0	4.0
Print Media Intvw.	4.8	9.0	0.0	11.2
Radio Interview	0.0	1.5	0.0	5.4
TV Interview	7.1	9.4	0.0	12.7
Press Av. or Conf.	19.0	19.1	0.0	11.6
Coffee, Recptn., Wlk. Tour	10.7	20.2	100.0	21.0
Total	100.0	100.0	100.0	100.0
N	84	267	1	276

Note: The figure refers to the percentage of total campaign events (N) reported in the *New York Times* and listed in daily schedules that candidates spent in different activities.

substantially more complete in the fall than the spring. But there also were significant fluctuations among candidates. While the *New York Times* reported 89 of Carter's 111 events (80.2 percent), it covered only 68.9 percent of Reagan's appearances and 31.5 percent of Anderson's visits. And vice-presidential candidates fared even more poorly; the newspaper covered 24.1 percent of Mondale's visits, 14.7 percent of Bush's, and 0.4 percent of Lucey's activities (illustrating how the press serves as a barrier to independent campaigns). Not surprisingly, the candidate (Carter) whose coverage was most complete displayed the highest match between press reports and travel schedules. But for campaigners having less complete coverage, press reports generated similar distortions in allocational patterns as found in the nominating process. There were also interesting contrasts between campaign stages in the use of the media. While candidates in the spring devoted a substantial percentage of their time to formal media interviews and press conferences, neither Reagan nor Carter did so in the general election. Instead they limited their media contacts to brief, impromptu press conferences when entering and leaving public appearances. In this way, party nominees tried to control their exposure to media questioning.

Of course, these conclusions should not be surprising. Based on what scholars know about press coverage, these patterns are typical.[16] Given media purposes (which differ substantially from scholarly ones), there is no reason for newspapers to treat nominating events in Idaho the same way they treat those in New York. And there is no reason for the media to cover candidates equally. After all, it would make little sense to treat Lucey with the same thoroughness as Reagan and Carter. But the important point of this comparison is that for scholarly purposes, press coverage is flawed. By comparing travel allocations as derived from the *New York Times* and daily itineraries that campaign organizations made available, it is clear that the press overreported campaign visits to its home and surrounding locations. Press coverage was also distributed in a way that some candidates and some activities received disproportionate coverage. So for allocational studies, there are good reasons to rely on candidates' itineraries (which I do in the following sections).

CONSTITUENCY ALLOCATIONS IN THE NOMINATING PROCESS

Since travel schedules list the audiences of campaign appearances, they provide a way of analyzing the constituencies that candidates wanted to rally. Table 5–3, which lists constituency allocations during the nominating process, shows several patterns. First, there were certain constituencies that all candidates visited regardless of party or coalitional strategy. The largest category of common visits was general audiences, those who were not identified with any particular interest groups or demographic blocs. Almost all the candidates devoted half their time to these people. For example, Anderson spent 46.4 percent of his time with this category while Reagan devoted 60.3 percent and Kennedy 56.5

percent of his time. College students and business audiences also were common constituencies for most campaigners (although I note later that the emphases on students varied with coalitional strategies). Surprisingly, there were no other campaign audiences that attracted a significant percentage of visits across the board. Perhaps in an era of candidate-centered coalitions, idiosyncratic coalitions are the norm, not the exception.

Second, certain constituencies clearly were party-related. Republican candidates visited service clubs with greater frequency than Democratic contenders. While Brown, Rosalyn Carter, and Mondale ignored service clubs completely and Kennedy allocated only 0.7 percent of his time to these people, Republicans gave them higher allocations: Anderson (5.4 percent), Bush (2.3 percent), Dole (5.5 percent), and Reagan (2.4 percent). Similarly, Republican campaigners (for obvious reasons) devoted more time than their Democratic colleagues to audiences that were identified on schedules as Republican party gatherings: Anderson (6.0 percent), Baker (16.0 percent), Bush (9.5 percent), Dole (11.5 percent), and Reagan (16.8 percent). Of course, there was a flip-side to these relations; Democratic aspirants had some constituencies which they visited more than Republicans did. For example, all of the Democratic campaigners (Brown, Rosalyn Carter, Mondale, and Kennedy) allocated time to black audiences, but only three (Anderson, Bush, and Dole) of the seven Republicans did. In addition, unions were a major recipient of campaign visits by Kennedy (7.6 percent) and Mondale (5.9 percent). But of the Republicans, only Baker (0.6 percent), Bush (0.2 percent), and Reagan (0.2 percent) spent time with union audiences. The Democratic candidates also spent more time than Republicans at Democratic party events: Mondale (9.6 percent), Kennedy (4.9 percent), Brown (3.8 percent), and Rosalyn Carter (3.3 percent). So while party coalitions may be weakening, constituency allocations still remain distinctive between Republican and Democratic contestants.

Third, scheduling patterns suggest a relationship between campaign visits and coalitional strategies. The candidates who attempted to remake party coalitions usually visited audiences that facilitated that strategy. For example, the most clearcut innovators (Anderson and Brown) spent the most time on collegiate audiences, a constituency characterized by youth, intensity, and weak political attachments. And as a clue to his disenchantment with the Republican party, Anderson spent less time than his counterparts on Republican audiences; he also visited both Republican and Democratic audiences. In addition, Dole devoted time to several constituencies not strongly emphasized by other Republicans: agricultural, veterans, and handicapped audiences. Finally, Crane and Reagan visited fundamentalist audiences in hopes of rallying those constituencies to the Republican cause.

Table 5-3
Constituency Allocations for Nominations

Constituency	Anderson	Baker	Bush	Connally	Crane	Dole	Reagan	Brown	R. Carter	Mondale	Kennedy
Black	0.8	0.0	0.2	0.0	0.0	0.6	0.0	0.8	0.6	0.5	1.5
Hispanic	0.0	0.0	0.0	0.0	1.0	0.0	0.2	0.0	0.0	0.5	0.5
Indian	0.0	0.0	0.0	0.0	0.0	0.0	0.0	0.0	0.0	0.0	0.2
Asian	0.0	0.0	0.2	0.0	0.0	0.0	0.0	0.0	1.1	0.0	0.0
Italian	0.0	0.0	0.0	0.0	0.0	0.0	0.2	0.0	1.1	0.0	0.2
Irish	0.0	0.0	0.0	0.0	0.0	0.0	0.0	0.0	0.6	0.0	0.0
Polish	0.2	0.0	0.2	0.0	0.0	0.0	0.4	0.0	0.0	0.5	0.5
Women	1.6	0.3	0.0	0.0	0.0	0.6	0.4	0.0	0.0	0.0	0.3
College	16.3	5.2	6.2	0.0	6.3	4.8	3.3	8.3	3.3	0.9	3.2
Elem + HS	1.4	1.7	1.1	0.0	2.1	1.8	3.5	0.8	0.0	9.6	2.0
Union	0.0	0.6	0.2	0.0	0.0	0.0	0.2	0.0	0.0	5.9	7.6
Business	10.4	7.3	10.7	2.4	16.7	17.0	6.2	3.0	7.8	5.5	6.6
Service club	5.4	2.9	2.3	0.0	1.0	5.5	2.4	0.0	0.0	0.0	0.7
Republican	6.0	16.0	9.5	1.2	9.4	11.5	16.8	0.0	0.0	0.0	0.7
Democratic	0.2	0.0	0.0	0.0	0.0	0.0	0.0	3.8	3.3	9.6	4.9
Rep. Women	0.6	1.2	0.5	0.0	1.0	1.8	0.7	0.0	0.0	0.0	0.0
Dem. Women	0.0	0.0	0.0	0.0	0.0	0.0	0.0	0.0	1.1	0.0	0.0
Sr. Citizens	0.6	0.3	0.9	0.0	0.0	0.0	0.4	0.0	5.0	1.4	2.9
Catholic	0.0	0.0	0.3	0.0	0.0	0.0	0.0	0.0	0.6	0.5	0.2
Jewish	0.2	2.0	0.2	0.0	1.0	1.2	0.0	0.0	1.1	1.8	3.2

Protestant	0.7	0.5	0.0	0.0	0.0	1.2	2.1	0.0	0.0	0.0	1.0
Fundmtlist	0.5	0.0	0.0	0.0	0.4	0.0	1.0	0.0	0.0	0.0	1.0
Sportsmen	0.7	0.5	0.6	0.0	0.7	4.2	1.0	0.0	0.9	0.3	0.0
Veterans	0.2	0.0	0.0	0.0	0.2	4.2	0.0	0.0	0.3	0.0	0.0
Medical	1.0	0.5	5.0	0.8	0.2	0.0	2.1	0.0	0.2	0.6	1.2
Agricultural	0.5	2.3	1.7	0.0	1.1	6.7	0.0	0.0	0.6	1.5	0.2
Pub. affairs	1.0	1.8	1.1	0.0	0.4	1.2	0.0	0.0	1.1	0.6	1.8
Municipal	0.7	0.9	0.6	0.0	0.2	0.6	0.0	0.0	0.0	0.0	0.2
Media Assn.	0.2	0.9	0.0	0.0	0.2	0.6	0.0	1.2	0.5	1.7	0.8
Lodges	0.3	0.0	0.0	0.0	0.2	0.6	0.0	0.0	0.2	0.0	0.0
Other ethnic	1.2	0.0	1.1	0.0	1.1	0.6	0.0	0.0	0.2	0.3	0.0
Child care	0.2	0.0	0.0	0.0	0.0	0.0	0.0	0.0	0.0	0.0	0.0
Environmental	0.3	0.0	0.0	0.0	0.0	0.0	0.0	0.0	0.0	0.0	0.2
Commnty, Act.	1.0	0.5	0.0	0.0	0.0	1.2	1.0	0.0	0.0	0.0	0.4
Legal	0.3	0.0	0.0	0.0	0.0	0.0	0.0	0.0	0.3	0.6	2.6
Unemployed	0.3	0.0	0.0	0.0	0.0	0.0	0.0	0.0	0.0	0.0	0.2
Energy	0.0	0.9	0.6	0.8	0.0	3.6	0.0	0.0	0.2	1.2	0.2
Humanitarian	0.0	0.5	0.0	0.0	0.0	0.0	0.0	0.0	0.2	0.3	0.0
Reform	0.0	0.0	1.1	0.0	0.0	0.0	0.0	0.0	0.2	0.0	0.2
Handicapped	0.0	0.0	0.6	0.0	0.0	1.2	0.0	0.0	0.0	0.0	0.0
Military	0.0	0.0	0.0	0.0	0.0	1.2	0.0	0.0	0.0	0.0	0.0
General	56.5	54.3	62.2	81.8	60.3	27.9	54.2	95.1	63.3	55.4	46.4
Total	100.0	100.0	100.0	100.0	100.0	100.0	100.0	100.0	100.0	100.0	100.0
N	593	219	180	132	453	165	96	82	663	343	502

Note: The figure refers to the percentage of total campaign events (N) listed on daily schedules that candidates spent on particular constituencies.

CONSTITUENCY ALLOCATIONS IN THE GENERAL ELECTION

Candidates faced a different situation in the general election than in the nominating process. For the first time, party competition was head to head. Instead of competing in separate party caucuses and primaries, campaigners needed to win support from a broad electorate. They also traveled with a large media entourage, a situation that enabled them to use campaign visits to communicate their symbolic concern with particular constituencies. Because of these features, it is not surprising that candidates allocated their time among constituencies in different ways than before. Table 5–4, which lists constituency allocations for the general election, shows the patterns of coalition-building by the three sets of campaigners. For Reagan and Bush, the priority constituencies were general audiences, Republicans, and business groups. However, beyond that point, each sought to mobilize distinctive coalitions. Reagan spent time with Catholics, Polish audiences, college students, senior citizens, Jews, and agricultural interests. Reagan also devoted more time than he had in the nominating process to blacks, Hispanics, Italians, and unions, among others. Meanwhile, Bush visited college students, senior citizens, sportsmen, farmers, public affairs organizations, and media associations. Like Reagan, he also increased his time with blacks and Hispanics. In contrast, Carter and Mondale devoted their time to general audiences, Democrats, businesses, students, and unions. Surprisingly, given their party's coalition, neither Democrat spent much time with women's organizations. Carter also did not spend a substantial amount of time with blacks (0.9 percent), compared to Reagan (0.8 percent) or Bush (1.7 percent), which makes one wonder whether parties take for granted voters who consistently support their candidates. Finally, Anderson and Lucey persisted in

Table 5-4
Constituency Allocations for General Election

Constituency	Reagan	Bush	J. Carter	Mondale	Anderson	Lucey
Black	0.8	1.7	0.9	0.9	2.5	0.0
Hispanic	1.2	1.7	0.0	0.0	0.0	0.6
Indian	0.4	0.0	0.0	0.0	0.0	0.0
Asian	0.0	0.0	0.9	0.0	0.0	0.0
Italian	0.8	0.4	0.9	0.0	0.0	0.0
Irish	0.0	0.0	0.0	0.0	0.0	0.0
Polish	1.6	0.0	1.8	0.0	0.6	0.0
Women	0.0	0.0	0.0	0.9	1.2	0.0
College	3.6	6.9	5.5	2.6	11.7	10.4
Elem + HS	1.2	1.3	0.0	4.4	1.2	1.8

Table 5-4 (continued)

Constituency	Reagan	Bush	J. Carter	Mondale	Anderson	Lucey
Union	2.0	0.4	4.5	7.9	1.2	1.8
Business	9.2	12.5	6.4	6.1	12.9	18.6
Service club	0.0	1.7	0.0	0.0	0.6	0.6
Republican	12.1	24.1	0.0	0.0	0.0	0.0
Democratic	0.8	0.0	17.3	8.8	0.0	0.0
Rep. Women	0.0	0.0	0.0	0.0	0.0	0.0
Dem. Women	0.0	0.0	0.0	0.0	0.0	0.0
Sr. Citizens	2.4	1.3	0.9	2.6	1.8	0.6
Catholic	2.4	0.0	0.0	2.6	0.6	0.6
Jewish	1.6	0.4	0.9	1.8	3.1	0.0
Protestant	0.0	0.4	0.0	0.0	0.6	0.0
Fundmtlist	0.4	0.9	1.8	1.8	0.6	0.0
Sportsmen	0.0	1.3	0.0	0.0	0.0	0.0
Veterans	0.0	0.4	0.0	0.0	0.0	0.0
Medical	0.0	0.0	0.9	0.0	0.6	0.0
Agricultural	2.0	3.0	2.7	1.8	0.0	7.4
Pub. affairs	0.4	2.2	1.8	0.9	1.2	0.6
Municipal	0.0	0.4	0.0	0.0	0.0	0.0
Media Assn.	0.0	1.3	0.0	0.0	1.8	1.8
Lodges	0.0	0.0	0.0	0.0	0.0	0.0
Other ethnic	0.8	0.4	0.0	0.0	0.6	0.0
Child care	0.0	0.0	0.0	0.0	0.6	0.0
Environmental	0.0	0.0	0.0	0.0	0.0	0.0
Commnty, Act.	0.0	0.0	0.0	0.0	0.0	2.5
Legal	0.0	0.0	0.0	0.0	0.6	0.0
Unemployed	0.0	0.0	0.0	0.0	0.0	0.6
Energy	0.0	0.4	5.5	0.0	0.0	0.6
Humanitarian	0.0	0.0	0.0	0.0	0.0	0.0
Reform	0.0	0.0	0.0	0.0	0.0	0.0
Handicapped	0.0	0.0	0.0	0.0	0.6	0.0
Military	0.0	0.0	0.0	0.0	0.0	0.0
Liberal Party	0.0	0.0	0.0	0.0	2.5	0.6
Gay	0.0	0.0	0.0	0.0	0.0	0.6
General	55.2	36.6	47.3	57.0	52.8	60.1
Total	99.9	100.0	100.0	100.0	100.0	100.0
N	239	232	110	114	163	163

Note: The figure refers to the percentage of total campaign events (N) listed on daily schedules that candidates spent on particular constituencies.

Anderson's nomination pattern, emphasizing general audiences, businesses, and (especially) students. As would be expected with independent candidates, neither devoted time to audiences clearly defined as Republican or Democratic. Instead, Anderson visited Liberal party audiences, blacks, Jews, public affairs organizations, and media associations, while Lucey devoted time to unions, farmers, media associations, and community activists. Lucey was also the only candidate who visited a homosexual audience (although Brown did so in his prenomination campaign).

These patterns suggest that candidates (especially Republican ones) scheduled appearances more broadly in the general election than nominating process. Owing to the breadth of the electorate in the fall and the minority status of the GOP, Republicans used the general election to broaden their base (with the result that party divisions were less apparent in the fall than the spring). However, constituency allocations were related to electoral strategies in the general election (as they had been in the nominating process). Coalitional innovators used campaign visits to signal their interest in key voting blocs. Candidates (such as Reagan and Anderson) who wanted to make inroads with Democratic constituencies (such as Catholics, ethnic voters, union members, Jews, and minorities) lavished personal time on these voters. In this way, presidential campaigning was an integral part of the coalition-building process.

CAMPAIGN VISITS AND COALITION-BUILDING

In summary, constituency allocations were a vital part of the coalition-building process. Analysis of the audiences on which candidates spent time reveals important clues about the electoral coalitions they attempted to develop. Political observers have often bemoaned presidential campaigning, saying that it represents nothing more than superficial and contrived events. But this interpretation ignores the substantive nature of campaign events. In a world of limited time, candidates must make choices. They must emphasize certain constituencies and de-emphasize others. These choices are not random decisions. Although there were certain constituencies for which all candidates competed, party affiliations and coalitional strategies influenced the allocations of time among various voters. Republicans and Democrats campaigned before different audiences in the nominating process. And candidates who wanted to mobilize unconventional voters or remake party coalitions visited constituencies that facilitated those strategies. For these reasons, candidate travels were not just media events; they were a vital technique for building coalitions.

In addition, this research suggests that strategies based on travel allocations are well suited to the new electoral system: the large number of primaries, the need to demonstrate popular support in a variety of settings, the requirement that dark horse candidates build their name recognition among the public, the necessity of building personal campaign organizations, and the need to symbolize one's concern with particular constituencies through campaign visits. Travel allocations make it possible for candidates to target certain constituencies. Unlike broadly based symbolic strategies, campaign organizers can distribute campaign visits in a discrete manner. And the fact that travel allocations allow candidates to communicate concern for particular audiences without also requiring policy means that candidates can attract support on the basis of personal qualities or style. Since many voters are not especially interested in politics but still may want to know that candidates share their values and understand their problems, campaign visits represent a valuable electoral tactic in contemporary campaigns.

But speaking more broadly, it should be apparent that constituency allocations have implications for party realignment. With the exception of James Sundquist, scholars have ignored the role of leadership in realignment and coalition formation. Typically, writers have investigated realigning elections at the level of voters. Yet one can argue that candidates play a major role in this process. Looking at 1980, it seems clear that leadership was crucial to Reagan's coalition. His landslide (and subsequent opportunities for realignment) did not arrive by accident. Instead, they developed as a result of his constituency allocations during the campaign. Reagan actively sought coalitional change as well as programmatic adjustments in the national agenda (see chapter 4). He made overt appeals to Democrats. He tried to rally "de-aligning" constituencies to his side. And he sought to bring new constituencies into the Republican party. In short, while Reagan's election victory arose as a protest vote against Carter and the poor state of the economy, the Californian deserves credit for a coalitional strategy that took full advantage of Carter's weaknesses. By actively pursuing vulnerable voting blocs, Reagan expanded his opportunities for realignment (even if he later lost those opportunities because of a lengthy recession).

Constituency allocations also are important for their policy consequences. Campaigns contribute to candidates' political understanding. Since electioneering forces them to allocate time among audiences, it shapes their perceptions of constituencies. When it comes time to distribute policy benefits, most leaders do not forget the battle lines of support and opposition. Few cases illustrate this point better than the weak relation between blacks and the Republican party. For several decades, blacks have not voted in large proportions for Republican presidential candidates. Consequently, many Republican organizers in 1980 wrote off the black vote. For example, one campaign manager honestly conceded, "We don't spend a lot of time campaigning for minorities because minorities don't vote in Republican primaries." And in Reagan's case, his campaign also did little to sensitize him to the plight of minority groups. By making no appearances before black audiences in the nominating process and by making a controversial appearance in the fall at a Mississippi county fair popularized by segregationists, Reagan made clear that blacks were not an integral part of his coalition. Unfortunately for blacks, the attitudes and priorities that developed during the campaign carried over into the Reagan Administration (as usually is the case). On racial matters, Reagan made decisions (tax breaks for segregated schools and lukewarm support for voting rights legislation) and appointments (William Bell for the Equal Employment Opportunity Commission and Samuel Hart for the Civil Rights Commission) that black leaders bitterly opposed.[17] Even more revealing, Reagan often expressed surprise when his actions provoked the fury of minority groups. While there may have been many reasons for these policy decisions, one cannot ignore the way Reagan's constituency allocations made him insensitive to minority concerns. Because he devoted little time trying to understand the problems of these groups (and substantial time trying to understand the views of those opposed to civil rights), his policy decisions bore the burden of that neglect. In this way, constituency allocations were intimately tied to the policy process.

NOTES

1. See Crotty, *Political Reform and the American Experiment*, pp. 193–237 and Witcover, *Marathon*, pp. 21–35.

2. See "1979 Travel Statistics," an unpublished campaign document that the George Bush for President Committee made available.

3. Stephen Brams and Morton Davis, "The 3/2's Rule in Presidential Campaigning," *American Political Science Review*, 68, no. 1 (March, 1974), pp. 113–134.

4. See Stanley Kelley, Jr., "The Presidential Campaign," in Paul David, ed., *The Presidential Election and Transition* (Washington, D.C.: Brookings, 1961), pp. 57–87 and Claude Colantoni, Terrence Levesque, and Peter Ordeshook, "Campaign Resource Allocation under the Electoral College," *American Political Science Review*, 69, no. 1 (March, 1975), pp. 141–154. Unlike Brams and Davis, who combined appearances of the presidential and vice-presidential nominees, Kelley analyzed them separately and found that each presidential contender used his running mate's schedule in different ways. For example, in 1960, Kennedy used his schedule to mobilize large, industrial states and Johnson's appearances to hold the South. In contrast, Nixon and Lodge allocated their time in a duplicative fashion. These differences suggest that researchers should not combine the appearances of presidential and vice-presidential contenders but rather should analyze them separately.

5. Aldrich, *Before the Convention*, and Brams and Davis, "Optimal Resource Allocation in Presidential Primaries," presented at the annual meeting of the American Political Science Association, Washington, D.C., August 28–31, 1980.

6. Time is one of the most valuable resources in presidential campaigns. In part, its value comes from its scarcity. However, its value also rises because of the control that campaign organizers have over scheduling. Unlike financial resources, which depend on willing contributors, time is contributed and therefore controlled by candidates.

7. Quoted in S. Rule, "Reagan Turns Down Invitation to Address N.A.A.C.P.," *New York Times* (July 1, 1980), p. 36.

8. See John Runyon, Jennefer Verdini, and Sally Runyon, *Source Book of American Presidential Campaign and Election Statistics, 1948–1968* (New York: Ungar, 1971).

9. For example, in addition to constituency allocations, one can study substate allocations (how candidates allocate their time among different cities or regions of a state) as well as allocations of candidate activities (how they distribute their time among fund-

raising, the media, and public speeches). While I briefly discuss the latter, I emphasize constituency allocations because of their substantive link to electoral coalitions.

10. The campaign organizations of all candidates except Brown, Connally, and Crane provided daily schedules. For these exceptions, I reconstructed their itineraries from a computerized information retrieval system, the Associated Press Political Databank.

11. Aldrich, *Before the Convention*, p. 70..

12. These categories were defined inductively from travel schedules. Since the list was designed to reflect the way campaign organizers see election constituencies, it includes a mix of demographic and issue constituencies.

13. Of course, candidate itineraries were not perfect sources of travel information. Although these itineraries were the final versions of the candidates' schedules (the ones distributed to the media and Secret Service), candidates did not always follow the letter of their schedules. In some cases, the schedules listed appearances that were canceled. In other cases, they omitted appearances organized at the last minute (one notable example being Anderson's late decision to attend a candidate forum held by Gunowners of New Hampshire, a well-publicized event that fueled Anderson's candidacy). However, these last-minute changes represented a small percentage of the candidates' total appearances. In addition, while the itineraries did not include all actual appearances, they did represent a complete list of intended appearances. Obviously, the final version included all events that the candidate and staff agreed were part of the itinerary.

14. The figures for Brown, Connally, and Crane were low because of reliance on the Associated Press Political Databank; daily itineraries were unavailable.

15. These comparisons did not include time that candidates devoted to activities other than public appearances, such as travel, personal time, and staff meetings (although their schedules listed these activities). When these things were included, candidates spent about half their time in the nominating and general election campaigns traveling between events.

16. For example, see Doris Graber, *Mass Media and American Politics* (Washington, D.C.: Congressional Quarterly Press, 1980).

17. See Adam Clymer, "Republicans Worry About Eroding Black Support," *New York Times* (April 14, 1982).

6

The Role of Political Symbolism

Symbolic strategies have been persistently popular with political leaders. Going back to the earliest days of the Republic, politicians have wrapped themselves in flag, country, and God. For example, John McDiarmid studied inaugural addresses from George Washington to Franklin Roosevelt and found frequent references to commonly perceived symbols: America, the founding fathers, freedom, religion, and the American people.[1] Periodically, leaders also have sought to develop "larger than life" images of themselves. Andrew Jackson campaigned as "Old Hickory," while Abraham Lincoln became known as the "Great Emancipator."

But despite the longtime use, symbolism recently has acquired negative connotations. Journalists and cartoonists deride symbolism as empty and meaningless. In their eyes, to employ symbolic gestures is to be manipulative or deceitful. Leaders who engage in symbolic behavior (such as Carter carrying his own luggage to show that he would not be an imperial president) are viewed with suspicion. Scholars have also attacked symbolism for being devoid of substance. Murray Edelman, the most prominent critic of symbolism, argues that leaders manipulate emotional symbols for their own benefit.[2] They use threatening events to make citizens fearful and politically docile and, according to Edelman, talk about broad symbols to avoid policy discussions.

In this chapter, I challenge the negative view of symbolism. First, I investigate the link between symbolism and the new electoral system. In outlining how leaders use and manipulate symbolism, Edelman describes it as a universal condition among leaders. Because he assumes that symbolic strategies come "naturally" to them, he does not consider why they employ symbolism or what conditions offer the greatest incentives for symbolic strategies. Since some political environments may be especially conducive to symbolic strategies, it is worthwhile to consider how the new electoral system affects leader perceptions of these strategies. Second, because Edelman describes symbolism as a blanket condition, he also does not investigate the limits of symbolic strategies. In reading his analysis of leader symbolism and "mass quiescence," one gets the impression that candidates employ symbolism without risks or limitations. However, as with many leader techniques, it is likely that symbolic strategies offer "double-edged" opportunities for presidential candidates. Finally, I argue that symbolism is not completely devoid of substance. Rather, candidates use symbolism to communicate substantive messages about themselves, their policies, and their visions. In fact, symbolic messages usually are consistent with candidates' coalitional strategies.

SYMBOLISM: DEFINITION AND TESTABILITY

Before investigating symbolism in the new electoral system, it is important to state what the term means. Scholars have used the concept of symbolism in two different ways. First, researchers traditionally defined it narrowly as references to commonly perceived *symbols*, such as God, country, and freedom. McDiarmid's analysis of verbal symbols used this approach as did Harold Lasswell, Daniel Lerner, and Ithiel de Sola Pool in their content analysis of press coverage.[3] In addition, Charles Goodsell's contemporary study of service and authority symbols in government offices focused narrowly on commonly perceived symbols (flags, uniforms, and so on).[4] Second, other scholars have defined the term more broadly as *symbolic behavior*. Murray Edelman did not limit his research to the study of flags, forefathers, and freedom (as previous writers did). Rather, he argued that political behavior can stand for or symbolize ideas other than its literal meanings.[5] As an example, Edelman argued that leaders try to develop particular images of themselves (such as the strong leader or the caring leader). But since these images usually bear little resemblance to what leaders actually plan to do, their behavior is deceptive and manipulative.

In comparing these approaches, it is apparent that they offer contrasting advantages. By emphasizing commonly perceived symbols, the traditional approach avoids the definitional problems that some say plagued Edelman's work. Since most observers agree that flags connote patriotism, country, and freedom, there are few disputes over their symbolic meanings. And because analyses rest on simple counts or references to symbols, scholars also avoid testability problems (another complaint about Edelman's work). With these strengths, it is little wonder that many scholars have defined symbolism narrowly. However, it should be clear that these advantages come at a price. Perhaps the primary virtue of Edelman's reformulation was its ability to raise new and interesting lines of analysis. Since he broadened the focus to symbolic behavior, he was able to discuss important normative questions about the implications of leader behavior for citizen beliefs, public policy, and the political system. Were leaders manipulative? Did they exploit crises for personal benefit? Did they manufacture images without limitations? And were they unaccountable to voters? These questions (which are crucial for democracy) went well beyond the range of traditional approaches to symbolism. Scholars who defined symbolism narrowly and counted verbal references to country and God in public speeches simply could not shed much light on these topics. In addition, Edelman's approach may be less subject to testability criticisms than is usually thought. Since Edelman's innovative reformulation in the early 1960s, research has arisen which, while not explicit tests of his framework, certainly bears on his conclusions (and illustrates that his work is testable). Edward Tufte's study of political control of the economy supports Edelman's contention that leaders manipulate the economy for their political benefit.[6] Meanwhile, Page's work on candidate rhetoric shows the limits of strategies of ambiguity; candidates rarely contradict their policy stands, and they cannot be ambiguous without risks to their credibility.[7] Despite these conflicting findings, the key point is that scholars have managed to test Edelman's conclusions.

In this analysis of campaign symbolism, I focused on the symbolic dimensions of candidate activities. Rather than counting references to God, freedom, and the nation (which would accomplish little), I asked the following questions: How did campaign organizers see political symbolism? When did they employ symbolic strategies and why did they use them? Were there any limits on these strategies or could they be used without risks? And what role did symbolism play in coalition-building? Since I was interested in leader perceptions of symbolism, I did not impose a narrow definition on campaign advisors. Instead, I let them define their use of symbolism. In this way, I tried to see symbolic strategies as they saw them.

SYMBOLISM AND THE NEW ELECTORAL SYSTEM

Symbolic strategies played a prominent role in a variety of campaign activities in 1980. To open their campaigns, candidates usually planned their announcements in symbolic settings. Because of the media coverage that accompanies candidacy announcements, political leaders saw them as the major opportunity in the prenomination period for public attention. Since announcements officially mark campaign kickoffs, candidates used them to set themes and overall images. As Richard Stearns, Kennedy's chief delegate director, noted: "an announcement speech is a staged event. You look for the right connotations in the way the staging is done." To illustrate his point, Stearns said that Kennedy chose an announcement location (under the bust of John Quincy Adams at Faneuil Hall in Boston's Quincy Market) with historical connotations:

Symbols are an attempt to reach back through associations that are comforting or inspiring to people. . . . [In choosing] Faneuil Hall in Boston to deliver his announcement speech, well, clearly you are reaching back to a symbol which, particularly after the bicentennial celebration, has a very strong historical connotation in people's minds.

Similarly, Kennedy's campaign manager, Paul Kirk, added that:

there was a lot of history involved in Massachusetts. . . . To some degree, the Republic was launched there and it was symbolic of what he felt about the spirit of the American people as it contrasted with what Carter had said about that [in the "malaise" speech]. . . . He also felt that to announce from his own home state in a setting that legitimately provided some history to it was better than doing what his brothers had done, doing it from the Senate caucus room.[8]

Campaigners also were aware of the symbolic dimensions of scheduling, media advertising, and campaign slogans. Jon Miller, Bush's deputy political director, described the symbolic value of travel allocations:

The purpose [of a campaign visit] is to, in a symbolic sense, show that you are concerned enough with the electorate to come to that area. That's probably the most important reason. For instance, we made a point of saying George Bush was the only candidate of either party who went to the upper peninsula of Michigan or to northern Michigan.

In addition, this awareness extended to Bush's media campaign. In describing the decision to de-emphasize Bush's Texas oil background (while emphasizing almost every other aspect of adult life), John Morgan, Bush's media advisor and demographer, explained: "We have never fostered that [oil man image]. In fact, I've stayed away from [advertising on] shows like *Dallas* because I don't want people to get the idea that he's a Texas wheeler dealer."

More generally, staff members employed campaign slogans to send symbolic messages to the public. Because they used these slogans on bumper stickers, media advertising, campaign posters, and in direct mail, they crafted them with great care. According to Doug Bailey, Baker's media advisor: "theme lines and slogans and bumper stickers and graphics and all the rest are part of an overall effort to communicate about your guy what you want people to believe." And Pat Caddell, Carter's pollster and advisor, said: "You always want the 'tag line' [of an ad] to reflect what you want people to take away if you could have your way." With these things in mind, Bailey devised a slogan for Baker ("Tough. Honest. Right for the 80's") that was intended to communicate the following symbolic messages:

We were trying to draw a contrast with Carter and a contrast with Reagan at the same time and perhaps a contrast with Connally. "Tough" means we're not like Jimmy Carter. "Honest" may mean to some people that we're not like John Connally. "Right for the 80's" means that we're not like Ronald Reagan. . . . I think if we had been successful in communicating broadly to the public a candidate who was tough, honest, and right for the 80's, we probably would've been successful in the campaign.

Hence, campaign organizers defined symbolism in broad terms. They were conscious of the symbolic potential of many electoral activities: candidacy announcements, scheduling, media advertising, and campaign slogans. In fact, it was rare when they did not think about the political connotations (or symbolic value) of their efforts. As Edelman has suggested, symbolism is a pervasive feature of political life.

Of course, it is hardly a novel idea to argue that presidential candidates communicate symbolically. These strategies have been popular for a long time because they have several qualities that are attractive to campaigners. First, their directness and emotional connotations enable candidates to communicate with large numbers of voters in a shorthand fashion. By using "code words" that particular voting blocs understand, presidential aspirants can woo voters without elaborate or complicated arguments.[9] As Walter McGuire, Brown's director of scheduling, said: "If you don't have enough time to talk to everybody for an hour, then you try to communicate through various means and symbolism is one of them." Similarly, Dan Swillinger of Anderson's campaign argued that symbols help to reduce the complexity of modern information flows:

Life is so complex that it is easier to deal with things in a symbolic way. . . . Labels and symbols take the place of what used to be more careful consideration. The whole information flow to any individual is ten times what it was ten years ago and probably a hundred times what it was twenty-five years ago. The exponential increase makes it very difficult and I think there is a certain amount of reducing things to their simplest symbol.

In addition, tactics based on political symbolism enable candidates to deliver multiple messages to audiences. Since symbolic gestures generally are broad and diffuse, they give candidates room for maneuver. As Richard Maullin, Brown's campaign cochairman, stated, this feature is particularly advantageous when candidates must speak to a large and diverse electorate:

When you have mass audiences watching your ads or watching your speeches and at the same time, knowing that we have an incredibly diverse social structure, you know you've got to say things in a way so that some people will quite understand what you are saying and others won't or maybe they'll understand it differently.

Finally, in a country where politics rarely has generated widespread public interest, symbolism enables candidates to develop favorable voter evaluations.[10] Les Francis, Carter's national chairman, noted that, "symbols generate feelings, hopefully positive feelings. . . . Any candidate uses the symbols . . . to convey a message [and] to generate warm and good feelings." And Robert Mosbacher, Jr., Baker's national political director, explained, "a lot of voters react in a gut way to how they feel about the candidate and what he represents to them. . . . I would suggest that a great many voters want to feel comfortable with the person as president. And symbols are often important to bolster or reinforce how one perceives the individual."

However, these qualities alone do not explain the prevalence of symbolic strategies in the new electoral system. Symbolism has always made possible shorthand communications between leaders and citizens. It also has been used to boost popular support on many occasions in history. More important is the way that the contemporary campaign environment accentuates the value of these qualities. As presidential campaigns move into a new era, symbolic strategies have become even more relevant for candidates. In asking campaign advisors about their rationales for symbolic strategies, they noted that mass media (particularly television) facilitate symbolism. Charles Black, Reagan's national political director, suggested that the mass media enable candidates to communicate particular images to voters:

There's a role for symbolism, particularly in the age of mass media. You are creating images. People don't base their vote purely on the issues; they also vote on the image of a guy. For example, Carter's theme in 1976 was "let's return honesty and the voice of the people to the White House, that sort of thing." So wearing blue jeans and walking down Pennsylvania Avenue at his inauguration, those sort of things were symbols that promoted that image. Of course, a person would never tell you that, "I voted for Jimmy Carter because he wears blue jeans instead of a coat and tie every day." But a person that says, "I voted for Jimmy Carter because he's one of us and he's an honest guy and listens to the people more than Jerry Ford," the blue jeans played a part in that. So images and personalities are created by symbols.

Similarly, Lyn Nofziger (Reagan's press secretary) claims that television has increased the importance of symbolic gestures: "A lot of people believe that Franklin D. Roosevelt could never be elected today because people would see him in a wheelchair and . . . the symbolism of that is a sign of physical inability to do the job. So I think television has made . . . symbolic gestures probably of greater importance than they ever were before." In part, the media heighten symbolic imagery because they emphasize headlines. As Doug Bailey noted:

Politics has increasingly become a game of television. Television is a visual medium. Television is also a headline medium. You don't get half an hour to explain your positions on things. You're lucky if you get thirty seconds, whether you paid for the time or it's on news coverage. Therefore, you're into headlines, you're into trying to communicate in shorthand language, you're trying to communicate by symbols.

However, Dan Swillinger also argues that news reporters stimulate symbolic appeals because of their need to summarize and translate the candidates' messages:

the candidate's message become translated into symbolic terms by the intermediaries which are principally television and newspapers. . . . Candidates get labels attached to them very quickly. . . . Anderson was the dark horse. . . . Connally was the candidate of the boardrooms. Reagan was the darling of the old right Republicans. Phil Crane was the new right. These guys all have . . . this baggage which to some extent was accurate but which became kind of a symbolic shorthand for describing their campaigns.

Thus, the mass media provide candidates with various incentives to communicate symbolically.

Staff members also found symbolic strategies attractive in the contemporary environment because of the high (and growing) levels of apathy and political disinterest. For example, Eddie Mahe, Jr., Connally's campaign manager, explained in rather graphic terms his rationale for symbolic strategies:

I think you have to go back to the voter first. If we buy thirty minutes of television time to explain John Connally's position on the issues, our rating would be three or four percent. . . . Thus, we are forced to use thirty-second spots because it's the only time we can catch them before they jump up after a program to go piss. If we go five minutes, we lose them. . . . In terms of reaching a mass electorate with thirty-minute, issue-oriented, substantive shows, you are not going to do it because they absolutely are not going to watch it. So what do we have to resort to? If we want to make a point on pollution, do we buy a thirty-minute show to explain pollution or do we go stand by a stinking river, throw a match in it, and watch it explode, and thereby show people that we're concerned about pollution? We are forced to symbolism because it's the only way to communicate with the American people.

Likewise, Doug Bailey discussed how voters reached decisions about candidates:

[I want to know that] that person is going to bring to bear in his decision-making process a set of values which he shares with me. I want to know, if the church is important in my life, I want to know that the church is important in that person's life. If my family is important to me and a sense of family is important to me, then I want to know that family is important to that person. And to the degree that he can communicate to me, believably and successfully, that the basic impulses, the basic priorities, the basic philosophy, the basic values of his life are like mine, that he's going to bring to bear the same kind of things in deciding those issues that I would bring to bear, therefore I can have confidence in his judgment. When you're talking about church and you're talking about personality, and you're talking about how you spend your off-hours and what kind of person you are, you're not talking substance, you're talking style. But it's terribly important to talk those subjects or to communicate on those subjects to give me the kind of confidence to vote for someone who is going to deal with complicated issues that I never will understand if they're explained to me ten hours a day.

And Gerald Rafshoon, Carter's media advisor, described the impact of voter apathy on electoral tactics: "They are apathetic and we have low voting turnout. You also have to assume that they're getting a lot of information from a lot of areas, so you have to hone in on just a few central themes and pound them over and over." As voter apathy, political disinterest, and public cynicism spread, candidates increasingly will use symbolism to build support.[11]

In summary, symbolism has several qualities that make it attractive to campaigners. Symbolic gestures serve as shorthand communications devices. Their diffuseness gives candidates rhetorical flexibility. And they enable candidates to boost their popular support. However, these features alone do not guarantee use of strategies based on political symbolism. Rather it appears that several qualities of the new electoral system encourage these strategies. First, many of the traditional tools with which candidates build support (notably party appeals) have become ineffective or risky. Second, the dominance of mass media, the need for polished media performances, and the penchant for symbolic labeling by news reporters place a premium on candidate style and image. Third, the need to communicate with a large and diverse electorate (particularly with open nominations and the large number of primaries) heightens the value of broad and diffuse symbols. Finally, citizen mistrust and disinterest encourage candidates to build popularity through symbolic avenues. In modern campaigns, presidential aspirants see symbolism as one way to develop favorable voter evaluations in hopes that positive evaluations will bring votes along as well.

THE LIMITS OF SYMBOLISM

Presidential contenders have many incentives to use symbolism. But there are no guarantees about these strategies. Contrary to Edelman's view, campaigners cannot use symbolism without limitations. Instead, symbolic strategies are ''double-edged'' opportunities that entail risks for candidates. While this notion flies in the face of Edelman's argument, there was evidence in 1980 of politicians who became prisoners of their symbolic images. One of the clearest examples was Brown (also known as Governor Moonbeam and the Peter Pan of politics). Brown began his campaign hoping to duplicate his 1976 success, when he won several primaries and attracted favorable media attention as a ''fresh face.'' Yet Brown's efforts to establish his unconventionality symbolically backfired. His African safari trip with Linda Ronstadt (ostensibly designed to solidify Brown's credibility in foreign affairs) did little to accomplish that aim. A visit with Indian Swami Mukhtanada also proved disastrous (Brown later defended it by saying, ''Swami Mukhtanada is not of the same rank or prestige as the Dalai Lama. But he is an important religious figure in his country. People meet with Billy Graham, the Pope, the Archbishop of a Greek Orthodox Church. It's rather ethnocentric to say one religious grouping is more important than another. Islamic leaders should be met with. This planet is very small.'')[12] And his multimedia production on the eve of the Wisconsin primary added to Brown's image as the ''flake'' candidate.[13] Despite Brown's efforts to control his symbolic image, his public profile proved unamenable to manipulation.

Meanwhile, Kennedy's campaign also suffered as a prisoner of symbolism, albeit in a different way than Brown's. Unlike the Californian, whose short tenure on the national political scene left him unknown to many voters, Kennedy was a familiar commodity. As the heir of an extraordinary political family, Edward Kennedy did not need to manufacture a political identity. Whether he liked it or not, Kennedy's image already existed. For some, he was the spoiled brat of the Kennedy family, a person whose rise to political prominence came from his name, not his achievements. Others saw him as the tragic victim of assassinations, Chappaquidick, and family problems. Still others viewed him as the impassioned defender of the disadvantaged. And in some quarters, he was seen as a dangerous threat to American capitalism. In short, few were neutral about Kennedy. While prominence often seemed advantageous, it came at a cost. As Garry Wills has argued in *The Kennedy Imprisonment*, Edward Kennedy in many ways was a prisoner of the past.[14] He was imprisoned by public expectations about Kennedy charisma. He was a prisoner of Kennedy ideology. And most important for the argument here, he was a captive of Kennedy style, image, and symbolism. Because of Camelot and the myths it entailed, Kennedy was expected in 1980 to act in certain ways—to be charismatic, articulate, liberal, and dashing. Actions that fell short (such as bumbling rhetoric) or veered in other directions (such as attempts to recast his liberalism) ran headlong into popular expectations. In these ways, Kennedy lacked the room for symbolic manipulation (or image transformation) that Edelman ascribed to political leaders.

In addition, campaigners who successfully developed symbolic images were undercut by changing political circumstances. As an example, Anderson's media style apparently served him well in the early primaries when it helped establish his symbolic differences with other Republican candidates. According to his advisor, Dan Swillinger:

the whole pitch of the Iowa debate was that he should be different. . . . That was the whole plan. . . . We compared briefing books and questions and answers and the single most important message that we tried to get through to him was "you've got to be different. Every time you answer a question, you've got to point out differences between you and all the others." . . . You know, when you are running in a seven-way primary—and that's what it would be in the first two primaries—you don't have to get a huge proportion of the vote in order to do very well.

Continuing, Swillinger said:

in his closing statement at the Iowa debate, he was very—he was almost emotional. Well, he *was* emotional. But he was very cranked up. He was very intense. And compared to the other six who were consciously trying to be very low key . . . he stood out both in terms of the way he answered questions, stood out in the substance of his answers, and also in the sort of personality he projected. . . . He was the hot guy for the hot media. And it worked out beautifully.

Given the multicandidate field in these primaries, Anderson needed only small vote totals to attract media attention and develop "momentum." But in the general election debate with Reagan, where the audience was broader, the stakes were higher, and Anderson needed more support to become viable, the media style that earned him praise earlier apparently turned viewers off. His direct mail advisor and "de facto" press secretary, Tom Mathews, evaluated Anderson's debate performance against Reagan this way:

He came across very hot and argumentative and full of facts and figures and people didn't like him. . . . Anderson lost the debate hands down except if any academic had been scoring it. . . . If Anderson in that debate had had the same kind of amiability and good humor and certainty and confidence that he had at the latter part of the campaign, I think he probably would have done himself an enormous amount of good. But he didn't. He was . . . too tight and too competitive.

In other words, the symbolic message that served him well in the early campaign environment when he needed only a small vote to gain media attention may have harmed Anderson during the general election. Similarly, Connally's symbolic emphasis on leadership aided him when the political environment cried out for strong leadership and the Democrats appeared ready to nominate Kennedy (in the fall of 1979). But this image failed when the situation shifted after the Iranian hostage takeover and the Soviet invasion of Afghanistan. According to Lance Tarrance, Connally's pollster, Connally believed initially that Carter's ineptness would lead to a general election between him and Kennedy:

When he announced in '79 and all through until the Iranian crisis, Kennedy was basically on a tremendous high at that point. Connally felt, whether it had religious connotations or not, destined to meet Ted Kennedy on the field of battle. And it would be somewhat like a "Star Wars" situation, one of those gargantuan battles of right versus wrong. Connally perceived Ted Kennedy as a real Darth Vader and Reagan, Carter, and all those people were really minor participants in this large, global war. He was destined to be there. He really felt that. In fact, he almost overdid it by telling everyone that Kennedy would be the eventual nominee. So by raising in a purposeful way the expectations that Kennedy was going to be the nominee, when Kennedy took his gigantic fall, thanks to Roger Mudd and Iran, then the context, the framework for Connally, really began to become muted. . . . Connally was as strong as there was weakness in Jimmy Carter, there was weakness in America, there was fear of Teddy Kennedy, particularly in the business community. . . . Connally was strong when those concerns, fears, and almost stigmas were in evidence. Once those changed, Connally had a tough time.

Thus, as the political situation changed, the symbolic message that seemed appropriate before the primaries lost its value; both Anderson and Connally lacked the flexibility to transform their symbolic appeals.

There were other examples in 1980 of limits on symbolic strategies. Contrary to the picture that Edelman painted, leaders could not be vague or deceptive without risks. With a vigilant press following their moves, campaigners who appeared to engage in manipulative behavior (like Bush sounding vague and Brown being expedient) were heavily criticized. Carter's use of the Iranian hostage crisis also serves as a case in point. While it is impossible to prove that the president manipulated this event for political advantage, the circumstantial evidence created the appearance of manipulation. These perceptions, which were prevalent among the media if not the public, damaged Carter's credibility. When negotiations were undertaken before the general election, many reporters were skeptical of Carter's motives (which certainly did not help the Georgian's reelection efforts). In these ways, the media acted as a check on symbolic behavior.

Because symbolism is limited, strategists sometimes tried to compensate by modifying their use of symbolic strategies. In recognition of the rapid pace of campaigns (which can render particular symbolic messages obsolete or ineffective), Reagan's organizers relied on flexible and "open-ended" slogans. Advisor Richard Wirthlin explained it this way:

When Peter Dailey came on board, we felt we needed a somewhat more flexible slogan. And his people came up with the slogan, "The Time is Now," which was tested and we found there was a number of things that could be done with that slogan: "The Time is Now to Make America Great Again," "The Time is Now to Make Government More Sensitive and Responsible," and so on. In other words, it was an open-ended slogan that could serve a variety of purposes. . . . Many of the dimensions of the campaign are both uncontrollable and unpredictable. Given an open-ended slogan, you can adapt that slogan to give you the maximum impact regardless of what the specific action parameters of the campaign turn out to be.

And Peter Dailey, Reagan's media advisor, added that:

What we wanted to do was to create a sense of urgency. . . . We also wanted an open-ended slogan that we could, as the campaign evolved, we could be more specific. If it evolved that strong leadership in the latter stage became an important aspect of the campaign, we could adjust it to say, "The Time is now for Strong Leadership, Reagan for President." We could move it around that way. And that's how it evolved later on.

But in making these adjustments, strategists ran the risk of sacrificing the unique qualities of symbolism: its simplicity and directness. By using symbolism for a variety of messages (instead of "pounding in" a few themes), campaigners inadvertently limited the effectiveness of their symbolic strategies.

In summary, symbolism represents a "double-edged" opportunity for presidential contenders. On the one hand, several features of the new electoral system (media dominance, widespread apathy, and need for popular support) encourage symbolic strategies. However, symbolism entails risks. Candidates can become prisoners of their symbolic images. Changing campaign dynamics may make particular symbolic messages ineffective. And campaigners who appear to abuse symbolic strategies may be denounced by news reporters. Despite Edelman's contention that leaders are the masters of symbolism, this research suggests that in certain ways, they also can become captives.

SYMBOLISM AND COALITIONAL STRATEGIES

Perhaps no question has divided political observers as much as the link between symbolism and "substance." Among early research on the subject, Harold Lasswell and his colleagues argued that symbolic appeals are consistent with leaders' substantive concerns because the appeals are linked intrinsically to the attitudes of those who use them.[15] In contrast, Edelman condemned leaders who employ symbolic strategies, arguing that symbolic appeals hide the leaders' true (or real) policy preference, thereby enabling them to manipulate the populace. Recently, Fenno and Page revived this debate by taking different positions on the nature of leader influence. Using the "presentation of self" perspective of Erving Goffman, Fenno claims that candidates seek to control the responses of others by expressing themselves in ways that leave "correct" impressions. However, unlike Edelman's ideas on symbolic manipulation, Fenno adds issue and district service elements to the act of presentation. These variations allow Fenno to reject Edelman's notion of arbitrary and unrestrained leadership manipulation. Rather than arguing that leaders present their messages unfettered by issues or service records, Fenno notes that these things mold candidate styles.[16] In contrast, Page appears to accept much of Edelman's argument. Unlike other theorists using economic reasoning, Page recognizes the danger of leadership manipulation and deception in models assuming unstable citizen preferences.[17]

Because scholars debate the substantive components of symbolism, I evaluate the link between symbolism and one dimension of "substance": candidates' coalitional strategies.[18] Few choices are more basic for campaigners than their coalitions. By emphasizing some constituencies and de-emphasizing others, candidates make decisions that influence (or reflect) their substantive leanings (see chapters 3 and 5). Not surprisingly, given the versatility of symbolism as a communications device, candidates interested in coalitional change used symbolism to communicate those interests to the public. Symbolic strategies were particularly relevant for coalitional change because their emotional connotations and shorthand format helped campaigners send messages to alienated, inactive, or dissatisfied voters.[19] To illustrate, Vicky Golden Markell, Anderson's original press secretary and scheduler, noted how her candidate's symbolic slogan, "The Anderson Difference," articulated their interest in putting together an unconventional coalition:

[when] we first tried to develop our ad campaign, [we] just kept saying that Anderson was so different than all the others. . . . [We asked ourselves] what makes him different? You know, he really is different. He really isn't your typical Republican and he really isn't your typical Democrat, and he just is different. And it just sort of came down to "The Anderson Difference." . . . Bob Sand said, "I like 'The Anderson Difference.' " We started talking and said, "yeah, that's pretty good." . . . "The Anderson Difference" . . . symbolizes that he really is different from all these other candidates.[20]

Crane also tried to communicate his coalitional strategy by building an image as the "Kennedy of the Right." According to Richard Williamson, his campaign manager, "The image we tried to project with Phil Crane was that he was a Kennedy of the right, that he was young, attractive, thoughtful, a conservative, and symbolically, he did it by a lot of gimmicks." And Laura Broderick, Crane's House press secretary, added, "He thought there was very much a potential out there for someone, very much like Jack Kennedy in '60, when people were looking for a fresh face, new times, new leadership, and new opportunities.''

These efforts to link symbolic appeals to coalitional strategies were not limited to dark horse candidates. The Republican frontrunner, Reagan, chose an announcement setting (New York City) that communicated symbolically his interest in broadening coalitional bases. John Sears, Reagan's campaign manager, explained the announcement location this way: "The first thing anybody has got to show is that he's a reasonable person. And if there is any doubt about that already, you've got to go out and erase that doubt.'' Similarly, Jim Lake, Reagan's press secretary, noted:

Ronald Reagan was the unfortunate inheritor of a lot of perceptions about conservatives, based on what people's view of conservatives have been over time going back to 1964. So we set out to demonstrate to people what Ronald Reagan was, that he was . . . much more careful, much more thoughtful, and a much more caring and practical man . . . than people in the East have been led to believe. . . . By having his announcement in New York, by making a significant effort to court the politicians in New York state to support his candidacy, by being willing to say, "I understand your problems up here" . . . that said something to people. [It said], "He's not a crazy man who doesn't want us or who wants to shove us off in a corner." . . . "Here's a guy who's practical."

In addition, Richard Wirthlin, Reagan's chief strategist in the general election, explained how the Republican convention motto, "Together, A New Beginning," underscored Reagan's coalitional strategy:

We felt we had to extend our appeal beyond the reaches of the Republican party. [When] you start with 12 percent of the electorate who identify themselves as strong Republicans, you don't win many elections. . . . So the words, "Together," was used as a vehicle to extend our reach out beyond the confines of the Republican party. . . . And the "New Beginning" element conveyed the feeling that America was not going down the proper road and that we did need to reassess the national agenda.

Since campaign leaders interested in forging realignments consciously devised symbolic slogans that communicated their coalitional strategies, scholars should not overlook the symbolic dimensions of realignments. As Bennett and Haltom argue for the 1896 period, realignments involve more than contrasting issue positions; candidates also distinguish themselves symbolically.[21] Of course, this does not mean that policy matters are unimportant in coalitional change. Rather, it suggests that style and image play a greater role than commonly assumed. Because candidates who want to restructure party coalitions use symbolism (as well as rhetoric and campaign visits) to communicate their strategies, it appears that realignments rest (at least in part) on symbolically induced perceptions. As Edelman found for other areas of political life, symbolism also plays a prominent role in efforts at electoral realignment.

SYMBOLISM AND PRESIDENTIAL CAMPAIGNS

In this chapter, I have analyzed several features of Edelman's work on political symbolism. While this research does not solve all the testability problems for which Edelman persistently has been criticized, it shows the applicability of his work to modern campaigns (he generally emphasized symbolism in government). During an era of open nominations, party decline, and media dominance, symbolic strategies represent one electoral tactic by which candidates attempt to boost popular support and build winning coalitions. Symbolism also provides candidates with an electoral tactic that is well suited to the dilemmas of modern candidates: the need to build coalitions in a period when coalitions are vital yet difficult to cement.

However, symbolic strategies are not without risks. Unlike Edelman, who implies that leaders use symbolism without limitations, I found that campaigners believe there are definite limits. Specifically, many of them argued that campaign dynamics shaped the effectiveness of particular symbolic messages. Symbolic images that seemed beneficial early in the campaign (such as Anderson's media style and Connally's leadership image) later undercut these candidates. The media also acted as a check on symbolic behavior. Candidates who appeared vague or deceptive received heavy criticism. And campaigners can become prisoners of their symbolic appeals. For these reasons, symbolism represents an electoral tactic that candidates must use with caution.

More important, though, is the link that I found between symbolic and coalitional strategies. In investigating the symbolic messages of various candidates, it was apparent that they devised symbolic appeals that communicated their coalitional strategies. The coalitional innovators (such as Anderson and Reagan) consciously developed slogans or chose announcements in locations that would "telegraph" their interest in remaking party constituencies. For example, Reagan's candidacy announcement (New York City) and slogan ("Together, A New Beginning") were intended to signal an outreach beyond the Republican party. In fact, the Californian's symbolism delivered messages that were remarkably similar to the ones present in his rhetoric and constituency allocations. Rather than being a tool for deceit, Reagan's symbolism meshed with his overall strategy.

In addition, his symbolism provided clues about the shape of the Reagan presidency. The message of his symbolism was twofold: to reshape the nation's political agenda and remake party coalitions. A look at the early days of the Reagan Administration shows that these messages were not misleading. His campaign symbolism fits with President Reagan's attempts to recast public policy and alter the role of the federal government. These findings suggest that one should not dismiss symbolism as mere imagery. Instead of being a leader plot to avoid accountability, campaign symbolism can tell observers something about prospective presidents.

NOTES

1. McDiarmid, "Presidential Inaugural Addresses: Study of Verbal Symbols," *Public Opinion Quarterly*, 1 (July, 1937), pp. 79–82. For a related study, see William Hayworth, "Analysis of Speeches in Presidential Campaigns, 1884–1920," *Quarterly Journal of Speech*, 16 (1930), pp. 35–42.

2. Edelman, "The Politics of Persuasion." For an alternative view, see Charles Elder and Roger Cobb, *The Political Uses of Symbols* (New York: Longmans, 1983).

3. Harold Lasswell, Daniel Lerner, and Ithiel de Sola Pool, *The Comparative Study of Symbols* (Stanford, Calif.: Stanford University Press, 1952).

4. Charles Goodsell, "Bureaucratic Manipulation of Physical Symbols," *American Journal of Political Science*, 21, no. 1 (February, 1977), pp. 79–92.

5. Given Edelman's obvious objections to the quantitative methods of modern behavioralism, it is ironic that the idea of behavioralism molded his study of symbolism and made it distinctive from earlier studies.

6. Edward Tufte, *Political Control of the Economy* (Princeton, N.J.: Princeton University Press, 1978).

7. Page, *Choices and Echoes in Presidential Elections*.

8. Ironically, Kennedy made use of these historical connotations in one of the nation's most successful urban redevelopment projects.

9. David Sears and his colleagues argue that the public responds symbolically to appeals that activate emotional and value-laden feelings. See Sears, Richard Lau, Tom Tyler, and Harris Allen, Jr., "Self-Interest versus Symbolic Politics in Policy Attitudes and Presidential Voting," *American Political Science Review*, 74, no. 3 (September, 1980), pp. 670–684 and Sears, Carl Hensler, and Leslie Speer, "Whites' Opposition to 'Busing': Self-Interest or Symbolic Politics," *American Political Science Review*, 73, no. 2 (June, 1979), pp. 369–384.

10. Richard Brody and Paul Sniderman find that the public does not view political problems as very important, thereby implying that issue and party appeals will not arouse the general public and that alternative strategies (including symbolism) may be effective. See their "From Life Space to Polling Place," *British Journal of Political Science*, 7 (1977), pp. 337–360.

11. C. Wright Mills predicted long ago that political leaders would try to raise their prestige in "nonpolitical" ways, such as traveling with celebrities from the fields of theater, music, and sports. See his *The Power Elite* (New York: Oxford University Press, 1956).

12. Wayne King cited this quote in "Brown Image Chief Problem: Exotic Interests Posing a Hurdle to Candidacy," *New York Times* (January 8, 1980), p. A16. When asked about this trip, advisor Walter McGuire conceded, "symbolically, he did one stupid thing and that was . . . the visit to the Eastern religious guy."

13. Noting his opposition to the production, McGuire explained the Wisconsin gala this way: "I thought it was stupid. I thought it reinforced everything bad. I mean, Brown basically was trapped in a dilemma. There was a fellow, Francis Coppolla, who was willing to front a lot of the money [for a statewide television broadcast] which we didn't have in the campaign. . . . But like all people in this position, he insisted on 100 percent control of that event. . . . Jerry Brown gave a thirty-minute speech which I think if you talk to journalists was one of his better speeches. It was not flaky at all. . . . But the surrounding stuff [the television visuals], he relied on Coppolla. . . . Brown

had no idea what was going to be behind his head, like the astronauts tumbling. . . .
So it was an unfortunate thing. We came out with more negatives. It was a disaster.''

14. Garry Wills, *The Kennedy Imprisonment* (Boston: Little, Brown, 1981).

15. Lasswell, Lerner, and Pool, *The Comparative Study of Symbols*, p. 29.

16. At one point, Fenno (*Home Style*, p. 134) notes, "issues have little autonomous effect on election outcomes. Rather issues are vehicles that some House members choose to convey their qualifications, their sense of identification, and their sense of empathy.'' But unlike Edelman, Fenno does not criticize candidates for using issues as avenues for sustaining identification, rather than as avenues of policy communication. Fenno later criticizes theorists who require policy congruence for representation and who denigrate as "symbolic'' any "extra policy'' bases of representation (ibid., p. 242). By claiming the legislator's presentation of self includes important aspects of legislative representation, Fenno tries to reconcile leader presentations with notions of democratic representation.

17. However, unlike Edelman, who concludes that the potential for manipulation makes the study of voting returns useless, Page accepts survey responses and voting patterns as valid indicators of citizen preferences.

18. Obviously, this does not provide a complete test of Edelman's ideas. Such an analysis would need to relate campaign symbolism to the candidates' "true'' policy preferences as well as leaders' actions in office.

19. For related thoughts, see Edward Carmines and James Stimson, "The Two Faces of Issue Voting,'' *American Political Science Review*, 74 (March, 1980), pp. 78–91.

20. While it is difficult to trace the direction of diffusion, several months after Anderson ran "Anderson Difference'' ads, a leading pharmaceutical company began television ads extolling the "Anacin Difference.''

21. Bennett and Haltom, "Issues, Voter Choice, and Critical Elections.''

7

Candidate Presentations and Audience Reactions

Political observers have recognized for a long time that campaigns and coalition-building are dynamic processes. Candidates continually seek to mold public perceptions of themselves—through their speeches, campaign visits, and symbolic appeals. But they also use campaigns to learn about constituencies. The new electoral system adds urgency to this process; since presidential aspirants must develop popular support in a variety of settings, the contemporary environment places a premium on communications between candidates and their constituencies.

Though this point may seem obvious, many scholars study political processes as static phenomena. With the exception of statistical studies on "reciprocal effects," voting researchers generally analyze the electorate without considering the effect that candidates have.[1] Instead, they investigate voters in isolation from candidates. Similarly, leadership studies often ignore the impact that campaigns have on candidates. Despite the fact that campaign audiences may influence candidate behavior, writers have not studied what campaigners learn from audiences.

In this chapter, I explore one aspect of the coalition-building process—how presidential contenders get feedback about their performances on the campaign trail. Few things are more important for campaigners than accurate feedback. Yet candidates rarely have clear and objective yardsticks for evaluating their public appearances. In the following sections, I suggest that one of the most immediate types of feedback that candidates have is the reactions of campaign audiences. Because of the lack of good alternatives, audience reactions are more important than generally believed.

THE NATURE OF CAMPAIGN COMMUNICATIONS

Scholars have investigated political communications from a variety of intellectual traditions. Lasswell laid the groundwork for the field of mass communications by conceptualizing the communications perspective as "Who says What in Which Channels to Whom with What Effects?''[2] Others (such as Kenneth Burke and W. Lance Bennett) have used linguistics and structural anthropology to study political rhetoric.[3] Still others (like Karl Deutsch) have employed a cybernetic view of communications to study learning through feedback.[4] And students of symbolism (Murray Edelman, Charles Elder, and Roger Cobb) have noted the importance of presentational styles for political leaders.[5]

Although these traditions differ in scope and method, each one agrees on a basic tenet: that communication is central to the political process. Leaders face a variety of tasks that involve communications—building popular support, developing a policy agenda, and attracting media attention. But one of their most difficult problems (and one that is critical for their ultimate success) is self-evaluation. Political appearances are dynamic events. As Fenno has pointed out using Goffman's "presentation of self" notion, campaign appearances are complex phenomena involving two-way communications between candidates and audiences. Candidates use speeches and public appearances to send messages to the public. Yet campaigners are not passive transmitters. They also monitor audience reactions to their speeches to make sure that crowds are receiving the appropriate messages.

This cycle of candidate presentations and audience reactions raises two complications for campaigners. First, as Xandra Kayden has noted, campaign activities take place under conditions of considerable uncertainty.[6] Campaigners are rarely certain about the issues to raise, the events to schedule, and the strategies to emphasize. Few things that candidates undertake while campaigning are done with great confidence about the results. For this reason, candidates have a rather high need for feedback while they are campaigning (to reduce the uncertainty of their strategic calculations). But the overall uncertainty of campaign decision-making also means that candidate feedback will be a vague and ambiguous process, one that lacks clear and definite standards of evaluation. Second, candidates have diverse constituencies in mind when they campaign. Although scholars subdivide these constituencies in different ways (citizens versus activists and media versus financial elites), it seems clear that campaigners must simultaneously appeal to various audiences. From a feedback perspective, the diversity of audiences is problematic. Candidates must decide from whom to receive feedback and, if there are different signals coming back from various audiences, they must decide how to synthesize the disparate results. Of course, in an electronic age, the mass media have become a critical constituency (perhaps the dominant one) for aspiring presidents. Media figures are important because they control channels of communications that reach mass audiences. The media also can make or break dark horse candidates by the amount of coverage they provide. The ascendancy of mass media in presidential elections suggests several roles for the media in the feedback process. Candidates may use media figures to gain feedback about public performances. The media may also facilitate the feedback process by helping campaigners interpret audience reactions. And finally, the media may communicate their evaluations of candidate performances to the public by the way they report campaign appearances.

To summarize, communications play an important role in political campaigns. Candidates communicate messages to various constituencies, which these audiences receive and interpret. At the same time, campaigners continually check audience reactions to make sure crowds (and the media) are receiving the correct signals. Although this research focuses only on part of the communications process (namely, candidate feedback during presidential races from campaign audiences), it provides a broad framework for analyzing electoral feedback mechanisms. In that way, this chapter attempts to illuminate the views of political leaders about campaign feedback.

CANDIDATES AND CAMPAIGN FEEDBACK

Presidential candidates need feedback on the campaign trail. However, in the world of campaign appearances, it is difficult to get objective feedback about performances. Public opinion surveys (one of the common monitoring devices in the new electoral system) offer little help in this area. Polls suffer from several drawbacks. They are expensive to conduct professionally, in terms of both time and money. They also do not measure very well the subtle features of campaign appearances, that is, the dynamics of candidate-audience interactions. And since many campaigners mistrust polling results (preferring more personal and less "scientific" methods), they do not rely heavily on public opinion surveys.[7] In addition, election returns are limited as learning devices.[8] For one thing, they occur too late to be of much help. Campaigners need assistance before, not after, the election. Elections also are relatively blunt instruments; winners are not always certain what they did in the way of campaign appeals and strategies that produced votes.

So where do campaign organizers turn? How do they receive regular feedback about presentations during their months on the campaign trail? There is substantial evidence from other research that campaigners prefer to learn experientially. Kingdon asked candidates in Wisconsin to rate the reliability of various information sources about public sentiments—polls, party people, volunteers, past statistics, and warmth of reception—and found that campaigners were more confident of impressionistic methods (such as warmth of reception, 57 percent favorable) than polls (13 percent favorable).[9] Fenno also argues that despite their unrepresentative character, personal constituencies are very influential in candidate thinking.[10] Supporters and intimates who have been loyal to the candidate over a long period of time seem to have extra clout with the candidate. Others have found examples of candidates who pulled media advertising off the air after receiving a handful of negative complaints from influential supporters.[11] Similarly, Arterton has shown how presidential campaigners take cues from media reporters; in 1976, when Carter was questioned about his lack of self-deprecating humor, he later worked funny stories about himself into his speeches.[12]

But these sources of information (political supporters, personal friends, and the media) are not the only avenues of self-evaluation. One can propose that

campaign audiences also act as feedback devices. Campaign appearances involve more than candidate presentations; they also generate behavioral responses from audiences (such as cheers, jeers, laughter, and applause). As
feedback mechanisms, audience reactions offer a number of advantages to candidates. Unlike polls, which take time, these reactions provide immediate feedback. Audience reactions also make possible personal evaluations of success.
Since many campaigners value impressionistic ways of judging public sentiments, crowd responses fit their preferences. In addition, since candidates can
measure reactions throughout their performances, crowd responses can serve as
continuous monitoring devices. Finally, audience reactions are unobtrusive
measures; campaigners can consider audience reactions without interrupting the
speech or making the audience aware of their evaluations. Hence, for candidates who spend a great deal of time campaigning, audience responses provide
immediate, personal, continuous, and unobtrusive means of measuring
performances.

Of course, just because campaigners may treat these reactions as instant
feedback devices does not make them valid indicators. From a social science
perspective, it is probable that audience reactions fall short as measures of crowd
sentiments. But despite this disclaimer, campaigners (and media reporters) often
fall back on observable reactions such as applause because there are no clear
alternatives that tap audience receptiveness. Barring other possibilities, politicians use what is readily available to gain much-needed information about campaign performances. Accordingly, the study of audience reactions may tell researchers something about what candidates learn during their public appearances.

THE STUDY OF AUDIENCE REACTIONS

To investigate audience reactions (as well as campaigners' perceptions of these
responses), I used a variation of Fenno's method of analyzing candidate behavior in House elections. Like Fenno, I focused on campaign behavior in the field,
arguing that researchers should investigate candidate presentations in the context of their constituencies. Accordingly, I spent twenty-four days traveling with
the major candidates during the early primaries. I also used Fenno's notion that
researchers should study both candidate appeals and audience reactions, not just
one in isolation from the other.[13] For my analysis of crowd reactions, I used
audience applause because campaigners and journalists (whether rightfully or
wrongfully) treat applause as a ''feeling thermometer'' of candidate popularity
(though they do so in an imprecise and unsystematic way). Judging from the
way the media report applause levels, they seem to place great stock in the
''warmth'' of audience receptions to various candidates.[14] Essentially, I treated
candidates' speeches as a series of verbal cues. When audiences applauded candidates, I noted two things. First, what was the length (in seconds) of the audience applause?[15] Since campaigners and media observers distinguish between
polite and enthusiastic applause, I used length of applause as a measure of the

intensity of feeling.[16] Second, what was the nature of the stimuli to which audiences responded? To see if crowds reacted most intensely when candidates discussed issues (or other topics), I classified campaign appeals in the sentence preceding audience applause into the following categories: specific policy proposals (policy discussions involving specific dollars, particular legislative remedies, or concrete policy actions); general problems or performances (discussion of general policy areas without specific recommendations); general goals (references to abstract concepts, such as freedom or liberty); personal qualities (for example, the candidates' qualities, such as honesty, competence, or principle); campaign phenomena (references to strategies, organizations, or the horse race), and party appeals (specific references to political parties or party leaders).[17] These procedures enabled me to determine which campaign appeals "moved" or "excited" audiences and hence, what rhetorical lessons candidates might have learned from their campaign appearances.[18]

For my data, I relied on audio tapes of 178 campaign speeches by different candidates in the primaries and general election. These tapes, which I made personally during field observation or obtained from news reporters covering the candidates, did not represent a random sample of campaign speeches. Instead, they deliberately represented settings that were theoretically interesting for the study of audience reactions. For example, the nomination stage tapes came mainly from key states (New Hampshire, Massachusetts, Illinois, New York, Wisconsin, Michigan, and Florida, among others), as did the general election tapes (Illinois, Ohio, Pennsylvania, Michigan, Texas, New Jersey, New York, Oregon, and others). In addition, I sought to represent the major candidates and to maximize the diversity of constituencies. When several candidates addressed the same audiences in candidate forums, I also (when possible) obtained audio tapes for all the contenders.

Admittedly, this methodology is somewhat experimental. Few scholars have collected data on audience reactions to candidate speeches. The general assumption is that these reactions have no enduring significance and that they reflect nothing more than superficial responses to campaign rhetoric. However, in the following section, I try to demonstrate that there was impressionistic evidence from the 1980 presidential campaign that campaigners and the media used audience reactions as one (but not the only) source of information.

PRELIMINARY EVIDENCE: CAMPAIGNER AND MEDIA PERSPECTIVES

Before investigating the applause of various campaign appeals, one should explore the perspectives of campaigners and the media about audience reactions. From my interviews with campaign advisors, it was apparent that *they* believed candidates relied on audience reactions as one source of information (although campaigners continually cross-checked audience responses with other feedback—personal contacts, media reports, fundraising, volunteers, and the like).

One aide said, in response to a question about how he knew when his candidate's speech was going well, "obviously, applause is one way you can measure crowd response," while another campaign official argued that it depended "on how they applaud, whether it's polite applause or they're jumping to their feet." Similarly, Kennedy advisor Richard Stearns pointed out, "you learn what sort of speech works if you have to go out and give it eight times a day for different kinds of audiences." And Peter Teeley, press secretary to Bush, expressed the idea in even stronger terms; he suggested that candidates alter the tone of the speech depending on audience receptiveness: "If you've got some line in a speech and when you deliver it, everybody starts booing, chances are you're going to drop it fast. . . . You learn from audiences and I think that the candidates learn during the time they're giving a speech." Continuing, Teeley explained:

let's say you're going out and you're really attacking the administration with some group. And if you are not [moving the audience], obviously nobody has to tell you that these people are not particularly excited about you tearing down the president or attacking some particular program or policy. So generally what will happen is that as the speech moves on, a candidate will lighten up in things of a partisan nature. Or it may start out in a very nonpartisan sense of hit and a quick pitch and it may be accelerated to get the audience going.

Audience reactions are important not merely because campaigners appear to use them as learning tools. Crowd responses take on additional importance because they color media interpretations of candidate popularity and performance (along with other impressionistic indicators—straw polls, quality of campaign organizations, and personal contacts around the country). For example, to illustrate Kennedy's poor start, the *New York Times* reported that the Massachusetts senator was "often getting more applause coming into a hall than he was getting coming out." And in its daily campaign report the newspaper also said: "George Bush, who defeated Ronald Reagan Tuesday in the Connecticut primary, has been hammering away at the Carter Administration's handling of the hostage situation in Iran with increasing frequency and toughness, and with that has come increasing audience applause."[19] These comments were not rare occurrences. Perusal of campaign coverage reveals that most stories of public appearances noted audience reactions, either generally or the response to particular candidate statements. In fact, campaigners who failed to arouse audience enthusiasm in their public appearances usually found the media reporting stories about "lackluster" performances or the candidates' inabilities to move audiences. Thus, crowd reactions gained importance far beyond appearances themselves; the media publicized weak responses throughout the land.

In 1980, two events illustrated most vividly the way that campaigners and the media depended on audience reactions—Kennedy's Democratic convention speech (which helped restore the senator's credibility as a public speaker) and the New Hampshire Gunowners' forum (which fueled Anderson's rise to prominence in the primaries).[20] The following sections describe in greater detail what these cases reveal about campaign processes.

Case 1: The Kennedy Convention Speech

The Kennedy race of 1980 proved to be the big surprise of the campaign season. Kennedy had started the contest with an air of expectancy. Since many Democrats appeared to concede that Carter could not gain reelection, Kennedy seemed to be the ideal replacement. However, as soon as he edged toward candidacy, disaster hit. His initial appearances showed a bumbling and inarticulate candidate, not the strong and experienced leader that observers expected. In addition, a prime-time television interview by Roger Mudd revealed a Kennedy hesitant to answer basic questions about his candidacy, Chappaquidick, and family life. But as the race developed, Kennedy improved his presentational style and eventually pushed his challenge to the floor of the Democratic nominating convention. Having decided to contest the nomination, Kennedy chose to make a dramatic break with the past. Rather than watching floor proceedings from a hotel suite, Kennedy announced that he would deliver a major speech on the convention floor in support of his platform planks (the first candidate to do so since Bryan with his "Cross of Gold" speech in 1896). With this decision, though, came uncertainty among his advisors about the content of the speech. Obviously, because it was breaking precedent and would take place before a national television audience, the speech would be one of the most important addresses of Kennedy's political career. Coming as it did at the end of an unsuccessful campaign, one that his supporters feared would end Kennedy's presidential aspirations, the Kennedy organization viewed the speech with utmost importance.

According to staff members inside the Kennedy campaign, one major debate concerned whether Kennedy should attack Reagan in the speech. Since some advisors viewed Carter as the major opponent, they felt that Kennedy should focus his criticisms on Carter and economic issues. In contrast, others believed he should criticize Reagan as a pretender to Democratic principles. Most interesting for this research is the way that Kennedy resolved this debate. Robert Shrum, one of the writers who drafted the convention speech, described how the candidate used audience reactions to settle the disagreement:

there were some people [in the campaign] who thought that he shouldn't go after Reagan in the speech. I thought that the simplest way to settle that argument was not to have a long discussion but to let him see how people reacted when he talked about Reagan. . . . On Sunday morning [before the convention] . . . I said to him, "why don't you as a third point in this thing, when you talk about the open convention, talk about the economic issue and then why don't you talk about Reagan." [So] he talked about the open convention and our people cheered; the Carter people sat on their hands. He talked about the economic issue, and our people cheered; the Carter people politely ap-

plauded. He talked about Reagan [and] the whole place went nuts. So he did continue
to talk about Reagan then from that point on at each delegation he went to. . . . Right
after the California thing, he came back upstairs before he went to the next thing and
he said, ''I think the Reagan stuff is going to do very well.'' And that ended that argument.

Needless to say, this decision turned out to be a resounding success. Kennedy's
remarks (especially his comments about Reagan) were cheered passionately by
Democratic delegates and moved many to tears. With the favorable impressions
created that night, this speech removed some of the negative images that arose
early in Kennedy's campaign (such as his poor speaking style and inability to
excite audiences). According to a *Newsweek* story about the speech:

In one night, with one superb speech that was by turns graceful, rousing, poetic and
defiant, Kennedy transformed what was supposed to have been a tearful last hurrah into
a triumphant call to arms, and he emerged as a more potent political figure than at any
point in his frustrated pursuit of the nomination. His failed campaign now seemed to
some to have been a shakedown cruise. He had developed his own political machine of
committed young operatives, he had learned the hard way the complex election rules
that his brothers never faced and perhaps he had finally found the right voice for his
liberal message.[21]

This case illustrates three points about campaigning. First, candidates rarely
have foolproof methods of gauging audience sentiments. In the absence of immediate, clear, and personal indicators of success, campaigners often fall back
on observable reactions, such as applause. While they are not able to form pre-
cise measurements, candidates know enthusiastic receptions when they receive
them; these reactions may shape their campaign presentations. In addition, audience reactions are important not just in day-to-day campaigning. Even when
candidates face momentous occasions (such as Kennedy speaking to the Democratic convention and a national television audience), they use crowd dynamics to make crucial decisions about their appeals. Finally, audience reactions
influence media interpretations of candidate presentations; enthusiastic receptions can lead reporters to favorable evaluations of political events.[22]

Case 2: The New Hampshire Gunowners' Forum

Audience reactions also played a role (albeit a different one than in the first
case) during another prominent campaign event in 1980—a presidential forum
that the Gunowners of New Hampshire sponsored. This event, which Anderson, Baker, Brown, Bush, Jack Carter, Connally, Crane, Dole, and Reagan at-
tended, was held February 18, 1980, one week before the crucial New Hampshire primary. Since all the candidates spoke for approximately five minutes
before the same audience, the forum represents a setting in which to analyze
audience reactions (as well as media reports of those reactions) and demonstrate
how one candidate (Anderson) used audience reactions to convey a particular
impression of himself (''The Anderson Difference'').

The timing of this event was crucial for Anderson's campaign. During this period, his candidacy was beginning to surge. Anderson's sparkling performance at the Republican debate in Iowa (January 5, 1980) introduced him to a national audience. At the same time, he was reaping favorable coverage from political columnists, reporters, and even cartoonists (such as Garry Trudeau in "Doonesbury"). As a result, a growing number of voters and contributors began to see Anderson as a distinctive candidate, one who would speak his mind freely and propose innovative solutions to controversial policy problems. But with the New Hampshire primary coming up (followed in rapid succession by Massachusetts, a "must" state for Anderson's candidacy), it was a critical time for Anderson.

According to his advisors, Anderson's staff originally had rejected the gunowners' invitation. Knowing that their candidate's anti-gun position would not be received favorably by the militant gunowners, they decided not to attend. However, when Anderson was campaigning in New Hampshire shortly before the event and heard that most of his competitors were going to participate (which also meant that reporters covering these candidates would be present), he overruled his staff and accepted the invitation. At the event, all the other candidates went out of their way to indicate their sympathies with the gunowners (with Reagan revealing his membership in the National Rifle Association, Connally discussing his gun collection, and Jack Carter talking about his father's love of hunting). Meanwhile, Anderson spoke strongly in favor of gun control. The crowd reactions were predictable. The audience interrupted Anderson repeatedly with boos, hisses, and cries of "throw the traitor out." In addition, the applause at the end of his presentation was noticeably shorter (6.5 seconds) than that for Connally (12.9 seconds) or the crowd's clear favorite, Reagan (whom the audience applauded for 17.5 seconds, the longest for any candidate that evening). But even more instructive than the audience reactions was the way reporters portrayed the event. With striking graphics and splashy stories, the media reported the gunowners' hostile reactions toward Anderson. In fact, Anderson's aides later argued that the national publicity generated from those antagonistic responses raised Anderson's stock with constituencies hostile to the gunowners and impressed by his willingness to stand up for what he believed. It also, according to his advisors, brought a much-needed infusion of campaign contributions to the organization. But speaking more broadly, this appearance demonstrates how presidential aspirants can use audience reactions (in conjunction with media reports of those responses) to communicate their coalitional strategies, either their warmth or distance from particular constituencies. In Anderson's case, he used the gunowners' forum to communicate the distinctive nature of his candidacy ("The Anderson Difference"). Therefore, this event shows that crowd responses represent something more than a means for self-evaluation; they also can become important strategic tools in the arsenals of resourceful candidates.

To summarize, there was evidence from the 1980 presidential contest that audience reactions played a complex role in the campaign process. At one level, campaigners (such as Kennedy at the Democratic convention) relied on these reactions as learning cues and instant feedback devices; rather than being criteria of the moment that had no enduring impact, crowd responses were a vital part of the campaign. However, the case of Anderson indicates that audience reactions also can serve broader purposes. Instead of operating directly as a means of candidate feedback (in the manner of a "stimulus-response" model), audience reactions may enable presidential aspirants to communicate certain impressions of themselves (in other words, candidates may manipulate as well as be manipulated by audience responses). As illustrated by Anderson, candidates can use audience reactions to send larger messages to relevant constituencies.[23]

In suggesting these points, it is important to note the exploratory nature of this project. Obviously, these findings do not prove that candidates relied on audience reactions. For one, the evidence is suggestive, not definitive. It also is indirect; the evidence relies on advisor statements, not candidate interviews. But despite the experimental nature of this research, the results do suggest that audience reactions are more important than commonly believed and that there is a need to explore them in greater detail. Accordingly, in the following section, I study the relation between audience reactions and campaign rhetoric to see what candidates might have learned during campaign appearances and what campaign appeals might have generated audience enthusiasm.

A FURTHER LOOK AT THE EVIDENCE: AUDIENCE REACTIONS AND CAMPAIGN APPEALS

Since campaigners appear to use audience reactions as feedback devices, it is important to determine whether audiences rewarded candidates for different kinds of campaign appeals. Table 7–1 lists observable reactions (applause, cheers, boos, or laughter) for the nominating period. Because candidates rely on different presentational styles, it is not surprising that audiences reacted in different ways to them. For example, Dole, the candidate who was best known for incorporating humor in his campaign speeches, generated the most laughter (55.6 percent of all his audience reactions). In contrast, more somber Republicans (such as Anderson, Bush, and Crane) produced less laughter but more applause. Among Democrats, Mondale generated a higher percentage of laughter (50.3 percent), while Rosalyn Carter and Kennedy received more applause, again reflecting style.[24]

Of course, these distributions of audience reactions tell us little about levels of audience reactions and their relation to campaign appeals. To investigate this relationship, I studied whether audiences applauded with different intensities for policy, general substance, parties, general goals, personal qualities, or campaign strategies. Since applause generally was the most frequent reaction candidates received, Table 7–2 lists mean applause (in seconds) for the six categories of campaign appeals in the nominating process. The most striking trend

Table 7-1
The Nature of Audience Reactions During Nominations

Reaction	Anderson	Baker	Bush	Connally	Crane	Dole	Reagan	Brown	R. Carter	Mondale	Kennedy
Applause	61.4	48.1	70.7	0.0	74.1	44.4	58.6	56.2	95.0	48.0	82.4
Cheers	3.0	1.9	4.3	0.0	0.0	0.0	2.5	1.7	0.0	0.0	0.0
Boos	0.0	0.0	0.0	0.0	0.0	0.0	0.4	0.0	0.0	1.7	0.4
Laughter	35.6	50.0	25.0	0.0	25.9	55.6	38.4	42.1	5.0	50.3	17.2
Total	100.0	100.0	100.0	0.0	100.0	100.0	100.0	100.0	100.0	100.0	100.0
N	101	160	140	0	27	9	237	121	20	175	221

Note: The figure refers to the percentage of audience reactions (N) that fell within each category.

Table 7-2
Campaign Appeals and Audience Applause During Nominations

Campaign Appeal	Anderson	Baker	Bush	Connally	Crane	Dole	Reagan	Brown	R. Carter	Mondale	Kennedy
Specific Policy	6.5	7.8	6.1	NA	4.9	3.5	7.2	8.3	6.8	7.9	9.9
General Problems	10.4	9.2	6.5		4.8	0.0	10.6	7.1	6.5	6.2	7.2
Goals	12.4	9.2	12.1		0.0	0.0	11.3	9.1	6.1	7.3	7.8
Personal Qualities	15.9	9.0	7.9		9.7	0.0	4.2	0.0	12.2	5.8	12.2
Campaign	11.5	7.7	7.2		10.4	0.0	9.9	4.5	0.0	5.2	7.9
Political Party	20.2	7.7	3.4		6.8	1.1	9.4	0.0	0.0	0.0	8.0
N	61	74	95	0	19	4	135	63	19	80	177

Note: The figure refers to the mean audience applause (in seconds) for each category of appeals.

among Republican contenders was that campaign audiences generally applauded less enthusiastically (i.e., shorter durations) for specific policy statements than other appeals. In Reagan's case, he received on the average of 7.2 seconds of applause for policy matters, but 11.3 seconds for general goals, 10.6 seconds for general problems, 9.9 seconds for campaign discussions, and 9.4 seconds for party appeals. Only in the case of personal qualities (4.2 seconds) did issue discussions generate longer applause. Similarly, Anderson generated less intense applause with specific policy statements (6.5 seconds) than with party appeals (20.2 seconds), personal qualities (15.9 seconds), goals (12.4 seconds), campaign discussions (11.5 seconds), and general problems (10.4 seconds). While one could go down the list, most Republicans generated less applause with policy than other appeals. Hence, there is support for the idea that audiences do not reward presidential candidates for discussing policy in detail. Instead, audiences encourage campaigners to discuss a variety of other topics.

On the Democratic side, there also is some support for this idea. For example, Kennedy generated an average of 9.9 seconds for specific policy statements but 12.2 seconds of applause for discussions of personal qualities. Rosalyn Carter averaged 6.8 seconds when discussing policy but 12.2 seconds with statements about personal qualities. And while the differences are not as large as with other candidates, Brown generated more applause on goals than policy. The only exception to this pattern was Mondale. Audiences rewarded him with enthusiastic applause more when he spoke about policy matters (7.9 seconds) than any other topic (goals, 7.3 seconds; general problems, 6.2 seconds; and personal qualities, 5.8 seconds). Although it is unclear why Mondale stood out, perhaps his representation of the incumbent president altered audience-candidate interactions. But otherwise, as with Republicans, audiences rewarded Democrats less for policy specificity than other appeals.

Overall patterns are not the only thing of interest. Since candidates apparently used applause as "learning cues," it also is important to see which policy stands generated the most enthusiastic receptions for various candidates (and whether these patterns varied by party). In Reagan's case, statements on welfare (10.7 seconds), defense (10.7 seconds), and the Olympics (9.1 seconds) were greeted most favorably. For Bush, it was government regulation (10.8 seconds), Iran (10.5 seconds), and social security (7.2 seconds). Audiences applauded Anderson the most on the SALT II treaty (11.9 seconds), social security (11.3 seconds), and government reorganization (8.9 seconds). In contrast, audiences rewarded Democrats for different issues than Republicans. Mondale was applauded for specific policy statements on the Soviet Union (9.6 seconds), unemployment (9.3 seconds), and energy and the Olympics (8.9 seconds). Meanwhile, Kennedy generated applause with statements on gun control (20.7 seconds), government spending (20.3 seconds), inflation (11.6 seconds), and the Equal Rights Amendment (11.2 seconds), while Brown did so on foreign policy (10.8 seconds), nuclear energy (10.6 seconds), and draft registration (10.3 seconds). In these ways, party shaped the lessons that candidates learned from their audiences; as one would expect given the differences in party coalitions, audiences rewarded Republicans for different issue stands than Democrats.

Turning to the general election, candidates face a different situation than in the nominating process. Normally, it is a two-candidate race, not a multican-didate contest as in the primaries (although in 1980, Anderson's independent candidacy gave voters a third choice). And since campaigners of opposing parties compete head to head for the first time in the election cycle, party loyalties exercise a different role in the electorate than they do in primaries (where parties hold separate nominating contests). Because of these features, it is important to investigate campaign appeals and audience reactions in the general election. Table 7–3 lists audience reactions (applause, cheers, boos, or laughter) to the major candidates in the fall campaign. As in the primaries, Anderson provoked the most somber reactions; he received the highest percentage of applause (91.5 percent) and the lowest percentage of laughs (6.3 percent). In contrast, both Reagan and Carter stirred a balance of applause (60.8 and 62.5 percent, respectively) and laughter (30.4 and 34.5 percent, respectively). Apparently, Anderson did not learn the lesson that candidates can use humor in strategic ways—to launch subtle attacks or to defend themselves. This failure may have contributed to media criticisms of Anderson's "tight" and "unrelaxed" campaign style. In addition, this table shows that (unlike nominations) all the major candidates were booed in the fall, perhaps reflecting the higher stakes of the general election and the intensity it inspired among activists. However, no candidate was booed as much as Reagan; 7.4 percent of his audience reactions were boos, almost double Carter's amount and much more than Anderson's percentage. While it is not clear what stirred these boos, Reagan may have generated them more than other candidates because of fears about his substantive views.

Table 7-3
The Nature of Audience Reactions During General Election

Reaction	Reagan	Carter	Anderson
Applause	60.8	62.5	91.5
Cheers	1.4	0.0	1.0
Boos	7.4	3.0	1.0
Laughter	30.4	34.5	6.3
Total	100.0	100.0	99.8
N	148	200	95

Note: The figure refers to the percentage of audience reactions (N) that fell within each category.

Looking at audience applause for campaign appeals, Table 7–4 lists the mean applause (in seconds) for various appeals in the general election. Candidates again generated the most intense applause with nonpolicy statements. Audiences applauded Reagan more for discussion of general goals (10.9 seconds) than specific policy (7.1 seconds). Carter stirred longer applause with party appeals (11.0 seconds), discussion of personal qualities (10.5 seconds), goals (10.2 seconds), and campaign strategy (9.3 seconds) than he did with specific policy commitments (8.1 seconds). Meanwhile, Anderson received slightly shorter applause from policy appeals (6.7 seconds) than discussions of general problems (7.1 seconds) or goals (7.0 seconds). As with the nominating process, audiences did not give candidates strong incentives for policy appeals. In addition, the particular policy statements that generated enthusiastic reactions differed between the party candidates. Reagan's longest applause lines concerned Iran (10.0 seconds), domestic issues (9.6 seconds), and defense (9.3 seconds). In contrast, Carter's top issues were unemployment (11.3 seconds), domestic issues (10.0 seconds), and the environment (9.6 seconds), and Anderson's "crowd-pleasers" included defense (13.2 seconds), education (10.0 seconds), and the environment (7.7 seconds). Thus, as in the primaries, audiences rewarded Republicans for stands on different issues than Democrats.

Table 7-4
Campaign Appeals and Audience Applause During
General Election

Campaign Appeal	Reagan	Carter	Anderson
Specify Policy	7.1	8.1	6.7
General Problems	7.9	6.2	7.1
Goals	10.9	10.2	7.0
Personal Qualities	7.5	10.5	5.4
Campaign	3.1	9.3	6.6
Political Party	0.0	11.0	0.0
N	85	113	72

Note: The figure refers to the mean audience applause (in seconds) for each category of appeals.

CONCLUSIONS

In this chapter, I have suggested two points. First, using interviews and field observation, I found impressionistic evidence that campaigners and the media relied on audience reactions as feedback devices; campaigners appeared to use them to monitor crowd receptiveness to their public addresses, while journalists used them as rough indicators of candidate performances. Second, the analysis of audience reactions to campaign appeals presents indirect evidence that crowds reward candidates more for nonpolicy than for policy appeals (both in nominating and general elections).

Of course, there may be alternative explanations for these reaction patterns. One could argue that applause reflects delivery style, not content and that the type of audience (such as labor, business, blacks, Catholics, and the like) might influence applause patterns. However, these possibilities seem unlikely. Candidates who used blustering styles probably do so for all campaign appeals, not just personal qualities, general goals, or policy statements. Hence, delivery style would not explain the consistently short applause for policy appeals. In addition, there is no reason to assume that audience type would lead to systematic differences in applause between rhetorical categories. Blacks should not be more (or less) likely than business audiences to applaud for policy commitments.

Since these findings are exploratory, it is important not to overstate their implications. After all, this work does not explore all the interesting questions raised by the subject of candidate feedback. A more complete analysis would study changes in candidate rhetoric over time. Does the amount of time in candidates' speeches dedicated to policy proposals decline as a function of the length of applause? Do candidates spend more time on policy proposals that draw applause and less time over the course of the campaign on proposals that do not fare so well? This research also does not consider all the ramifications of Fenno's notion of two-way communications between candidates and audiences. Do candidates react to audience applause by tailoring their speeches? To what extent do audience reactions influence general campaign strategy, issue positioning, and candidate beliefs about policy (which would influence conduct in office)?

Although this research did not investigate these topics in detail, one can speculate about their implications for presidential campaigns. Because audiences did not reward candidates for policy appeals, crowds may supply part (but not all) of the reason for the lack of policy discussions in presidential campaigns. Candidates may not discuss public policy because audiences do not encourage them to do so. Study of audience reactions shows that campaigners will not generate the same enthusiasm and intensity with policy statements as they do with goals or personal qualities, among other topics. Since lack of enthusiasm casts doubt on candidates' campaign performances and usually finds its way into media coverage, candidates take risks arising from the campaign context when they discuss policy matters. So observers bemoaning low levels of policy specificity must consider the opportunity structure confronting candidates if they want to improve campaign discourse.[25]

At a more general level, this research illustrates the importance of candidate feedback in presidential campaigns. Candidates do not campaign in a vacuum. Rather, elections require that they meet constituents, hear complaints, and articulate political positions. In turn, audiences give campaigners informal feedback through the warmth of their reactions. While audiences are not random samples of public opinion, they are one of the few learning avenues that candidates have outside their peer groups (that is, the media, advisors, and intimates at home). For this reason, campaigners sometimes equate audiences with "public opinion" or "the people." And the lessons that they learn often stick with leaders. To illustrate, right-wing audiences for over twenty years have cheered Reagan when he attacked "godless totalitarians" in the Soviet Union and "welfare cheats" at home. These positive reactions probably reinforced Reagan's intuitive beliefs about public policy and encouraged him once in office to seek fundamental changes in government policy. Similarly, political observers have noted Reagan's tendency to say things that sound outrageous to the political establishment. But what these people fail to realize is that conservative audiences persistently have encouraged Reagan to make these claims. Although he now holds national office, Reagan's learning and rhetoric were shaped by the right-wing dinner circuit. What sounds outrageous to liberals and moderates probably brought Reagan enthusiastic applause from his "personal constituencies." In these ways, crowd dynamics may have influenced Reagan's views, and therefore have played a role in the policy process of the Reagan Administration.

The 1980 race also shows some of the dilemmas of leadership. Since leaders take cues from impressionistic sources (such as audience reactions, advisors, personal constituencies, and the media), much of their feedback comes from unrepresentative avenues. In terms of democratic theory, these learning patterns are troublesome. Ideally, candidates should use campaigns to discover what is on voters' minds and to build popular majorities. But with candidates' heavy reliance on personal impressions, there is always the risk that their campaigning will lead them to learn the "wrong" lessons. Enthusiastic responses from personal constituencies on the campaign trail may encourage them to legislate in ways that are not supported by public opinion. While the returns are not complete for the Reagan Administration, one can speculate that the 1980 campaign (along with Reagan's large election margin over Carter) may have led him to overestimate public support for fundamental policy revisions.[26] Americans may cheer homilies about big government, yet scream bloody murder when their benefits are reduced. Leaders who fail to recognize the limits of their learning patterns may risk political suicide if they overreach their political support.

NOTES

1. Studies of reciprocal effects include John E. Jackson, "Issues, Party Choices, and Presidential Votes," *American Journal of Political Science*, 19 (1975), pp. 161–185; Gregory Markus and Philip Converse, "A Dynamic Simultaneous Equation Model of Electoral Choice," *American Political Science Review*, 73 (December, 1979), pp. 1055–1070; and Benjamin Page and Calvin Jones, "Reciprocal Effects of Policy Preference, Party Loyalties and the Vote," *American Political Science Review*, 73 (December, 1979), pp. 1071–1089.

2. Harold Lasswell, "The Structure and Function of Communication in Society," in Lyman Bryson, ed., *The Communication of Ideas* (New York: Harper, 1948).

3. See Kenneth Burke, *A Grammar of Motives* (Berkeley: University of California Press, 1969) and W. Lance Bennett, "The Paradox of Public Discourse," *Journal of Politics*, 42 (August, 1980), pp. 792–817.

4. Karl Deutsch, *The Nerves of Government* (New York: The Free Press, 1963).

5. Edelman, "The Politics of Persuasion" and Elder and Cobb, *The Political Uses of Symbols*.

6. Kayden, *Campaign Organization*.

7. In the 1980 presidential contest, only Bush, Carter, and Reagan had extensive polling operations. For a variety of reasons (for example, mistrust of polls and the expense of polling), the other contenders relied on polls less frequently. For example, Kennedy advisor Robert Shrum noted that his candidate was "very skeptical of polls" and rarely looked at them. Connally pollster Lance Tarrance echoes this description, saying his man was "very personally hesitant about polls." Advisors to several other candidates also expressed similar thoughts.

8. See Hershey and West, "Single-Issue Groups and Political Campaigns."

9. John Kingdon, *Candidates for Office* (New York: Random House, 1966), p. 91. Reprinted by Robert Erikson, Norman Luttbeg, and Kent Tedin in *American Public Opinion*, 2nd ed. (New York: John Wiley, 1980), p. 253.

10. Fenno, *Home Style*, pp. 24–27.

11. Sabato, *The Rise of Political Consultants*, pp. 133–134, reported that Baker pulled presidential campaign ads featuring his Watergate hearings performance after a few calls from Republicans. And Hershey and West, "Single-Issue Groups and Political Campaigns," found that McGovern (in his 1980 senatorial campaign) removed ads after calls from "intimates" at home.

12. Arterton, "Campaign Organizations Confront the Media-Political Environment," p. 13.

13. Implicit in Fenno's notion of presentation of self is the similar idea that candidates monitor audience reactions to their speeches to make sure that viewers are receiving the "correct" messages.

14. Television and movie producers also have used audience applause to indicate levels of warmth. The early 1960s television show, *Queen for a Day*, used sound-level meters to measure the popularity of each show's contestants. Following on-stage interviews with each contestant, the audience expressed its preference through applause. The contestant receiving the loudest applause would be named queen for a day and would receive cash prizes. In a more recent saga, *Take the Money and Run*, Woody Allen portrays an inept bank robber (Virgil Starkland) who used the applause of banking officials to determine which gang (of two groups of robbers simultaneously attempting to rob a bank) completes the robbery. Predictably, Allen's gang loses the "vote" by a large margin.

15. Originally, I tried to measure both length (using a stopwatch) and loudness (using a sound-level meter). However, after extensive testing, I dropped the sound-level meter because of problems in the measurement of sound. First, since auditoriums in which presidential candidates speak differ considerably in their acoustics, it was impossible to compare the loudness of audience applause in different auditoriums. Second, because applause consists of intermittent clapping, the sound of applause is unstable and hard to measure in a reliable way. Fortunately, the length measure does not suffer from similar problems.

16. This analysis is not the first to report length of applause as a measure of intensity. In the Soviet Union, transcripts of speeches by party leaders note at appropriate times during speeches the following categories of audience reactions: applause; prolonged applause; stormy, prolonged applause, and stormy, prolonged applause turning into an ovation. From time to time, the *Congressional Quarterly Weekly Report* also shows when applause interrupts the speeches of American presidents. Finally, television networks sometimes report the number of times that the president is applauded during State of the Union addresses as well as the lines that drew enthusiastic reactions.

17. In this content analysis, I followed the categories of Page and the standard distinctions of voting research (party, issues, and candidate qualities). The sentence preceding the audience reaction was the unit of analysis.

18. John Wahlke argues that much behavioral research is actually pre-behavioral. Rather than measuring behavior directly, many researchers rely on attitudinal or mentalistic measures. Since several researchers have matched perceptions to a variety of sensory processes (loudness of sound, pain, taste, and line length), one can argue that researchers need to go beyond self-reporting. Hence, this research seeks to develop a behavioral measure of audience reactions. See John Wahlke's "Pre-Behavioralism in Political Science," *American Political Science Review*, 73 (March, 1979), pp. 9–31.

19. See the "Campaign Digest," *New York Times* (March 28, 1980), p. A24.

20. In addition, Witcover reports that Reagan shifted his policy emphasis from domestic to foreign concerns (specifically, from social security and welfare cheats to the Panama Canal Treaty, detente, and Henry Kissinger) in the 1976 campaign because of audience reactions. Apparently, Reagan and his advisors were impressed by the overwhelming crowd response to speeches he delivered in Florida on these subjects. See Jules Witcover, *Marathon*.

21. "A New Ted Kennedy?" *Newsweek* (August 25, 1980), pp. 31–33.

22. Kennedy aides privately speculated that if their candidate had made his remarks critical of the shah of Iran in a public meeting, instead of a press interview, favorable audience reactions might have led political observers to report the comments more positively than they did.

23. Essentially, these two mechanisms are separate questions. The first case sees audience reactions as a factor impinging on candidate behavior. The second case notes the ways candidates can manipulate audience reactions for their own purposes. Although these processes may overlap to some degree, the remainder of this chapter tests ideas at the first level only.

24. One might note that there are problems of cultural assumptions in this analysis. What are the differences between applause, cheers, boos, and laughter? Despite possible variations in the way reactions are interpreted in different societies, there is little evidence of substantial variation within the American setting. In this research, I concentrate on applause because it occurred more frequently than laughter.

25. As an example, sponsors of presidential debates have shown sensitivity to the impact of audience reactions by forbidding applause, cheers, boos, and laughter during debates.

26. Other reasons also may have contributed to this situation—Reagan's ideology, his coalitional base, and media coverage during the early part of his administration.

strategies. Similarly, there is a growing body of research that documents the consequences of campaigns for voting behavior. For example, Page found that candidate "choices" and "echoes" influenced voters' policy options.[6] James Kuklinski and Darrell West found that campaign context was important for economic voting. Owing to the quality of challengers, presence of national issues, and election visibility, voters in Senate elections more frequently held candidates accountable for economic policy than they did in House contests.[7] And Gary Jacobson and Samuel Kernell demonstrate that candidates' decisions to run (and contributors' decisions to finance them) determined the competitiveness of congressional elections.[8] These projects share the notion that campaigners can aid (or hinder) voters in the ballot box. Candidates can clarify (or fuzz) issues. They can influence where voters lay the blame for economic performances. Since campaigns set the boundaries of voter choices, electioneering activities cannot be ignored. Similarly, campaigns are important for public policy. Skeptics have often derided campaign commitments as no more than vote-getting illusions. According to this view, electoral promises have about as much chance getting fulfilled as Brooke Shields has getting invited to the Vatican in her Calvin Kleins. But research on past presidents has shown moderately strong relations between campaign commitments (as made in speeches and party platforms) and executive enactments. Fishel's analysis of administrations from Kennedy to Reagan discovered that presidents enacted from 60 to 70 percent of their promises.[9] Pomper, Kessel, and Ginsberg also suggest that campaigns provide relevant policy guides.[10]

Because public policy lies at the heart of politics, political observers need predictive tools that are linked to policy matters (and not just psychological processes). While there are no magic formulas or neat typologies, this research suggests ways of finding clues about presidential candidates. First, core constituencies are crucial for campaigners. Candidates do not enter presidential contests with blank slates. They have electoral histories that influence their views of constituencies and policies. As Fenno has discussed, core constituencies are particularly important because they are the loyalists who have supported the candidate throughout his political career (and probably were instrumental in giving him his first victory). They helped finance the candidate. They served as volunteers or advisors. And they publicized the candidate's name. By finding the supporters whom candidates most value, writers will discover something about campaigners' substantive priorities. In Reagan's case, right-wing groups were his core constituencies. These people brought Reagan into politics. After hearing his 1964 speech on behalf of Goldwater, they drafted him for a California gubernatorial race. Since then, in times of crises, Reagan has returned to these electoral roots. When his 1976 presidential effort faltered, he reached out to his conservative supporters for badly needed money. And after his surprise upset by Bush in the 1980 Iowa caucuses, Reagan paid more attention to conservatives. He fired the person (John Sears) responsible for ousting conservative advisors and returned Martin Anderson, Lyn Nofziger, and Michael Deaver to his campaign. With the conservatism of his core constituencies, observers should not have been surprised at the ideological tenor of Reagan's administration. Also, when his presidency encountered serious trouble in 1982, Reagan reemphasized his conservative roots. He endorsed tax credits for parochial schools, voluntary prayer in schools, and a balanced budget amendment.

Second, coalitional strategies play an important role in candidate thinking. Campaigners must make decisions about their constituencies. Since they cannot win the support of everyone, presidential aspirants must allocate their time and resources; these allocations reveal the people and causes having the highest priorities with candidates. There were two pillars of Reagan's coalitional strategy—conservative core constituencies and disenchanted Democrats. While there was some policy tension between these camps, potential conflicts were reduced because Reagan emphasized conservative Democrats—right-to-life activists, union members who felt alienated from union leaders, pro-gun advocates, and those upset over the decline of American values. Likewise, some constituencies (notably blacks) were consciously excluded from Reagan's coalitional strategy. Reagan did not visit black audiences during the nominating campaign and made little effort to understand their concerns. With these coalitional priorities, it was little wonder that Reagan pursued the policies he did. His social conservatism, fiscal frugality, and militant anti-communism flowed from the Californian's coalitional strategy (as well as his policy beliefs).

Third, the way campaigners communicate their coalitional strategies to the public provides clues about prospective presidents. Once candidates choose coalitional strategies, they must inform the relevant constituencies (voters, opinion leaders, financial contributors, convention delegates, and the media). In studying communications devices, it was apparent that candidates relied on a variety of electoral tactics—rhetoric, campaign visits, and symbolism. Most important for prediction, candidates used these tactics in mutually reinforcing ways. By and large, campaigners communicated their coalitional strategies through the issues they addressed, the audiences they visited, and the symbolic appeals they generated. Contrary to conventional wisdom about the inconsistencies of electoral tactics, candidates employed these avenues in consistent ways. Accordingly, their analyses tell us relevant things about would-be presidents. To illustrate, Reagan's communications reflected his coalitional strategy. By the topics he discussed—poor economic performance, the inefficiencies of government, overregulation, weak military strength, and lax moral standards—Reagan addressed the concerns of constituencies important to his coalition. His campaign visits also conveyed his interest in (or distance from) certain voters. And Reagan's symbolism communicated his attempts to broaden coalitions and redefine political agendas. Rather than being meaningless fluff, Regan's rhetoric and symbolism were vital to his coalition-building and agenda-setting. They also provided substantive clues about his presidency.

Finally, audience reactions tell us about presidential learning. It is difficult for candidates to get clear feedback on the campaign trail. Consequently, contenders must fall back on impressionistic sources, such as audience reactions. These reactions influence campaigners' rhetoric as well as their particular policy appeals. Since audience receptiveness molds candidate thinking, study of reactions shows the lessons that candidates learn while campaigning. Like other candidates, Reagan found in general that audiences did not enthusiastically reward candidates for policy commitments. Instead, they cheered discussions of general goals, personal qualities, and past performance. But this does not mean that audience reactions bore no relation to substantive matters. For more than twenty years, right-wing audiences have cheered Reagan passionately for anti-government and pro-defense rhetoric. These reactions undoubtedly reinforced Reagan's intuitive policy beliefs. And since campaigners often equate impressionistic audience reactions with "public opinion," Reagan's campaign appearances probably encouraged him to seek fundamental changes in government policy. In these ways, crowd dynamics influenced Reagan's views and therefore played a role in public policy.

To summarize, there are no foolproof methods of predicting leader behavior. But campaigns supply relevant information about presidential candidates. Campaigners' core constituencies and coalitional strategies tell observers which people the candidates most value and in this way reveal something about their substantive priorities. Since leaders carefully guard the constituencies they have cultivated over time, their perceptions do not change radically. The way candidates communicate their coalitional strategies to the public also provides clues about policy and coalitional intentions. Analyses of rhetoric, campaign visits, and symbolism show the overall directions of future administrations. And audience reactions demonstrate the lessons that candidates learn on the campaign trail. Through careful study, campaign researchers can discover important clues about prospective presidents.

LEADERSHIP AND COALITION-BUILDING

This research is also relevant for leadership and coalition-building. Many writers seek to understand politics by studying broad social and economic forces. For example, political sociologists investigate the significance of social classes and organizations. Meanwhile, political economists analyze the impact of aggregate economic patterns. Although these approaches offer important insights, they ignore the role of leadership in modern politics. Scholars have ignored leaders for various reasons. Some believe that leadership is irrelevant, that it does not matter whether Republicans or Democrats hold government authority. Since members of both parties accept what Theodore Lowi calls the new public philosophy of government activism, there will be no fundamental reversals of public policy in different administrations.[11] Rather leaders will exercise influence only at the margins of politics when they make incremental adjustments. Leadership research also declined because of the shortcomings of the historical "elite studies" (represented by the work of Gaetano Mosca, Vilfredo Pareto, Robert

Michels, C. Wright Mills, G. William Domhoff, and Thomas Dye).[12] Whether intended or not, many of these analysts adopted conspiratorial tones. By emphasizing small groups of people who were homogeneous, autonomous, and self-perpetuating, these writers created such a distorted picture of leaders that their field lost credibility. It was easy to challenge the conclusions by finding leaders who did not share political beliefs or did not come from similar backgrounds. Exhausted by conflicting results, elite studies became a research graveyard.

Of course, the field eventually was revived. Rechristened as "leadership studies," this area gained new life. Rather than dividing people into elites and masses and trying to prove the monolithic nature of elites, contemporary writers redirected their efforts. What was the essence of leadership? What qualities did leaders need to be effective? How did political institutions affect leadership? Perhaps best illustrated by James MacGregor Burns, the new generation of leadership studies started with the assumption that leaders could exercise influence in subtle ways.[13] They did not need to be a "power elite" to be politically important.

However, these researchers erred in one respect. Though they argued that leaders were important, they ignored leadership in campaigns (instead concentrating on institutional leadership). This omission is troubling because in the new electoral system, campaigns represent one of the few times when leaders have the attention of opinion leaders and (part of the) general public. According to Tucker, the basic tasks of leadership are "to define the collective situation, to design ways of dealing with it, and to mobilize support for the diagnosis and proposed mode of response."[14] In the old electoral system, where contests were short and predictable (owing to the strong grip of political parties), campaign leadership may have been less crucial for institutional leadership. Since the Democratic party dominated political institutions, leaders had ready-made coalitions available to them. They also had a tailor-made agenda, as the New Deal agenda defined policy problems and solutions. But in the new electoral system, campaigns are crucial to leadership. Presidential contests represent periods when leaders establish political agendas and build electoral coalitions. Since party coalitions have weakened and policy agendas have taken on complex and sometimes intractable issues (such as energy, abortion, and civil rights, among others), leaders can not lie low during campaigns. Instead they must try to define problems in ways that are favorable to them. They also must develop popular and legislative support for their programs. Candidates who fail to define their visions or create stable coalitions (as Carter failed to do in 1976) will be unable to lead effectively once they gain office.

In looking at the Reagan presidency, one cannot help but see the importance of the 1980 campaign for his governing efforts. Although he discussed specific policy matters in less than 15 percent of his public statements (see chapter 4), he used the campaign to develop the broad contours of his administration. As noted in the previous section, his campaign visits revealed much about his coalitional efforts—the people whose support he most valued. Meanwhile, his rhetoric and symbolism showed that he meant to undertake a major reassessment of the national political agenda—to question the activist role of government, roll back social legislation and federal regulations, and strengthen military capabilities against the specter of Soviet communism. These clues were more than image-making. They demonstrate the impact of Reagan's campaign on governance. Reagan's campaign set his early legislative agenda—tax cuts, budget reductions, and funding increases for the military. The campaign also produced Reagan's closest presidential advisors. Looking at the White House and cabinet, many of Reagan's campaign advisors became his presidential advisors (suggesting the role of campaigns in executive recruitment).

In addition, the 1980 race molded Reagan's beliefs. One of the burning questions after the election was whether Reagan had a mandate for major policy changes. Survey research by Warren Miller, Arthur Miller, and Martin Wattenberg indicated that he did not.[15] However, in policy terms, the "reality" question turned out to be less important than the fact that Reagan, his staff, the national media, and many legislators *believed* he had a mandate and acted accordingly. Because Reagan thought the election ratified his call for a strong defense and reduction in social programs, he proposed and fought for fundamental changes in public policy (many of which Congress implemented). As is often the case in Washington, the perceptions became the new reality.

In short, campaign leadership was very important to Reagan's coalitional efforts and his early legislative successes. Because of his coalitional and programmatic leadership during the campaign, Reagan positioned himself well for institutional leadership. He used the campaign to hone the vision and support necessary for presidential leadership. He devoted time and resources to building the grass roots of the Republican party. He also succeeded in preelection negotiations with congressional Republicans to forge a legislative consensus around his budget plans. Instead of being irrelevant for governance, the 1980 presidential campaign was intimately tied to Reagan's presidential performance.

Of course, it is not clear at this point what the long-term significance of the Reagan Administration will be. Reagan's victory in 1980 gave him unusual opportunities for enduring party changes. His success in attracting Democrats and Independents, the magnitude of his electoral margin (almost ten percentage points), and the Republican capture of the Senate for the first time since 1954 put him in an attractive position for realignment. But as with any prospective realigner, the election represented only an opportunity. As president, he needed to secure his position through innovative actions. During the first year of his administration, Reagan seemed well on the way to realignment. With the help of conservative Democrats, he pushed major policy changes through Congress. Social programs were cut, federal regulatory efforts were streamlined, and part of the tax burden was lifted. Political observers heralded a new era for government. However, in late 1981 the ceiling started to collapse. A recession raised unemployment (and government deficits) to record levels. And polls predicted that poor economic performance as well as doubts about Reaganomics would undercut future Republican prospects.[16]

This progression of the Reagan Administration illustrates the factors that limit the success of budding realignments. Realignment is a process that takes place over several elections. Realigners must combine a winning election, governing successes, and more election victories. One without the other is not adequate. Realignments also depend on the actions of the opposition party. "In-parties" do not control their fates. Rather "out-parties" influence the pace and direction of realignments through their strategic decisions. The degree to which the "outs" are conciliatory or confrontational (as Republicans were in 1934) clarifies the choices available to voters. Since Democrats in 1981 made efforts to compromise their differences with Reagan (and in fact tried to outbid him on tax cuts), they may have undermined his opportunities to crystallize public sentiments behind him. In addition, the analysis of realignment is influenced by the level at which one studies the process. Realignments involve different political levels: voters, leaders, and policy agendas. Voter realignments represent permanent changes in party identifications. For candidates to secure their electoral positions, they need people who will support them election after election (through thick and thin) and who will elect other members of their party. In Reagan's case, the 1980 election boosted the number of Republican identifiers (as measured through public opinion polls). But these gains turned out to be temporary. A year after the election, party affiliations resembled preelection levels (indicating that Reagan did not succeed in winning permanent friends for the Republican party among the general public). Of course, even if realignments fail among voters, it is possible for there to be enduring changes among leaders (that is, a "top-down" realignment). One of the keystones of Reagan's legislative strategy was maintenance of the conservative coalition. By combining Republican support with Southern Democrats in the House and holding his Republican majority in the Senate, Reagan wanted to have "de facto" government control. In these efforts, Reagan has been fairly successful. Although high deficits and budget cutbacks threatened his legislative majority, this coalition has endured remarkably well. Perhaps it represents a leadership realignment in Congress along ideological grounds. Finally, policy realignments refer to enduring adjustments in political agendas. Whatever Reagan's success with voters and Congress, there have been major changes in leader beliefs about public policy. For the first time in many years, there is serious debate among academics, legislators, and reporters about public philosophies. What should the role of government be? And how can government best perform its essential duties? While the new public philosophy of government activism has not been repealed, the effectiveness of government action is being debated by opinion leaders. Even if Republicans lose seats in future elections, Reagan's policy realignment may be his long-term contribution to party coalitions.

CANDIDATES AND ELECTORAL REFORM

Most research on presidential campaigns ends by considering reform propos-als; this study will do likewise. Many observers have criticized the new elec-toral system, with comments like the nominating process is too long and com-plicated; candidates dominate campaigns to the virtual exclusion of party leaders; process takes precedence over substance in elections; and coalitions are difficult to build.[17]

However, much of this analysis ignores the role of candidate perceptions in the process. Scholars generally have concentrated on the objective impact of reform: Will elimination of the electoral college help or harm racial minorities? What is the impact of finance rules on businesses and labor unions? Do winner-take-all primaries distort nominating contests? While these questions are im-portant, they miss a crucial link in the reform process—the perspectives of leaders. Writers often have commented on the poor performance of journalists and re-searchers in forecasting the consequences of reform.[18] The general tendency after seeing reforms in action is to bemoan their "unintended consequences." For example, who foresaw that requirements specifying demographic "quotas" at national nominating conventions would spur the growth of primaries? And who believed that the existence of numerous primaries would encourage prominent politicians to challenge presidential renominations?

Although it is easy to throw stones after the fact, the poor job of forecasting reform consequences points to a fundamental shortcoming among students of reform—the failure to consider the impact of reform on leaders. Specifically, how do reform proposals shape the way candidates see their political opportu-nities and risks? Do particular reforms foreclose some strategies while making others possible? How do reforms affect the way candidates play out their am-bitions in the electoral process? Because the failure to consider leader perspec-tives is partly responsible for "unintended consequences," it is important to discuss reform from the standpoint of campaigners.

The most prominent reforms deal with delegate selection procedures. Since the rise in the number of primaries and decline of party leaders, observers have proposed various reforms: abolition of open primaries, shortening the nominat-ing period, reducing the number of primaries, and guaranteeing convention seats for party and elected officials, among others.[19] In general, these proposals are designed to strengthen party professionals in the delegate selection process. But the question remains how these changes will affect candidate perceptions of the nominating process. What options do these reforms foreclose and what strate-gies or opportunities do they make possible?

This research indicates that these structural changes will probably reinvigo-rate party regulars in presidential campaigns. By abolishing open primaries, candidates in each party's primaries no longer would be able to appeal to par-tisans from the other party. For example, candidates in Democratic primaries would be unable to solicit Republican votes in the nominating process. Because this reform would help to insure purer party candidates, that is, those who were acceptable to party identifiers, it would strengthen political parties. In addition, shortening the primary season and guaranteeing convention seats for party officials might accomplish the same purpose. By bringing party leaders back into the nominating convention (and presumably reducing the number of "amateurs") and compressing nominating decisions, party regulars would gain influence.[20]

However, these changes may also produce a variety of other consequences (some of which are undesirable). For example, in chapter 2, I discussed how campaign processes mold perceptions of opportunities and risks. Specifically, the existence of open primaries, lengthy nomination processes, and weak political parties encouraged dark horse candidates for the presidency as well as nominating challenges to the president. Do we want to give up the diversity of choices that are now available to voters? Do we want to return to a pattern in which presidents or their handpicked successors automatically won their party's nomination while the prenomination frontrunner in the "out" party became that party's nominee? While some observers may answer in the affirmative, it should be clear that these reforms will entail costs. The electorate will have fewer choices in the primaries. The nominating process will be more predictable than it is now. And certain types of candidates (namely dark horses and party mavericks) will be foreclosed.[21]

These reforms might also decrease the coalitional options available to voters. Since the open nominating process has encouraged candidates to attempt coalitional innovations (see chapter 3), it is probable that steps away from openness would remove some of the incentives candidates have for coalitional change. Scholars have often argued that strengthening the role of party officials in delegate selection would reinvigorate the party system. At one level, this analysis is correct. Giving party regulars a stronger role in candidate selection strengthens the *existing* party system. But in the long run, these moves might weaken parties. By reducing the opportunities that candidates have for realignments, these reforms might undercut the system's capacity to realign parties. Hence, strengthening the influence of *current* party leaders (many of whom are cautious on policy matters and protective of the political status quo) would undermine the regenerative functions of party realignment, thereby harming *future* party systems.

Finally, these reforms might change the way political leaders play out their ambitions in the electoral process. In the contemporary period, the open nominating process and weakness of political parties have removed some of the traditional restraints on ambitions. With the current nominating process, presidential candidates can disregard party leaders and elected officials, apparently without damaging their chances for nomination. Prominent leaders can also challenge presidential renominations without fear of retribution. While some observers may see these developments as threatening the stability of the political system, one can argue that these challenges offer hope of renewal. In many respects, contested nominations, dark horse candidates, and third party challengers are healthy developments because they broaden the political agenda and reinvigorate the party system. Perhaps the greatest threat to the American political system today is not the open nominating process but public apathy, mistrust, and cynicism. Voting turnout has declined to its lowest level in decades. Public confidence in political leaders and government institutions is not exceptionally high. To the extent that the new electoral system brings candidates to the forefront, places ideas on the political agenda, and gives voters a choice between meaningful options, we should applaud and cherish that system.

NOTES

1. James David Barber, *The Presidential Character: Predicting Performance in the White House* (Englewood Cliffs, N.J.: Prentice-Hall, 1972).

2. Barber also distinguished "passive-positives" (those with high needs for approval) from "passive-negatives" (leaders serving out of a sense of duty).

3. In fact, the typology has gained such popular acceptance that some candidates have maneuvered for the favored "active-positive" designation.

4. For more extensive critiques, see Jeffrey Tulis, "On Presidential Character," in Joseph Bessette and Jeffrey Tulis, eds., *The Presidency in a Constitutional Order* (Baton Rouge: Louisiana State University, 1981) and Marjorie Hershey, *Running for Office* (Chatham, N.J.: Chatham House, forthcoming).

5. Ceaser, *Presidential Selection*.

6. Page, *Choices and Echoes in Presidential Elections*.

7. Kuklinski and West, "Economic Expectations and Voting Behavior in United States House and Senate Elections."

8. Gary Jacobson and Samuel Kernell, *Strategy and Choice in Congressional Elections* (New Haven, Conn.: Yale University Press, 1981).

9. Fishel, *From Presidential Promise to Performance*.

10. Pomper, *Elections in America*; Kessel, "The Seasons of Presidential Politics"; and Ginsberg, *The Consequences of Consent*.

11. Theodore Lowi, *The End of Liberalism*, 2nd ed. (New York: W. W. Norton, 1979).

12. For summaries of these works, see Robert Putnam, *The Comparative Study of Political Elites* (Englewood Cliffs, N.J.: Prentice-Hall, 1976) and Kenneth Prewitt and Alan Stone, *The Ruling Elites* (New York: Harper and Row, 1973).

13. James MacGregor Burns, *Leadership* (New York: Harper and Row, 1978). See also Robert Tucker, *Politics as Leadership* (Columbia: University of Missouri Press, 1981) and William Welsh, *Leaders and Elites* (New York: Holt, Rinehart and Winston, 1979).

14. Tucker, *Politics as Leadership*, p. 114.

15. Warren Miller, "Policy Directions and Presidential Leadership: Alternative Interpretations of the 1980 Presidential Election," paper presented at the annual meeting of the American Political Science Association, New York, September 3–6, 1981 and Arthur Miller and Martin Wattenberg, "Policy and Performance Voting in the 1980 Election," paper presented at the annual meeting of the American Political Science Association, New York, September 3–6, 1981. Of course, one can ask whether elections ever

produce mandates in the classical sense. Roosevelt's 1932 "mandate" arose from a campaign that was not dominated by the issues and one where Roosevelt did not lay out the specifics of the New Deal. In addition, Roosevelt undoubtedly benefited from protest votes against Hoover. So even though Reagan's "mandate" might not have satisfied strict requirements, it may have been as clear as Roosevelt's was.

16. In the 1934 midterms, Roosevelt was able to cement his realignment despite a dismal economy. But he did it by promoting hope for future economic performance (the dismal present notwithstanding). It remains to be seen whether retrospective or prospective voting will govern Republican changes in the future.

17. James W. Ceaser, *Reforming the Reforms* (Cambridge, Mass.: Ballinger Publishing Co., 1982).

18. Crotty, *Political Reform and the American Experiment*, p. 277.

19. In 1982, the Democrats (following recommendations from the Hunt Commission) enacted these proposals for future campaigns.

20. Of course, chances for participation do not mean that elected officials will use these opportunities. As Drew, *Portrait of an Election*, pp. 20–23, has pointed out, many elected officials are now choosing noninvolvement in delegate selection because of fears that divisive battles will damage them politically.

21. These results suggest the important impact that electoral institutions have on candidate thinking and behavior.

Appendixes

Interview List

John Anderson

      Clifford Brown, Research Director, September 6, 1980
      Edward Coyle, Deputy Campaign Manager, June 23, 1980
      Elizabeth Hager, New Hampshire Coordinator, June 12, 1980
      Vicky Golden Markell, Press Secretary and Scheduler, June 2, 1980
      Tom Mathews, Direct Mail, November 12, 1980
      Michael McLeod, Campaign Manager, July 19, 1980
      Dan Swillinger, Campaign Manager, July 17, 1980
      Kirk Walder, Political Staff, August 8, 1980

Howard Baker

      Doug Bailey, Media Advisor, July 31, 1980
      Tom Griscom, Press Secretary, December 12, 1979
      Andrew Lawrence, Regional Political Coordinator, December 19, 1979
      Richard Lugar, Campaign Chairman, December 17, 1979
      Robert Mosbacher, Jr., Political Staff and Fundraising, December 12, 1979
      Bill Roesing, Strategist, August 14, 1980
      David Spear, Scheduling, August 15, 1980
      Don Stansberry, Director of Scheduling, December 12, 1979
      Wyatt Stewart, Campaign Manager, August 12, 1980
      Sara Tinsley, Political Staff, December 12, 1979
      Bill Tucker, Deputy Manager for Convention States, August 14, 1980

Jerry Brown

      Joe Beeman, New England Coordinator, July 29, 1980
      Richard Maullin, Campaign Cochairman, September 12, 1980
      Walter McGuire, Director of Scheduling, August 8, 1980
      Tom Quinn, Campaign Manager, November 19, 1980
      Richard Silberman, Campaign Cochairman, September 22, 1980

George Bush

      Jeb Bush, Political Staff, June 13, 1980
      Mary Gall, Research Staff, December 12, 1979

David Keene, National Political Director, April 15, 1980
Jon Miller, Deputy Political Director, May 28, 1980
Kate Moore, Scheduling, April 11, 1980
John Morgan, Media and Demography, May 15, 1980
Susan Morrison, Deputy Communications Director, December 18, 1979
David Sparks, Deputy Political Director, May 28, 1980
Pete Teeley, Press Secretary, June 26, 1980
Margaret Tutweiler, Director of Scheduling, April 11, 1980

Jimmy Carter

Ben Brown, Deputy Campaign Manager, December 13, 1979
Pat Caddell, Pollster and Strategist, February 3, 1981
Michelle Clause, Press Operations, December 11, 1979
Malcolm Dade, Deputy Campaign Chairman, May 22, 1980
Evan Dobelle, Campaign Manager, December 11, 1979
Tom Donilon, Delegate Operations, September 25, 1980
Les Francis, Political Director, July 21, 1980
Ralph Gerson, Special Assistant, June 26, 1980
Gwen Hemphill, Political Operations, December 11, 1979
Robert Keefe, Political Coordinator, November 12, 1980
Tim Kraft, Campaign Manager, September 5, 1980
Linda Peek, Campaign Press Secretary, December 19, 1979
Gerald Rafshoon, Media Advisor, January 15, 1981
Diana Rock, Deputy Campaign Manager, December 18, 1979
Kevin Smith, Scheduling, December 11, 1979

John Connally

Chip Andrews, New Hampshire Coordinator, December 19, 1979
William Chasey, Political Staff, December 13, 1979
Mopsi Fahey, Political Staff, December 19, 1979
Sam Hoskinson, Research Director, December 19, 1979
Charles Keating, Campaign Manager, October 5, 1980
Ladonna Lee, Special Projects, December 20, 1979
Eddie Mahe, Jr., Campaign Manager, December 10, 1979
Jackie Nystrom, Deputy Manager, December 13, 1979
Lance Tarrance, Pollster, August 28, 1980
Mark Weinberg, Press Staff, December 13, 1979

Philip Crane

Laura Broderick, Press Secretary, August 11, 1980
Jerry Harkins, Campaign Manager, August 18, 1980
Richard Viguerie, Direct Mail, September 9, 1980
Richard Williamson, Campaign Manager, September 19, 1980

Robert Dole

John Crutcher, Campaign Manager, August 9, 1980
Mari Maseng, Political Staff, August 15, 1980
Anne McLaughlin, Campaign Treasurer, August 15, 1980
Betty Meyer, Scheduling, August 20, 1980

Edward Kennedy

Ron Brown, Deputy Campaign Chairman, July 16, 1980
Richard Drayne, Press Secretary, December 14, 1979
Peter Hart, Pollster, December 19, 1980
Joanne Howes, Deputy Campaign Chairman, June 20, 1980
Paul Kirk, Campaign Manager, September 17, 1980
William Oldaker, Legal Counsel, June 10, 1980
Tony Podesta, Scheduling, September 16, 1980
Robert Shrum, Speech Writer, September 12, 1980
Stephen Smith, Campaign Chairman, October 31, 1980
Richard Stearns, Delegate Selection, July 23, 1980
Carl Wagner, National Political Director, May 21, 1980

Ronald Reagan

Charles Black, National Political Director, December 17, 1979
Anderson Carter, Field Director, November 7, 1980
Peter Dailey, Media Advisor, February 19, 1981
Frank Donatelli, Regional Political Coordinator, June 20, 1980
Ken Klinge, Regional Political Coordinator, December 10, 1979
Jim Lake, Press Secretary, August 7, 1980
Drew Lewis, Deputy Chairman, August 20, 1980
Lyn Nofziger, Press Secretary, September 19, 1980
John Sears, Campaign Manager, July 31, 1980
Roger Stone, Regional Political Coordinator, December 10, 1979
William Timmons, Convention Manager, March 16, 1981
Richard Wirthlin, Pollster and Strategist, February 19, 1981

Notes on Campaign Research

> Susan Stamberg of National Public Radio: "To me, that's the secret of good interviewing: listening. I must have done 7,000 interviews in the first ten years of 'All Things Considered.' And my best interviews are the ones in which I listen most carefully: for new ideas, new perspectives, but also for slips of the tongue, slips of logic; for contradictions, enthusiasm, tension; for what's not being said; for silences, too, and what they reveal. 'Manic-depressive listening,' a reporter once called it." [1]

Leadership studies offer a mixture of joys and sorrows. The primary opportunity of analysis based on interviews and personal observation is the chance to see presidential races through the eyes of campaign organizers. Frequently, scholars have ignored this perspective, arguing that politicians are too involved in the process to have useful perspectives or that their views are based on faulty perceptions. While there is evidence that campaigners develop beliefs that sometimes bear little resemblance to objective conditions, it is precisely those thoughts that are relevant for the political process. Perceptions that influence candidate behavior are important even if they are based on incorrect information. For writers to disregard this view is to miss some of the ways that leaders shape voter choices and set limits on the political agenda.

But study of candidates and their advisors requires a special blend of patience, forebearance, and understanding of the time pressures under which campaigns take place. Advisors lead hectic lives. When candidates move into active campaigning, it is common for staffs to work grueling hours (which in conjunction with low salaries explains why campaigns are staffed with young people). As one campaigner put it, looking back on the experience: "I was leaving here at 7:15 in the morning and not getting home ever before 8:30 at night and that was six days a week. Sometimes on Saturdays, I could slip out at 6 or 6:30. And Sundays were usually spent there from one to six. . . . My husband works. We used to meet each other for lunch occasionally but it was really getting rough. I don't know how people do it." Another described the job this way: "It's fourteen hours a day nonstop. . . . It's a total commitment. I mean, you have no life of your own practically if you're dedicated. . . . It's like resurrecting a corporation every night that you know is going to end six weeks later."

Because of the heavy workload, academic interviews pose particular problems for campaigners. Interviews require them to set aside chunks of time (usually forty-five minutes or an hour). In the rapidly changing world of campaign organizations (where there are five crises a day) the loss of flexibility represents a major commitment by staff members. One advisor noted that, "you've got so many demands upon your time that if you set up an interview with one person, then you have to do it with all the other people. . . . [We are] constantly being asked to do an interview. . . . We have five or six requests for interviews and CBS and NBC are rolling in every week. It's really hard to set aside a block of time and be able to hang onto it." Interviews also take campaign officials away from their primary task—winning elections. Unlike media interviews, which pay off in free publicity, academic interviews contribute little to getting votes (although they may be useful in long-term image development). During the trying days of December, 1979, a Kennedy spokesman stated the dilemma bluntly: "It's very difficult for me or anyone else to ask our people in the field to sit down and talk to you for forty-five minutes when what they're out there for is to try to do some very hard and slogging work. You could take up hours and hours . . . when they really ought to be out there doing campaign work." And perhaps most problematic from the standpoint of campaigners, they have no way of gauging interviewers' publishing prospects. An hour-long interview is a resource commitment with uncertain payoff. "[We] never know whether a book will see the light of day or whether it'll be written," was the way one person voiced this concern.

Despite these problems, it is possible to encourage cooperation in ways that create the fewest difficulties for campaigners.[2] The best advice on gaining access is to start early in the campaign. I made my first contacts with campaign officials in September, 1979, several months before the first delegate test.[3] Since most of the organizations still were being staffed, it proved to be an ideal time to "get in on the ground floor." Because the campaign was in the early stage, staff members had not shifted into the "frenetic activity" that characterizes active campaigning. The media (always a formidable competitor for the scarce time of advisors) also had not descended on these organizations. Of course, most staffs suffered extensive turnover as the race progressed (which leads many observers to conclude that campaign organizations are not worthy of study). But in "tracking" personnel changes during the campaign, it was apparent that turnover was related to coalition-building. Candidates who wanted to mobilize certain constituencies or broaden their bases often did so by bringing representatives of those groups into their campaigns. As an example, Reagan's personnel shifts reflected his coalitional efforts— the early maneuvering between Sears and conservatives who resisted Sears's moderating influence, the dumping of Sears and his allies and the resurrection of Martin Anderson, Lyn Nofziger, and Michael Deaver in February, 1980, and the efforts to bring the campaign operatives of defeated Republican rivals into Reagan's general election organization. Similarly, Anderson's staff went through outreach efforts. Before the primaries, Anderson drew staff from his previous races and Ripon Society contacts. When he chose to leave the Republican party and launch an independent candidacy, he broadened his base by bringing aboard Edward Coyle (of Morris Udall's 1976 presidential campaign), Michael Fernandez (of Brown's staff), and Patrick Lucey (of Kennedy's campaign), among others. Eventually, David Garth brought some of his staff members into Anderson's "National Unity" campaign. This link between personnel changes and coalitional strategies shows how interviewing can produce substantive insights.[4]

In addition, scholars should use a "pyramiding" approach to solicit interviews. To be successful at gaining access, researchers need legitimacy. The usual academic credentials (such as rank, publications, and professional activities) offer some help. But politicians are often unable to judge these credentials. Generally, they do not know the difference between assistant and associate professors. They also can not distinguish the *American Political Science Review* from other publications. Because of their limited information about the academic world, campaigners prefer cues that arc familiar to them—their friends and acquaintances in Washington. However, if one lacks political connections (as is true for many scholars), the alternative is to make early contacts in the middle levels of campaign organizations and rely on these people to work up through the organization. To illustrate, I took down the names of all the people I met during September, 1979 visits to Washington campaign offices. Working with these preliminary contacts (all of whom received follow-up thank you notes), I sent letters requesting December interviews to top campaign advisors (and mentioned that I already had met some of their staff members). The text is printed here:

Dear _____,

I am writing to ask if I might interview you at your Washington office. I am . . . at Indiana University and am writing a book on the 1980 presidential campaign. I hope to interview all the major campaign officials of the _____ campaign about their perceptions and electoral strategies.

In early September, I made a preliminary visit to _____ headquarters and talked with _____, one of your regional political coordinators. His information about organizational structure and staff responsibilities proved especially useful for my research.

I plan to be in Washington from December 10 through December 20. Since I will interview individuals in a number of organizations, I am trying to coordinate my schedule by arranging the _____ interviews either for _____, _____, or _____. If you are willing to be interviewed, I would appreciate it if you would notify me (through the enclosed postcard) and indicate the time that is most convenient for you. I estimate that each interview will take between 35 and 45 minutes.

I look forward to hearing from you and thank you in advance for your time.

Of the seventy-one advisors in various campaigns who received this letter, twenty-two responded with interview commitments, four declined interviews at that time, and the others did not respond. However, on arrival in Washington, follow-up phone calls increased the December interviews to twenty-seven, including several campaign managers, press secretaries, and national political directors. Later, in May, 1980, a move to Washington to begin a research fellowship at the Brookings Institution facilitated the interviews. Although originally I used personal letters to request interviews, the Brookings affiliation enabled me to request interviews over the phone, obviously a much quicker route. Since the results seemed to be as good, if not better, than mail requests, I used the phone for the remainder of the interview requests (but almost all of the interviews themselves were conducted in person).

Most important for gaining access, researchers should be sensitive to campaign dynamics. As with any job, there are ebbs and flows in campaign activities. The worst times to seek interviews are around crucial primaries and caucuses and throughout the general election campaign. During these periods, campaigners are busiest and need control of their schedules. Requests for interviews generally go unanswered or are seen as intrusive. In contrast, advisors are much more accessible in the preprimary period, summer doldrums, and post-general election days. Surprisingly, one of the best times for interviews in unsuccessful campaigns is the week losing candidates withdraw from campaigning. At this time, organizers need someone to talk to (since the media vanish overnight). Many of them become reflective as they relive the ups and downs of their campaigns. And they are often willing to analyze their efforts with more detachment than before. As one Bush official said shortly after his candidate withdrew, "I'm being much more open with you now than I would have been two weeks ago" (or, he neglected to say, would be two months later when Bush became the vice-presidential nominee). Of course, there always are exceptions. Some advisors are difficult to reach at any time. Several of my interviews took over twenty phone calls to arrange. But researchers should not feel reluctant to be persistent. Secretaries sometimes can become allies in the battle for interviews. If you convince them your project is respectable, they may be willing to plot ways of getting interviews with their bosses.[5]

There also appears to be a relationship between interviews and campaign roles. Press people are difficult to hold for blocks of time. Since their jobs make them the campaign's formal link to the outside world, they are the most frazzled people in campaigns. Most of them start their days facing dozens of phone messages (requests for interviews, background information, or travel credentials). And throughout the day, these stacks get larger, not smaller. Press advisors also are more difficult to interview than political advisors. Since their job is information regulation and they are used to speaking in guarded manners, press officials are not very forthcoming about electoral strategies (as opposed to political strategists, who want to insure credit for their products). So role theory is relevant to campaign research.

Once interviews are arranged, new problems arise. As Fenno has noted, much of campaign research is exploratory.[6] Rather than testing explicit hypotheses and working deductively, "soakers" and "pokers" formulate their questions inductively. Although this approach is not cost-free (for example, these projects may require longer gestation periods than research evaluating ready-made ideas), there can be unexpected benefits. In my analysis, several things that were relevant for research strategies came out of early interviews and personal observation. First, I started the interviews with a structured, but open-ended, questionnaire. However, interviews with advisors in different campaign organizations showed that a general set of questions for all candidates and all organizational positions was not adequate.[7] Too often, questions that elicited useful information from press secretaries did not do so with pollsters or research directors. Or questions that were relevant for challengers or dark horses did not generate interesting responses from frontrunners. Consequently, as the early interviews progressed, I converted the questionnaire into a "semi-structured" format and (depending on the interviewee) added questions suitable for his or her campaign tasks.

Second, the early interviews convinced me that tape recorders do not inhibit interviewees. While this conclusion runs against the grain of conventional wisdom on "elite" interviewing, it may reflect the level of election I investigated and the period of the study.[8] Many of the pieces written on leader interviewing were published during periods when the media were less omnipresent than they are in contemporary elections (especially at the presidential level). Accordingly, political leaders had little experience with microphones and perhaps were reluctant to talk openly on tape. But in the contemporary era, the media are so pervasive that advisors have considerable experience before microphones. At press conferences and rallies, the only thing that exceeds the notebooks among reporters is the tape recorders. Standing in the press area, one often feels as if he is at a Sony, not a political, meeting. Campaign organizers also are veterans of several elections, something that gives them additional experience with recording equipment. Of course, one can never prove that tape recorded information has the same flavor as nonrecorded sessions (since the two states are impossible to achieve at the same time, the electronic equivalent of Heisenberg's Uncertainty Principle). But the forthrightness with which my subjects discussed personnel, strategies, and even their own candidates, suggests that tape recorders are not major obstacles. Tape recorders are also far superior to memory or sketchy notes in reconstructing quotations. Not only do recorders enable scholars to develop verbatim transcripts, they allow them to check their own judgments on the importance of particular statements. Sometimes discussions that seemed inconsequential during interviews gained new meaning the next day or even several months after the interview.

Third, the early interviews enabled me to explore possible data sources (as well as their availability). Often in field research, one starts the process interested in certain questions but unsure of the available evidence. In my interviews, campaigners helped shape the research strategy that emerged. In particular, they confirmed my preliminary belief that candidate-audience interactions (reported in chapter 7) were important. Hence, a data source (audience applause) that scholars previously have not tapped became part of this research. My campaign travels (twenty-four days in New Hampshire, Massachusetts, Vermont, and Illinois) also alerted me to a data source that previously had not been part of the project. While observing candidates in their public appearances and press conferences, I discovered that because of the need to coordinate campaign visits with the Secret Service and the media, presidential candidates compile minute-by-minute travel schedules. As discussed in chapter 5, these itineraries list not only allocations among different states (which scholars previously have analyzed), but also provide a variety of additional information: the city of the appearance, the type of campaign event, and (most important) the constituency that the candidate addresses. Since researchers have ignored how candidates allocate their scarce travel time among different groups or how these allocations relate to coalitional strategies, this observation made me aware of an underutilized data source. In addition, campaign travels enabled me to observe the rhetoric and presentational styles of different candidates. Although one can follow campaign rhetoric through news accounts, these articles do not always reveal the subtle ways in which candidates address audiences—the verbal inflections, the facial expressions, and the presentations of self. Even though there is no easy way to quantify these nuances or even to communicate them as qualitative data, their observation contributed to my understanding of campaign dynamics.[9]

Finally, my interviews allowed me to compare phone versus in-person interviews. Most of my interviews took place at the offices of campaign advisors. However, for the handful of staffers who were not located in Washington, I conducted lengthy interviews over the phone. While scholars have debated the relative advantages of phone and personal interviews, there did not appear to be noticeable differences between the two types. In general, one can attribute this finding to the experiences that advisors have with phones. Since most of them spend hours on the telephone (either conferring with subordinates across the country or being interviewed), phone interviews are familiar and comfortable. Unlike participants in public opinion surveys who lack these experiences and therefore may be reticent in phone interviews, campaigners speak freely on the phone. Advisors also are cosmopolitan people. In contrast to House candidates, whom Fenno found to be "locals" (using Robert Merton's terminology), professionals in presidential elections have broad orientations.[10] They are not rooted in single congressional districts; instead they often have worked for candidates in different states. For example, pollsters and media advisors may consult with ten or fifteen races each year. This background gives them experience with phones that other activists may lack. But there are some problems with phone interviews that are minimized with personal interviews, namely the need to coordinate interview times. When one has an office appointment, the interviewer's physical presence helps to keep waiting time to a minimum (which usually varies from twenty to sixty minutes). In contrast, with phone interviews, the opportunities for delay beyond the appointment time are considerable. Perhaps my most memorable experience with this dilemma came when I left my home phone number with a secretary in Denver who promised me her boss (a prominent campaign official) would call around 9:00 P.M. Washington time. However, it was 1:30 A.M. when a ringing telephone dragged me out of bed to begin what turned into an hour-long interview. Fortunately, the interview proved interesting enough to justify the unusual time. But despite Fenno's admonition that field research is a "young person's" game, as a twenty-six-year-old researcher at the time of this project, I remained convinced that field research requires more youth than even young people have.[11]

NOTES

1. Susan Stamberg, *Every Night at Five* (New York: Pantheon, 1982), p. 148.
2. Advisors also have several incentives to share experiences with researchers. Like most people, they love to talk about themselves and their work. In addition, some of them want to maintain good relations with opinion leaders, especially those who write the history books. And their need for legitimacy may make them accessible to scholars. As with any profession, their motives are diverse, and writers wanting access must experiment with different "pitches" to find out what works.
3. At this time, I visited the Washington headquarters of the major candidates and sought brief conversations (not formal interviews) with middle-level officials, such as press aides and administrative assistants. Fortunately, the Washington office for most candidates housed their political and press operations. While occasionally candidates had offices located in their home bases, such as Los Angeles for Reagan and Houston for Bush, these "headquarters" normally served only the functions of finance, administration, and (sometimes) scheduling. It was the Washington office that contained the strategy center, especially for elected office-holders.
4. This also shows that field research is a skill that requires extensive preparation. Rather than being the antithesis of methodology, careful research design is as much a part of methodology as statistical analysis.
5. Secretaries were often the unspoken (and unacknowledged) heroes of this project. They helped bring recalcitrant advisors to the phone. They arranged interviews. They filled me in on their boss's idiosyncrasies. And in some cases (after repeated phone calls), they even became friends. For their assistance, I thank them.
6. Fenno, *Home Style*, pp. 250–251.
7. I also learned to be wary of titles in campaign organizations. If researchers are not careful about specifying duties, they can end up with fifty-eight political advisors in every organization.

Campaign Chronology

Fall, 1977—Bush formation of Fund for Limited Government
January 22, 1978—Reagan formation of Citizens for the Republic
June 9, 1978—Democratic National Committee revision of 1980 rules
July 19, 1978—Crane formation of Exploratory Committee
August 2, 1978—Crane announcement speech
October 17, 1978—Dole formation of Exploratory Committee
January 5, 1979—Formation of Bush Exploratory Committee
January 24, 1979—Connally announcement speech
January 31, 1979—Formation of Baker Exploratory Committee
March 3, 1979—Formation of Carter Exploratory Committee
March 7, 1979—Formation of Reagan Exploratory Committee
May 1, 1979—Bush announcement speech
May 14, 1979—Dole announcement speech
June 8, 1979—Anderson announcement speech
June 24, 1979—Americans for Democratic Action "Draft-Kennedy" Resolution
July 6–11, 1979—Carter's Camp David "domestic summit"
July 15, 1979—Carter's "American malaise" speech
July 19, 1979—Carter's cabinet shake-up
July 30, 1979—Formation of Brown Exploratory Committee
August 31, 1979—Announcement of Soviet troops in Cuba
October 11, 1979—Connally's Mideastern policy speech
October 19, 1979—Ford rejection of presidential bid
October 25, 1979—First official Kennedy fundraiser
October 29, 1979—Formation of Kennedy Exploratory Committee
November 1, 1979—Baker announcement speech
November 3, 1979—Maine GOP Conference straw vote
November 4, 1979—Iranian takeover of American Embassy
November 4, 1979—Roger Mudd interview of Kennedy
November 7, 1979—Kennedy announcement speech
November 8, 1979—Brown announcement speech
November 13, 1979—Reagan announcement speech
November 17, 1979—Florida Republican State Convention straw vote
November 18, 1979—Florida Democratic State Convention straw vote

December 2, 1979—Kennedy's criticism of shah of Iran
December 4, 1979—Carter announcement speech
December 12, 1979—Connally decision to forego federal matching funds
December 26, 1979—Soviet invasion of Afghanistan
December 28, 1979—Carter withdrawal from Iowa Democratic debate
January 2, 1980—Mailing of first federal checks to candidates
January 3, 1980—Carter request to defer SALT II debate
January 5, 1980—Republican debate in Iowa (without Reagan)
January 21, 1980—Iowa precinct delegate caucuses
January 28, 1980—Kennedy's Georgetown speech
February 2, 1980—Arkansas Republican District Committee meetings
February 10, 1980—Maine Democratic municipal caucuses
February 16, 1980—Arkansas Republican State Committee meetings
February 17, 1980—Puerto Rico Republican primary
February 18, 1980—New Hampshire Gunowners candidate forum
February 20, 1980—Republican debate in Manchester, New Hampshire
February 23, 1980—Republican debate in Nashua, New Hampshire (Bush and Reagan)
February 26, 1980—New Hampshire primaries
February 26, 1980—Reagan firing of top staff
February 27, 1980—Dole stops active campaigning
March 1, 1980—Carter's United Nations "mistake"
March 2, 1980—Ford pondering of presidential bid
March 4, 1980—Massachusetts and Vermont primaries
March 5, 1980—Baker withdrawal
March 8, 1980—South Carolina Republican primary
March 11, 1980—Florida, Georgia, and Alabama primaries
March 13, 1980—Republican debate in Chicago, Illinois
March 15, 1980—Dole withdrawal
March 15, 1980—Ford decision not to run
March 16, 1980—Puerto Rican Democratic primary
March 18, 1980—Illinois primaries
March 25, 1980—New York and Connecticut primaries
April 1, 1980—Wisconsin and Kansas primaries
April 1, 1980—Brown withdrawal
April 5, 1980—Louisiana primaries
April 17, 1980—Crane withdrawal
April 22, 1980—Pennsylvania primaries
April 23, 1980—Republican debate in Houston, Texas
April 24, 1980—Anderson announcement of Exploratory Committee for Independent
    Candidacy
April 24, 1980—Abortive Iranian rescue mission
April 28, 1980—Carter visit to Texas military base (first campaign trip)
April 30, 1980—Carter announcement of resumption of campaign appearances
May 3, 1980—Texas primaries
May 6, 1980—Primaries in District of Columbia, Indiana, North Carolina, and Tennes-
    see
May 13, 1980—Maryland and Nebraska primaries
May 20, 1980—Oregon and Michigan primaries

May 26, 1980—Bush withdrawal

May 27, 1980—Idaho, Kentucky, and Nevada primaries

June 3, 1980—Primaries in California, Montana, New Jersey, New Mexico, Ohio, Rhode Island, South Dakota, and West Virginia

June 5, 1980—Meeting between Carter and Kennedy

June 5, 1980—Meeting between Reagan and Ford

June 12, 1980—Jordan move to Carter Campaign Committee

July 1, 1980—Anderson's formal announcement of independent candidacy

July 14–17, 1980—Republican National Convention

July 23, 1980—Billy Carter's "Libyan" affair

July 25, 1980—Democratic "open convention" meeting

August 11, 1980—Kennedy withdrawal

August 11–14, 1980—Democratic National Convention

September 1, 1980—Traditional beginning of general election campaign

September 21, 1980—Anderson-Reagan debate (without Carter)

October 28, 1980—Carter-Reagan debate in Cleveland, Ohio (without Anderson)

November 1–4, 1980—Last-minute negotiations over Iranian hostages

November 2, 1980—Final poll predictions of close race in popular vote

November 4, 1980—General election

December 15, 1980—Meeting of state electoral colleges

January 20, 1981—Inauguration Day

Election Returns in the Nominating Process

State	Turnout	Brown	Democrats Carter	Kennedy	No Preference
Iowa (1/21)	NA		59.1	31.2	9.6
Puerto Rico (D-3/16)	870,235	0.2	51.7	48.0	
New Hampshire (2/26)	111,930	9.6	47.1	37.3	
Massachusetts (3/4)	907,332	3.5	28.7	65.1	2.2
Vermont (3/4)	39,703	0.9	73.1	25.5	
Alabama (3/11)	237,464	4.0	81.6	13.2	0.7
Florida (3/11)	1,098,003	4.9	60.7	23.2	9.5
Georgia (3/11)	384,780	1.9	88.0	8.4	1.0
Illinois (3/18)	1,201,067	3.3	65.0	30.0	
Connecticut (3/25)	210,275	2.6	41.5	46.9	6.4
New York (3/25)	989,062		41.1	58.9	
Kansas (4/1)	193,918	4.9	56.6	31.6	5.8
Wisconsin (4/1)	629,619	11.8	56.2	30.1	0.4
Louisiana (4/5)	358,741	4.7	55.7	22.5	11.6

State	Turnout	Brown	Democrats		No Preference
			Carter	Kennedy	
Pennsylvania (4/22)	1,613,223	2.3	45.4	45.7	5.8
Texas (5/3)	1,377,354	2.6	55.9	22.8	18.7
Dist. of Columbia (5/6)	64,150		36.9	61.7	
Indiana (5/6)	589,441		67.7	32.3	
North Carolina (5/6)	737,262	2.9	70.1	17.7	9.3
Tennessee (5/6)	294,680	1.9	75.2	18.1	3.9
Maryland (5/13)	477,090	3.0	47.5	38.0	9.6
Nebraska (5/13)	153,881	3.6	46.9	37.6	10.4
Michigan (5/20)	78,424	29.4			46.4
Oregon (5/20)	343,050	9.7	58.2	32.1	
Arkansas (5/27)	448,290		60.1	17.5	18.0
Idaho (5/27)	50,482	4.1	62.2	22.0	11.8
Kentucky (5/27)	240,331		66.9	23.0	8.0
Nevada (5/27)	66,948		37.6	28.8	33.6
California (6/3)	3,323,812	4.0	37.7	44.8	11.4
Montana (6/3)	125,002		51.6	37.2	11.2
New Jersey (6/3)	560,908		37.9	56.2	3.5
New Mexico (6/3)	157,499		41.9	46.1	6.1
Ohio (6/3)	1,183,499		51.0	44.1	
Rhode Island (6/3)	38,327	0.8	25.8	68.3	2.0

State	Turnout	Brown	Democrats Carter	Kennedy	No Preference
South Dakota (6/3)	67,671		45.9	48.2	5.9
West Virginia (6/3)	314,985		61.9	38.1	
TOTAL	19,538,438	2.9	51.2	37.6	6.6

Republicans

State	Turnout	Anderson	Baker	Bush	Connally	Crane	Reagan	No Preference
*Iowa (1/21)	106,608	4.3	15.7	31.5	9.2	6.7	29.4	1.7
Puerto Rico (2/17)	186,371		37.0	60.1	1.1			
New Hampshire (2/26)	147,157	9.8	12.9	22.7	1.5	1.8	49.6	
Massachusetts (3/4)	400,826	30.7	4.8	31.0	1.2	1.2	28.8	0.6
Vermont (3/4)	65,611	29.0	12.3	21.7	1.3	1.9	30.1	
South Carolina (3/8)	145,501		0.5	14.8	29.6		54.7	
Alabama (3/11)	211,353		0.9	25.9	0.5	2.4	69.7	
Florida (3/11)	614,995	9.2	1.0	30.2	0.8	2.0	56.2	
Georgia (3/11)	200,171	8.4	0.8	12.6	1.2	3.2	73.2	
Illinois (3/18)	1,130,081	36.7	0.6	11.0	0.4	2.2	48.4	
Connecticut (3/25)	182,284	22.1	1.3	38.6	0.3	1.0	33.9	2.3
Kansas (4/1)	285,398	18.2	1.3	12.6	0.7	0.5	63.0	2.4
Wisconsin (4/1)	907,853	27.4	0.4	30.4	0.3	0.3	40.2	0.3
Louisiana (4/5)	41,683			18.8			74.9	5.3

*Dole received 1.5 percent of the vote in Iowa.

Republicans

State	Turnout	Anderson	Baker	Bush	Connally	Crane	Reagan	No Preference
Pennsylvania (4/22)	1,241,002	2.1	2.5	50.5	0.9		42.5	
Texas (5/3)	526,769			47.4			51.0	1.5
District of Columbia (5/6)	7,529	26.9		66.1		3.6		
Indiana (5/6)	568,315	9.9		16.4			73.7	
North Carolina (5/6)	168,391	5.1	1.5	21.8	0.7	0.3	67.6	2.7
Tennessee (5/6)	195,210	4.5		18.1		0.8	74.1	2.5
Maryland (5/13)	167,303	9.7		40.9		1.3	48.2	
Nebraska (5/13)	205,203	5.8		15.3		0.5	76.0	
Michigan (5/20)	595,176	8.2		57.5			31.8	1.7
Oregon (5/20)	304,647	10.1		34.7		0.7	54.5	
Idaho (5/27)	134,879	9.7		4.0		0.8	82.9	2.6
Kentucky (5/27)	94,795	5.1		7.2			82.4	3.3
Nevada (5/27)	47,395			6.5			83.0	10.5
California (6/3)	2,512,994	13.6		4.9		0.9	80.2	
Montana (6/3)	76,716			9.7			87.3	3.0
New Jersey (6/3)	277,977			17.1			81.3	
New Mexico (6/3)	59,101	12.1		9.9		7.5	63.7	2.2
Ohio (6/3)	854,967			19.2			80.8	
Rhode Island (6/3)	5,335			18.6			72.0	6.5
South Dakota (6/3)	88,325	6.3		4.2		0.5	82.1	5.8

Republicans

State	Turnout	Ander-son	Baker	Bush	Connally	Crane	Reagan	No Prefer-ence
West Virginia (6/3)	133,871			14.4			85.6	
TOTAL	12,785,184	12.3	1.4	24.0	0.6	0.8	59.7	0.5

Note: The figure refers to the vote percentage for all major presidential contenders. The percentages may not add up to 100 percent because votes for minor candidates were not included. Totals are based on official returns, except for Oregon, California, Montana, New Mexico, Ohio, South Dakota, and West Virginia, where only unofficial returns were available.

Source: Congressional Quarterly Weekly Report, July 5, 1980, pp. 1870–1871.

General Election Returns

State	Ronald Reagan (Republican)		Jimmy Carter (Democrat)		John Anderson (Independent)	
	Votes	%	Votes	%	Votes	%
Alabama	654,192	48.8	636,730	47.5	16,481	1.2
Alaska	86,112	54.5	41,842	26.4	11,156	7.0
Arizona	529,688	60.6	246,843	28.2	76,952	8.8
Arkansas	403,164	48.1	398,041	47.5	22,468	2.7
California	4,524,835	52.7	3,083,652	35.9	739,832	8.6
Colorado	652,264	55.0	368,009	31.1	130,633	11.0
Connecticut	677,210	48.2	541,732	38.5	171,807	12.2
Delaware	111,252	47.2	105,754	44.8	16,288	6.9
District of Columbia	23,313	13.4	130,231	74.9	16,131	9.3
Florida	2,046,951	55.5	1,419,475	38.5	189,692	5.2
Georgia	654,168	41.0	890,955	55.8	36,055	2.2
Hawaii	130,112	42.9	135,879	44.8	32,021	10.6
Idaho	290,699	66.4	110,192	25.2	27,058	6.2
Illinois	2,358,094	49.7	1,981,413	41.7	346,754	7.3
Indiana	1,255,656	56.0	844,197	37.6	111,639	5.0
Iowa	676,026	51.3	508,672	38.6	115,633	8.8
Kansas	566,812	57.8	326,150	33.3	68,231	7.0
Kentucky	635,274	49.0	617,417	47.7	31,127	2.4
Louisiana	792,853	51.2	708,453	45.8	26,345	1.7
Maine	238,522	45.6	220,974	42.3	53,327	10.2
Maryland	680,606	44.2	726,161	47.1	119,537	7.8
Massachusetts	1,056,223	41.8	1,053,800	41.7	382,539	15.2
Michigan	1,915,225	49.0	1,661,532	42.5	275,223	7.0
Minnesota	873,268	42.6	954,173	46.5	174,997	8.5
Mississippi	441,089	49.4	429,281	48.1	12,036	1.4
Missouri	1,074,181	51.2	931,182	44.3	77,920	3.7
Montana	206,814	56.8	118,032	32.4	29,281	8.1
Nebraska	419,214	65.6	166,424	26.0	44,854	7.0
Nevada	155,017	62.5	66,666	26.9	17,651	7.1

State	Ronald Reagan (Republican)		Jimmy Carter (Democrat)		John Anderson (Independent)	
	Votes	%	Votes	%	Votes	%
New Hampshire	221,705	57.7	108,864	28.4	49,693	12.9
New Jersey	1,546,557	52.0	1,147,364	38.6	234,632	7.9
New Mexico	250,779	55.0	167,826	36.8	29,459	6.5
New York	2,893,831	46.7	2,728,372	44.0	467,801	7.5
North Carolina	915,018	49.3	875,635	47.2	52,800	2.9
North Dakota	193,695	64.2	79,189	26.3	23,640	7.8
Ohio	2,206,545	51.5	1,752,414	40.9	254,472	5.9
Oklahoma	695,570	60.5	402,026	35.0	38,284	3.3
Oregon	571,044	48.3	456,890	38.7	112,389	9.5
Pennsylvania	2,261,872	49.6	1,937,540	42.5	292,921	6.4
Rhode Island	154,793	37.2	198,342	47.7	59,819	14.4
South Carolina	441,841	49.4	430,385	48.2	14,153	1.6
South Dakota	198,343	60.5	103,855	31.7	21,431	6.5
Tennessee	787,761	48.7	783,051	48.4	35,991	2.2
Texas	2,510,705	55.3	1,881,147	41.4	111,613	2.5
Utah	439,687	72.8	124,266	20.6	30,284	5.0
Vermont	94,628	44.4	81,952	38.4	31,761	14.9
Virginia	989,609	53.0	752,174	40.3	95,418	5.1
Washington	865,244	49.7	650,193	37.3	185,073	10.6
West Virginia	334,206	45.3	367,462	49.8	31,691	4.3
Wisconsin	1,088,845	47.9	981,584	43.2	160,657	7.1
Wyoming	110,700	62.6	49,427	28.0	12,072	6.8
	43,901,812	50.7	35,483,820	41.0	5,719,722	6.6

Note: Based on official returns from the fifty states and the District of Columbia. The percentages may not add up to 100 percent because votes for minor candidates were not included. The total popular vote was 86,513,296.

Source: Congressional Quarterly Weekly Report, January 17, 1981, p. 138.

Bibliographical Essay

Research on political campaigns has been rather sparse until recently. Unlike the outpouring of materials on voting behavior and public opinion, the study of candidates and campaigns generally has been left to journalists, participants, and ''how to'' specialists. However, in the late 1960s, several works appeared that helped fill this gap. David Leuthold studied ten California congressional races from 1962 in his *Electioneering in a Democracy* (New York: John Wiley, 1968); John Kingdon's *Candidates for Office* (New York: Random House, 1968) explored the beliefs and strategies of Wisconsin candidates in 1964; Karl Lamb and Paul Smith investigated presidential organization styles from 1964 in their *Campaign Decision-Making* (Belmont, Calif.: Wadsworth, 1968); John Kessel studied Republican strategies during 1964 in *The Goldwater Coalition* (Indianapolis, Ind.: Bobbs-Merrill, 1968), and Robert Huckshorn and Robert Spencer analyzed congressional challengers in their *The Politics of Defeat* (Amherst: University of Massachusetts Press, 1971).

Since that time, there has been an increasing body of scholarship on campaigns. Robert Agranoff's edited work, *The New Style in Election Campaigns*, 2nd ed. (Boston: Holbrook, 1976) was a useful contribution to the literature. Meanwhile, Richard Fenno's *Home Style* (Boston: Little, Brown, 1978) studied the presentational styles of eighteen House members campaigning for reelection, and Benjamin Page's *Choices and Echoes in Presidential Elections* (Chicago: University of Chicago Press, 1978) investigated the way candidates and parties structure voter options. Finally, Louis Maisel provided an insightful analysis of congressional challengers in his *From Obscurity to Oblivion* (Knoxville: University of Tennessee Press, 1982).

Not surprising, given the renewed interest in campaigns, research on presidential races has proliferated rapidly (with 1980 being no exception). At last count, over a dozen scholars and journalists have contributed books on the 1980 presidential contest. These books generally fall into one of four categories. First, there are the journalistic productions. Best typified by the last installment of Theodore White's saga of presidential campaigns, *America in Search of Itself* (New York: Harper and Row, 1982), these works largely provide descriptive accounts of the personalities and power struggles of modern campaigns. Although White has held the corner on this market for a long time, he had several competitors in 1980: a *Washington Post* team (David Broder and colleagues) produced *The Pursuit of the Presidency 1980* (New York: Berkley Books, 1980); a *New York Times* group (Hedrick Smith and colleagues) wrote *Reagan: The Man, The Presi-*

dent (Elmsford, N.Y.: Pergamon, 1981); Elizabeth Drew compiled her *Portrait of an Election* (New York: Simon and Schuster, 1981), and Jack Germond and Jules Witcover collaborated on *Blue Smoke and Mirrors* (New York: Viking Press, 1981).

Second, there are the "instant analysis" books edited by academic scholars: Gerald Pomper's *The Election of 1980* (Chatham, N.J.: Chatham House, 1981); Ellis Sandoz and Cecil Crabb, Jr.'s *A Tide of Discontent* (Washington, D.C.: Congressional Quarterly Press, 1981), and Austin Ranney's *The American Elections of 1980* (Washington, D.C.: American Enterprise Institute, 1981).

A third category of work falls within the area of primary sources. Rather than analyzing the campaign, two books provided transcripts of discussions among campaign advisors about the race: John Foley, ed., *Nominating a President* (New York: Praeger, 1980) and Jonathan Moore, ed., *The Campaign for President* (Cambridge, Mass.: Ballinger Publishing Co., 1981).

Finally, there are several in-depth academic studies that provide intensive analysis of selected aspects of the campaigns: Paul Abramson, John Aldrich, and David Rohde study voting behavior in *Change and Continuity in the 1980 Elections*, revised edition (Washington, D.C.: Congressional Quarterly Press, 1983); Paul Smith develops a cybernetic model of campaign decision-making in *Electing a President* (New York: Praeger, 1982); Herbert Alexander investigates campaign finance in *Financing the 1980 Election* (Lexington, Mass.: Lexington Books, 1983), and Williams Adams explores the role of the mass media in his edited book, *Television Coverage of the 1980 Presidential Campaign* (Norwood, N.J.: Ablex Publishing Co., 1983).

Beyond these treatments of the 1980 race, there are a number of books that deal with various dimensions of political campaigns. In the following section, I list some of these books by category (although in the interest of brevity, I generally cite only the more recent contributions to the literature).

MEDIA: One of the most interesting books in this area is Thomas Patterson's *The Mass Media Election* (New York: Praeger, 1980). Using panel surveys in two cities and a content analysis of media coverage, Patterson shows how media can influence voter beliefs as well as the factors that limit media influence. James David Barber (*Race for the Presidency*, Englewood Cliffs, N.J.: Prentice-Hall, 1978) and Edwin Diamond (*Good News, Bad News*, Cambridge, Mass.: MIT Press, 1978) conduct excellent analyses of the media as strategic actors in election campaigns. And Timothy Crouse provides an insightful discussion of news reporters in the 1972 presidential contest with his book, *The Boys on the Bus* (New York: Ballantine, 1972).

CONSULTANTS: The classic in this area is Stanley Kelley's *Professional Public Relations and Political Power* (Baltimore, Md.: Johns Hopkins, 1956). More recent accounts of consultants can be found in Dan Nimmo, *The Political Persuaders* (Englewood Cliffs, N.J.: Prentice-Hall, 1970) and Larry Sabato's enjoyable book, *The Rise of Political Consultants* (New York: Basic Books, 1981).

CANDIDATES: With the exception of Fenno's *Home Style* and Page's *Choices and Echoes in Presidential Elections*, little has been published in this area. However, two of the more important contributions have been Gary Jacobson and Samuel Kernell's *Strategy and Choice in Congressional Elections* (New Haven, Conn.: Yale University Press, 1981) and Marjorie Randon Hershey's *Running for Office* (Chatham, N.J.: Chatham House, forthcoming), which applies social learning theory to Senate campaigns in 1980.

DELEGATE SELECTION: The transformation of the nominating process has been well documented in books such as William Keech and Donald Matthews, *The Party's Choice*

(Washington, D.C.: Brookings, 1976), James Ceaser, *Presidential Selection* (Princeton, N.J.: Princeton University Press, 1979), and James Davis, *Presidential Primaries* (Westport, Conn.: Greenwood Press, 1980). But two recent pieces that are especially relevant include John Aldrich, *Before the Convention* (Chicago: University of Chicago Press, 1980) and James Lengle, *Representation and Presidential Primaries* (Westport, Conn.: Greenwood Press, 1981).

NOMINATING CONVENTIONS: The subject of conventions has received scant attention. However, two exceptions include Dennis Sullivan, Jeffrey Pressman, and F. Christopher Arterton, *Explorations in Convention Decision-Making* (San Francisco: Freeman, 1976) and Jeane Kirkpatrick, *The New Presidential Elite* (New York: Russell Sage, 1976).

MONEY: The standard in this area is Gary Jacobson's *Money in Congressional Elections* (New Haven, Conn.: Yale University Press, 1980). Also see Herbert Alexander's series of studies on campaign finance and the regular publications of the Federal Election Commission.

Index

About the Author

DARRELL M. WEST is Assistant Professor of Political Science at Brown University. His articles have appeared in *American Political Science Review, American Journal of Political Science, Social Science Quarterly,* and other periodicals.